Fundamental Analysis

FOR

DUMMIES®

Fundamental Analysis FOR DUMMIES®

by Matt Krantz

WILEY

John Wiley & Sons, Inc.

Fundamental Analysis For Dummies®

Published by
John Wiley & Sons, Inc.
111 River St.
Hoboken, NJ 07030-5774
www.wiley.com

Copyright © 2010 by John Wiley & Sons, Inc., Hoboken, New Jersey

Published by John Wiley & Sons, Inc., Hoboken, New Jersey

Published simultaneously in Canada

For general information on our other products and services, please contact our Customer Care Department within the U.S. at 877-762-2974, outside the U.S. at 317-572-3993, or fax 317-572-4002.

For technical support, please visit www.wiley.com/techsupport.

Wiley publishes in a variety of print and electronic formats and by print-on-demand. Some material included with standard print versions of this book may not be included in e-books or in print-on-demand. If this book refers to media such as a CD or DVD that is not included in the version you purchased, you may download this material at http://booksupport.wiley.com. For more information about Wiley products, visit www.wiley.com.

Library of Congress Control Number: 2009936811

ISBN: 978-0-470-50645-5 (pbk); ISBN 978-0-470-57320-4 (ebk); ISBN 978-0-470-57321-1 (ebk); ISBN 978-0-470-57322-8 (ebk)

Manufactured in the United States of America

10 9 8 7 6 5

WILEY

About the Author

Matt Krantz is a nationally known financial journalist who specializes in investing topics. Krantz has been a reporter and writer for USA TODAY since 1999. He covers financial markets and Wall Street, concentrating on developments affecting individual investors and their portfolios. His stories routinely signal trends investors can profit from and sound warnings about potential scams and things investors should be aware of.

In addition to covering markets for the print edition of USA TODAY, Matt writes a daily online investing column called "Ask Matt," which appears every trading day at USATODAY.com. He tackles questions posed by the Web site's giant audience and answers them in a plain-English and straightforward way. Readers often tell Matt he's the only one who has been able to finally solve investing questions they've sought answers to for years.

Matt has been investing since the 1980s and has studied dozens of investment techniques while forming his own. Before joining USA TODAY, Matt worked as a business and technology reporter for *Investor's Business Daily* and was a consultant with Ernst & Young prior to that.

He earned a bachelor's degree in business administration at Miami University in Oxford, Ohio.

Matt is based in USA TODAY's Los Angeles bureau. When he's not writing he's either spending time with his wife and young daughter, running, mountain biking, or surfing.

Dedication

This book is dedicated to my wife Nancy, who has helped me do my best, my parents for urging me to do my best, my grandparents for inspiring me to do my best, and my daughter Leilani for giving me a reason to do my best.

Author's Acknowledgments

Taking on a project with the size and scope as this book would have been overwhelming without the help of key people along the way. My wife, Nancy, is always there ready with an encouraging pat or a suggestion for the perfect word that is eluding me. My assignment editor, David Craig, and other USA TODAY editors have been supportive of my writing and journalism career from the start. Steve Minihan, a financial advisor and professor for UCLA Extension, has provided invaluable instruction and analysis skills. Fane Lozman shared his options expertise.

The team at Wiley has also been very supportive, including: Acquisitions Editor, Erin Calligan Mooney; Project Editor, Jennifer Connolly; and Technical Reviewer, Paul Mladjenovic. And again, a big thanks to Matt Wagner, my literary agent, for letting me know about this opportunity.

Finally, I wanted to thank my family for giving me the tools and determination to pursue my interest in writing and investing. My mom and dad taught all their kids they could achieve their goals if they always did their best and never stopped trying to get even better. And my grandparents are models of long-term success I continue to strive for.

Publisher's Acknowledgments

We're proud of this book; please send us your comments at http://dummies.custhelp.com. For other comments, please contact our Customer Care Department within the U.S. at 877-762-2974, outside the U.S. at 317-572-3993, or fax 317-572-4002.

Some of the people who helped bring this book to market include the following:

Acquisitions, Editorial, and Media Development

Project Editor: Jennifer Connolly

Acquisitions Editor: Stacy Kennedy and Erin Calligan Mooney

Copy Editor: Jennifer Connolly

Assistant Editor: Erin Calligan Mooney

Editorial Program Coordinator: Joe Niesen

Technical Editor: Paul Mladjenovic

Editorial Manager: Jennifer Ehrlich

Editorial Supervisor: Carmen Krikorian

Editorial Assistant: Jennette ElNaggar and David Lutton

Cover Photos: © iStock

Cartoons: Rich Tennant (www.the5thwave.com)

Composition Services

Project Coordinator: Sheree Montgomery

Layout and Graphics: Ashley Chamberlain, Melissa K. Jester, Mark Pinto

Proofreader: Jennifer Theriot

Indexer: Infodex Indexing Services

Publishing and Editorial for Consumer Dummies

Diane Graves Steele, Vice President and Publisher, Consumer Dummies

Kristin Ferguson-Wagstaffe, Product Development Director, Consumer Dummies

Ensley Eikenburg, Associate Publisher, Travel

Kelly Regan, Editorial Director, Travel

Publishing for Technology Dummies

Andy Cummings, Vice President and Publisher, Dummies Technology/General User

Composition Services

Debbie Stailey, Director of Composition Services

Contents at a Glance

Table of Contents

Part III: Making Money from Fundamental Analysis ... 157

Chapter 10: Looking for Fundamental Reasons to Buy or Sell......159

Chapter 11: Finding a Right Price for a Stock Using Discounted Cash Flow..177

Chapter 12: Using the Annual Report (10-K) to See What a Company Is Worth 193

Introduction

*I*f someone gave you a dollar for every newfangled stock-picking method invented every year, well, you probably wouldn't need a book on investing. You'd already be rich.

Investors are constantly barraged with new ways to pick stocks and buy stocks. There's no shortage of pundits, professional investors, and traders who all claim to know the best ways to invest. The trouble is, most of their advice is conflicting and often confusing.

Maybe it's this constant swirl of investment babble that tempted you to pick up this book. And if so, you made a wise decision. This book will help you get back to the basics of investing and understanding business. Rather than chasing hot stocks that whip around, *Fundamental Analysis For Dummies* will show you how to study the value of a business. You'll then use that information to make intelligent decisions about how to invest.

While faddish stock-picking systems come and go, fundamental analysis has been around for decades. The ability to pore over a company's most basic data and get a good idea of how a company is doing, how skilled the management team is, and whether or not a company has the resources to stay in business is a valuable skill to have.

Fundamental analysis is best known as a tool for investors trying to get a very detailed assessment of what a company is worth. But you might be surprised to learn you don't have to be an investor to use fundamental analysis. If you buy a warranty from a company and want to know if the company will be able to honor it, that calls for fundamental analysis. If you just want to know "how well" a company is doing, you might also want to use fundamental analysis. And journalists, too, can use fundamental analysis to find stories that will interest readers.

The aim of this book is to show you what fundamental analysis is and help you use it as a way to better understand business and investment.

About This Book

Fundamental Analysis For Dummies is one of the most approachable texts to tackle this somewhat complex topic. Rather than bog you down with the nitty-gritty details that academics pull their hair over, I've attempted to lay out all the main topics and techniques you'll need to apply fundamental analysis to a variety of business tasks.

And while fundamental analysis is useful for anyone with an interest in business, I appreciate the fact you are likely hoping to make some money from fundamental analysis. And for that reason, the book is largely targeted toward investors who are either hoping to use fundamental analysis to manage their portfolios or to enhance their current system of selecting stocks.

As the author, I can share the tricks, tips, and secrets I've learned from a career writing about online investing for readers just like you. In the course of writing for USA TODAY, including a daily online column about investing called "Ask Matt" at USATODAY.com, I've answered thousands of reader questions that may be the same ones you have.

Fundamental Analysis For Dummies gives you all the tools you need to access fundamental data, process them, and make decisions. The book, however, stops short at showing you how to actually buy or sell stocks by choosing a broker and entering orders. If you're interested in the actual process of buying or selling stocks, that topic is covered exhaustively in my *Investing Online For Dummies* (Wiley).

Conventions Used in This Book

I want to help you get the information you need as quickly as possible. To help you, I use several conventions:

- ✔ Monofont is used to signal a Web address. This is important, since there are so many Web addresses in the book.
- ✔ *Italics* signal a word is a unique and important term for online investors.
- ✔ **Boldfaced** words make the key terms and phrases in bulleted and numbered lists jump out and grab your attention.
- ✔ Sidebars, text separated from the rest of the type in gray boxes, are interesting but slightly tangential to the subject at hand. Sidebars are generally fun and optional reading. You won't miss anything critical if you skip the sidebars. If you choose to read the sidebars, though, I think you'll be glad you did.

What You're Not to Read

This book is a reference, which means you don't have to read it from beginning to end (any more than you have to read a dictionary from beginning to end to get what you need from it). If you're in a hurry, you can even skip certain pieces of information and still get the gist of what you need. Here's what you can safely skip:

- **Anything marked with a Technical Stuff icon:** For more on this icon, see the "Icons Used in This Book" section, later in this Introduction.

- **Text in gray boxes, which are known as sidebars:** Sidebars contain interesting — but not essential — information.

- **The copyright page:** Sure, the publisher's attorneys' feelings will be hurt, but you can skip the fine print without missing out on anything important. Shh! I won't tell.

Foolish Assumptions

No matter your skill or experience level with investing, you can get something out of *Fundamental Analysis For Dummies.* I'm fully aware that for a vast majority of the public, the sight of tables of numbers in an annual report is boring at best — and scary at worst. The first part of the book is designed for you if you're curious about fundamental analysis and wondering why it's a common tool used by successful professional investors. Hoping to spare you from technical terms, I stick to plain English as much as possible. (When I have no choice but to use investing jargon, I tell you what it means.) But I also assume more advanced investors might pick up this book too, looking to discover a few things they didn't already know about fundamental analysis. The book takes on more advanced topics as you progress through it, and it carefully selects online resources that will add new tools to your investing toolbox.

How the Book Is Organized

All the chapters in this book are self-contained and can be read by themselves. If you've been dying to learn how to do a discounted cash flow analysis, go on, skip ahead and dive in. Believe it or not, the discounted cash flow analysis is one of the most common things USA TODAY readers ask me about. Jump around. Flip through. Scan the index and find topics you've been dying to read about for years. And don't fear that you'll get in over your head if you read the back of the book first. If there are concepts you need to know at any point, I've carefully added references to those pages in the book, so you can jump around. This book is a reference, and you shouldn't feel as if you need to suffer through topics you already know or don't care to know. With that said, though, the book is assembled in a logical order. My goal is to start simple, and then ramp things up as the book goes on.

The book is divided into five parts, and the following sections give you a brief description of what you can find within each part.

Part I: What Fundamental Analysis Is and Why You Should Use It

If you've heard investors talk about fundamental analysis, but were never quite sure what it was, this part is for you. You'll discover not only what fundamental analysis is, but also why it's so powerful. You'll even find out how fundamental analysis might help boost your investment success even if you have other methods of buying and selling stocks. After reading the chapters in this part, you should have a good idea of what's entailed in fundamental analysis and how it can benefit you.

Part II: How to Perform Fundamental Analysis

Here's where we roll up our sleeves and start getting into specifics. Fundamental analysis starts with the fundamental data companies provide about themselves. You'll uncover what kinds of data companies generate and provide to the public, as well as what the numbers mean. And rather than setting you on a wild goose chase to find the data yourself, I give you very specific instructions on the best ways to retrieve all the fundamental data you'll need. In this part, too, you'll get an understanding of how to start not just reading fundamental data, but digging in and gleaning insights from them.

Part III: Making Money from Fundamental Analysis

Look. I'm not going to flatter myself and believe you're reading this book because you want to read all my clever analogies. You're probably interested in fundamental analysis because you want to make money or at least get a better understanding on how to gauge the health and success of companies. Investors who use fundamental analysis to get a solid understanding of businesses and their values get a huge advantage over those who blindly chase stocks. In this part, you'll get exposed to some of the more advanced techniques fundamental analysts use to get insights about companies that aren't apparent to some investors.

Part IV: Getting Advanced with Fundamental Analysis

The chapters in this part take fundamental analysis even further, highlighting some of the more thorough techniques available. You'll find how to analyze an industry, the broad economy, and even how to marry fundamental analysis with other methods of evaluating investments.

Part V: The Part of Tens

The tens chapters break down concepts in a top-ten list structure. You can discover what financial secrets fundamental analysis allows you to uncover (Chapter 20), you can zero in on the things you should look at when analyzing a company (Chapter 21), and you can find out once and for all what fundamental analysis *can't* do (Chapter 22).

Icons Used in This Book

When you're flipping through this book, you might notice several icons that catch your attention. That's done on purpose. I use several distinct icons to alert you to sections of the book that stand out. Those icons are

These icons highlight info that you should etch on the top of your brain and never forget, even when you're getting caught up in the excitement of fundamental analysis.

Read these sections to quickly pick up insider secrets that can boost your success with fundamental analysis.

Some of the things covered in the book get a bit hairy and complicated. This icon flags such sections for two reasons. First, you may decide to avoid the headache and skip over them, since the info isn't vital to your understanding of fundamental analysis. Second, the icon is a heads-up that the paragraph is probably loaded with investment jargon. Don't be embarrassed if you need to read the section a second or third time. Hey, you didn't want this book to be too easy, did you?

Avoid the landmines scattered throughout Wall Street that can decimate your good intentions at building wealth with these sections.

Where to Go from Here

If you're a new investor or just curious about fundamental analysis, you might consider starting from the beginning. That way, you'll be ready for some of the more advanced topics I introduce later in the book. If you've already been using fundamental analysis or wondering if fundamental analysis might enhance a strategy you think is working for you, you might skip to Part II. And if you're dying to know about a specific topic, there's nothing wrong with looking up those terms in the index and flipping to the appropriate pages.

Part I

What Fundamental Analysis Is and Why You Should Use It

The 5th Wave   By Rich Tennant

"Fundamental analysis, Grace. Learn all you can about a company before investing in it. Even a bridal gown company."

In this part . . .

If you're not sure what fundamental analysis is or how it can help you invest, this part is for you. In this part, I define fundamental analysis and explain how understanding how a company makes money can help you make money. You find out how fundamental analysis compares with other ways of investing and get a quick description of how some successful investors put fundamental analysis to work. Lastly, give you a quick rundown on the accounting that companies use to record their fundamentals for all to see.

Chapter 1

Understanding Fundamental Analysis

*B*efore you gulp down that neon-colored energy drink or pour yourself a bowl of super-sweetened cereal that looks like it was made by Willy Wonka himself, you probably do something first. More times than not, you just might take a glance at the nutrition label that spells out what's in the box.

You might not know what guar gum, guarana, or other ingredients that often show up on the labels of such processed foods are, but you can get a pretty good idea of what's good for you and what's not. If a bottle of apple juice, for instance, has a list of ingredients longer than your arm and is filled with stuff you can't pronounce, you know you're not drinking squeezed apples. Being aware of what's in a food may or may not sway your decision to eat it, but at least you know what you're putting into your body.

Companies and stocks, too, come with similar labels. All companies that are *publicly traded,* or that lure money from the investing public, are required to disclose what they're all about. Just as food processors must list all the ingredients that go into their products, companies must tell investors what they're composed of.

Unfortunately, though, a giant multinational company can't put all the information investors need to know inside a tiny rectangle as food companies can. Instead, the key elements that make up a company are broken down at length in a series of *financial statements* and other sources of fundamental data.

Reading these critical financial statements and gleaning insights from them are the most basic goals of fundamental analysis. Fundamental analysis is the skill of reading through all the information companies provide about themselves to make intelligent decisions. Just as you'd want to know what's in that Frankenfood you're about to bite into, you want to know what's in an investment you're thinking about adding to your portfolio.

Why Bother with Fundamental Analysis?

You might wonder why you need to hassle with fundamental analysis. After all, at every family picnic there's undoubtedly the loudmouthed relative who's filled with all sorts of can't-go-wrong stock tips. Why bother with technical things like net income or discounted cash flow analysis when you can just turn on the TV, write down a couple of stock symbols, buy the stocks and hope for the best?

Similarly, you might figure learning how companies operate is just needless information. After all, you don't need to know about fuel injection systems, suspensions, and car battery technology to drive a car. And you don't need to know what's going on behind the curtain to enjoy a play. Some investors figure they can just pick a couple of hot stocks, buy them, and drive off to riches.

If the vicious bear market that began in 2007 taught investors anything, it's that blindly buying stocks just because you might "like" a company or its products was hardly a sound way to tune up a portfolio. Chasing hunches and personal opinion about stocks is often not a great way to invest, as you'll find out in Chapter 20.

Some of the real values of fundamental analysis

Ever notice how there's always a new wonder diet promising to make you skinny, and a new pill to make you healthier? More times than not, though, it seems these things never work. Getting healthy comes back to the basics — a balanced diet and exercise.

The same goes with investing. Believe it or not, investing can be somewhat full of fads. There's always a new investment pundit or economist with a new way to pick winning stocks. And just as an hour on the treadmill will do you more good than a bottle full of miracle pills, successfully choosing stocks often comes back to fundamental analysis.

Fundamental analysis is the classic way to examine companies and investments for a variety of reasons, including the fact it is:

- ✔ **Based on fact, not opinion:** It's easy to get caught up in general enthusiasm about what a company is doing or the products it's selling. But fundamental analysis blinds you to this investment hype and gets you focused on cold-hard business realities. It doesn't matter if all the kids in your neighborhood are buying a company's products, if the company isn't making any money at selling them.

- ✔ **Good at pinpointing shifts in the business' health:** If a company's success is starting to fade, you'll see it show up on the fundamentals. No, there won't be a giant sign saying "Sell this stock." But there are clues if you know how to look, as you'll discover in Chapter 18. Companies are required to disclose key aspects of their business, so if there's a problem, a fundamental analyst will often be early at spotting some trouble.

- ✔ **All about execution:** Companies' CEOs are usually good at getting investors focused on the future and how things are going to get better next quarter. But the fundamentals are based in reality. Just think of children who say how hard they're working at school. The report card is still the tangible evidence of how things are actually going.

- ✔ **A way to put price tags on companies:** What's a painting worth? What's a used car worth? Just as with anything else with subjective value, the price is generally what someone is willing to pay for it. The stock market, an auction of buyers and sellers, does a good job putting price tags on companies. But fundamental analysis gives you another way to see just how much investors, by buying or selling stock, are paying for a stock.

Driving home an example

One of the best recent examples of how fundamental analysis can help you and your portfolio is General Motors. For decades, GM represented the might of U.S. industriousness, know-how, and creativity. GM commanded a massive market value of $3.5 billion in 1928, says Standard & Poor's. I'll step you through what market value means in more detail in Chapter 3, but for now, just know that GM was the most valuable company by far in 1928.

GM vs. Ford

Even months before GM filed for bankruptcy protection, fundamental analysis could have served you well.

Back in January 2009, seeing both GM and Ford facing intense financial strain, many investors wondered if either one was worth taking a bet on. Some helpful fundamental analysis tools, including an analysis of the statement of cash flows, could have determined whether you lost a fortune or enjoyed a big gain.

I'll show you how to read the statement of cash flow in detail in Chapter 7. But for now, I'm just giving you a real example of why fundamental analysis matters to whet your appetite. At the beginning of 2009, both Ford and GM were constantly in the news. Both faced a tough business climate and both had depressed stock prices: Ford began 2009 at $2.46 a share and GM $3.65.

But a quick fundamental analysis showed Ford was the much better bet. Ford ended the quarter with $27.5 billion in cash and burnt $600 million in cash. Don't let the numbers scare you at this point. I'm just exposing you to a basic free cash flow analysis, as you'll learn about later. Just for now, know that at the quarterly rate, Ford had enough cash to last nearly 46 quarters.

Over at GM, however, the company ended the quarter with just $15.9 billion in cash. Meanwhile, it burnt through $8.9 billion during the quarter. A fundamental analyst knew right away the company wasn't going to make it through the year at that rate. That's critical information to have known.

Knowing how to do this one type of fundamental analysis may make a world of difference for investors. In the following six months, shares of Ford jumped 149% to $6.13. Ford also did not accept government funding assistance. Meanwhile, shares of GM crashed 79% to 75 cents.

Makes you want to read the rest of the book, doesn't it?

For decades, investors figured a dollar invested in GM was money in the bank. The company slugged through upturns and downturns and was a lasting power that helped drive the U.S. economy. The company kept paying fat dividends and kept powering profits higher.

But investors who blindly bet GM would remain a lasting force and ignored the fundamental signs of trouble suffered a brutal blow on June 1, 2009. On that day, which will forever remain one of the lowlights of capitalism, GM became the fourth-largest public company to seek bankruptcy protection, according to BankruptcyData.com. Shares of GM stock collapsed to just 75 cents a share, down 97% from their level just three years before.

Fundamental analysis may not have helped you predict this shocking outcome of GM. Concrete elements from the company's financial statements, though, could have tipped you off to just how challenged GM was well before it became a penny stock.

Putting fundamental analysis to work

It's easy to get consumed with the fast-money trading aspects of stocks. Exciting TV reports about stocks on the move and companies that have new products practically turn investing into a sporting event. In fact, if you listen to some traders talk, they rattle off companies' ticker symbols in rapid-fire delivery just as sports fans talk about teams. Flashing arrows and rapid trading can become an addiction for people who get into it.

And it's exactly the headache and insanity fundamental analysis is trying to help you avoid. After all, stocks rise and fall each minute, day, and week based on a random flow of news. The constant ups and downs of stocks can sometimes confound logic and reason. Many readers of my Ask Matt column at USATODAY.com are baffled when a stock falls even after the company reports what appears to be good news. Trying to profit from these short-term swings is a game for gamblers and speculators. It's futile on a long-term basis.

But that's not to say investing is gambling. Remember that those stock symbols you see flashing red and green aren't dice, horses, or cards. They're more than just the two, three, or four letters of their ticker symbol.

When you buy a stock, you're buying a piece of ownership in companies that make and sell products and services. You're buying a claim to the companies' future profits. Owning a piece of a real business over time isn't gambling, it's capitalism.

Fundamental analysis forces you to focus on investing in businesses, not stocks. You're not buying a lottery ticket, but a piece of ownership in a company.

If jumping in and out of stocks at the right time isn't the way to riches, then what is the trick to successful investing? The answer is to stop thinking of stocks as just symbols that gyrate each day. The goal of fundamental analysis is to help you step away from the short-term trading and gambling of stocks. Instead, you approach investing as if you're buying a business, not rolling the dice.

Fundamental analysis ideally helps you identify businesses that sell goods and services for more than what they paid to produce them. Fundamental analysis is your tool to evaluate how good a company is at turning raw materials into profits.

Certainly, famed investor Warren Buffett is one of the best-known users of fundamental analysis. You will read more about how Buffett applies fundamental analysis to investing in Chapter 3.

No matter how you choose investments currently, you can likely apply fundamental analysis. Even if you're the kind of investor who likes to buy diversified mutual funds and hold onto them forever, called a *passive investor,* it can be helpful to understand basic financial characteristics of the companies.

Knowing what fundamentals to look for

Knowing what makes a company tick isn't as convoluted as it may sound. Companies are so regulated and scrutinized, all the things you need to pay attention to are usually listed and published for all to see. Generally, when you hear about a company's fundamentals, the key elements to be concerned with fall into several categories including:

- **Financial performance:** Here you're looking at how much a company collects from customers who buy its products or services, and how much it keeps in profit. Terms you probably hear quite a bit about, such as *earnings* and *revenue*, are examples of ways fundamental analysts evaluate a company's financial performance.

- **Financial resources:** It's not enough for a company to sell goods and services. It's not even enough to turn a profit. Companies must also have the resources to invest themselves and keep their businesses going and growing. Aspects of a business, such as its assets and liabilities, are ways to measure a company's resources.

- **Management team:** When you invest in a company, you're entrusting your money with the CEO and other managers to put your cash to work. Fundamental analysis helps you separate the good managers from the bad.

- **Valuation:** It's not enough to identify which companies are the best. What's a "good" company anyway? Definitions of "good" can run the gamut. You also need to consider how much you're paying to own a piece of a company. If you overpay for the best company on the planet, it's still likely you'll end up losing money on the investment. You'll read more about this in Chapter 10 and Chapter 11.

- **Macro trends:** No company operates in a vacuum. A company's performance is highly influenced by actions of competitors or the condition of the economy. These broad factors need to be incorporated into fundamental analysis, as you'll discover in Chapter 15 and Chapter 16.

Knowing what you need

One of the great things about running as a hobby is all you need is a pair of decent shoes. And basketball? Just grab a ball and find a hoop. No fancy equipment is required. The same goes with fundamental analysis. Much of the data you need is provided free by companies and can be accessed in seconds from any computer connected to the Internet.

Fundamental analysis can get pretty involved. But at its most basic form, there are just a few basic ideas behind fundamental analysis, including:

- ✔ **Awareness of the benefits of fundamental analysis:** Since fundamental analysis takes some know-how and time spent learning a bit, you'll want to know ahead of time why you're going to the trouble. Chapter 2 and Chapter 3 highlight the payoff of fundamental analysis. Even if you're a passive investor, or one who simply buys a basket of stocks and holds on, there are reasons why fundamental analysis might be worth your while.

- ✔ **Retrieval of financial data:** Getting all the key data you need to apply fundamental analysis is easy, if you know where to look. Chapter 4 gives you quick tips on how to round up all the data you'll need.

- ✔ **Basic math:** There it is: The M word. There's no way around the fact there will be some number crunching involved in some aspects of fundamental analysis. Don't worry, I'll guide you to help keep the math as painless as possible. One of the key tools you'll need is for trend analysis, which you will read about in Chapter 4.

Knowing the Tools of the Fundamental Analysis Trade

You can read all sorts of books on home repair and even take a trip to your hardware store and buy lots of screws, nails and glue. But none of that effort will benefit you unless you have a tool-belt of hammers and the knowledge of how to get started and put your plan into reality.

The same importance of execution is part of fundamental analysis. You may appreciate the importance of fundamental analysis and may even be able to download fundamental data from Web sites or from a company's annual report. But you need to have the tools to analyze the fundamentals to get any real value from them.

Staying focused on the bottom line

If there's one thing investors may agree is of upmost importance, it's the company's profitability. When it comes down to it, when you invest in a stock you're buying a piece of the company's profitability. Knowing how to read and understand how much profit a company is making is very important when it comes to knowing whether or not to invest.

The income statement, described in full detail in Chapter 5, will be your guide when you're trying to determine how profitable a company is. What might also surprise you is that the income statement can tell you a great deal about a company, in addition to just how much income it brings in.

Sizing up what a company has to its name

During times of intense financial stress, investors often make a very important mental shift. They're not so concerned about making money as they are about just getting their money back. Similarly, when things get tough in the economy, investors are less interested in how profitable a company is and are more mindful of whether a company will survive.

When you're trying to understand the lasting power of a company, fundamental analysis is of great value. By reading the company's *balance sheet,* you can get a rundown of what a company has — its *assets* — and what is owes — its *liabilities.* Monitoring these items give you a very good picture of how much dry powder a company has to endure a tough period. Chapter 6 explores the balance sheet in more detail.

Burn baby burn: Cash burn

One of the biggest killers of companies, especially smaller firms just starting out, is cash flow. While a company might have a great product concept, excellent management, and even dedicated financial backers, timing is everything. If a company is using up cash to pay its bills and employees but not bringing in enough cold hard cash from customers, it can run into a giant financial headache very quickly.

If there's one thing I hope you pick up from this book, it's how fundamental analysis helps you keep a close eye on how much cash is coming into and out of a company. Monitoring cash flow is critical to know if a company is running perilously empty on cash, which you'll dig into in more detail in Chapter 7. But cash flow is also a very important way fundamental analysis helps you put a price tag on a company, as you will find out about in Chapter 11.

Financial ratios: Your friend in making sense of a company

As you flip through the book and jump around to different topics that interest you, you might be a bit bewildered by just how many pieces of data fundamental analysts must deal with. You've got the financial statements that measure just about every aspect of the company. It can be intimidating to decide what numbers matter most and which ones can be ignored.

Financial ratios will be a great help here, as you'll see in Chapter 8. These ratios draw all sorts of fundamental data from different sources and put them into perspective.

Financial ratios are also important because they form the vocabulary of fundamental analysts. If you're ever at a cocktail party where analysts are talking about gross margins and accounts receivable turnover, I want you to be prepared. By the way, that sounds like a pretty boring party.

I'll show you a whole host of financial ratios in Chapter 8 that are the favorites used by many fundamental analysts. You'll soon be using seemingly unrelated pieces of financial data about a company to glean some very important conclusions about the company.

Making Fundamental Analysis Work For You

Imagine a young child who memorized an entire dictionary, but can't use a single word in a sentence. That's a basic analogy of some investors' fundamental analysis knowledge. You might, too, know some things about the income statement and balance sheet and have a great knowledge of what's contained in the statements. But when it comes to applying your know-how, that can be a bit trickier.

Putting fundamental analysis in action requires taking everything you know about a company and mixing in some estimates and best guesses about the future to arrive at a decent expectation of whether or not to invest in a company.

Using fundamentals as signals to buy or sell

Buying a stock at the right time is very difficult. But knowing when to sell it is even tougher. And while fundamental analysis won't tell you the exact best time and day to buy or sell, it can at least give you a better understanding of things to look out for when it comes to making decisions.

If you're a passive investor and buy large diversified baskets of dozens of stocks, you can afford to buy and hold stocks. Even if one company runs into big-time trouble, it's just one holding in a large basket of stocks. However, if you choose to invest in individual stocks, monitoring the fundamentals is critical. If you start noticing a company's trend deteriorating, you don't want to be the last investor to get out.

The perils of ignoring the fundamentals

Blindly following a company and investing in its stock can be very dangerous. Table 1-1 shows a list of a few major U.S. stocks that were worth $100 a share or more at the beginning of 2000, but saw their share prices fall to below $10 a share by the start of 2009. Ouch!

Table 1-1	Watch Out! A Falling Knife!	
Stock	*Stock price 12/31/1999*	*Stock price 1/1/2009*
JDS Uniphase	$645.25	$3.65
InfoSpace	$535.00	$7.55
Blue Coat Systems	$326.72	$8.40
Ciena	$201.25	$6.70
Sun Microsystems	$154.88	$3.82

*Source: Standard & Poor's Capital IQ

If there's a primary goal of fundamental analysis, it's avoiding stock disasters like the ones listed above. Losses that large are nearly impossible to recover from in a single person's lifetime. You can read more about why avoiding investment disasters is so critical in Chapter 18.

Using fundamental analysis as your guide

As Table 1-1 shows, investing in individual stocks is very risky. Losses can be sizeable. That's why you want to invest with your eyes wide open. Just as you probably wouldn't dare fire a loaded weapon or jump out of an airplane without proper training, the same goes with investing in individual stocks.

Luckily, fundamental analysis provides investors with a host of very specific tools to help them protect themselves. And while the tools of fundamental analysts aren't foolproof, as you will see in Chapter 22, they give investors guidance of when a stock might be getting a little dangerous or the underlying trends might be changing.

You'll find complete explanations of some of the most powerful tools used by fundamental analysts in this book. Chapter 11, for instance, will be very valuable to you since it shows you how to use a company's cash flow as a way to measure its value. And in Chapter 12, you'll discover how the pros spin through the annual reports they receive from companies.

Chapter 2

Getting up to Speed with Fundamental Analysis

Try to remember what it was like being a beginner at something you're good at now. Whether it was karate, ballet, or basketball, as a beginner, you may have been tempted to bypass all the basics and go straight for the advanced techniques. For instance, it's natural to want to try breaking boards with your bare hands or doing pirouettes or slam-dunks on your first day of trying something new.

Good coaches, though, encourage you to slow down and start from the very beginning. It's almost always best to start working on the basic karate stances, ballet poses, and basketball dribbling before even thinking about moving to the showy and advanced aspects of each sport.

Beginning investors often experience a similar overconfidence at first. Many hope they can skip mundane things — like reading accounting statements, understanding basic financial ratios, and calculating discounted cash-flow models — and get right to the exotic rapid-fire trading. It's tempting to think you can trade complex securities, dabble in highly volatile stocks, and dart in and out of investments with ease right away. Sadly, though, investors usually lose money when they try to get too advanced too soon. And unfortunately, there's no coach to cool off investors who are just starting out.

So, consider this book to be your coach as you begin. Starting with this chapter, this book will introduce you to the basic skills that make up fundamental analysis. The basics explained in this chapter will set you up for taking fundamental analysis to the next level in chapters deeper in the book.

What Is Fundamental Analysis?

Ask 20 people how they choose their investments, and you'll probably hear 20 different methods. Some like to buy stocks recommended by a friend or broker. Others think it's wise to invest in companies making products they personally enjoy and use. A few even consult with astrologers (seriously). What most people, though, have in common is that they feel they're always paying too much for stocks and selling them when they're too cheap.

Perhaps you swing between different investment strategies like some folks switch diets to lose weight. Experimenting with different ways of picking stocks may have worked fine as stocks made breathtaking advances in the 1990s. But the crash of 2008 changed everything, making 2008 a harsh reminder that it's possible to overpay for stocks. Not realizing that ahead of time can be hazardous to your portfolio, and perhaps after losing money a few too many times, you're looking for a method with a little more science behind it.

That's where fundamental analysis comes in. Fundamental analysis is one of the most sound and primary ways to evaluate investments. As a fundamental analyst, you carefully and thoroughly study every aspect of a company's operations. Much of your analysis will be focused on financial statements companies provide, as described briefly in this chapter and in more detail later in this book.

Going beyond betting

If you're like most investors, even the words fundamental analysis may turn you off a bit. Fundamental analysis sounds somewhat stuffy and academic. And it's true that fundamental analysis finds much of its roots in academia. But you might be surprised to find you probably are using some basic forms of fundamental analysis in your life, perhaps even in places you wouldn't expect.

One of my favorite examples of where a type of fundamental analysis is used is at the horse races. Before a race, you'll notice groups of bettors doing some serious work trying to pick the day's winning horses. Some may pore over the life histories of horses in the race, getting to know the jockeys and their techniques, and even studying how wet or dry the track is.

While investing isn't exactly like horse racing, the analogy is a helpful way to understand fundamental analysis. For instance, some fundamental analysts will study a company like a bettor will study a horse. How successful has the company been recently, and is it healthy and well-cared for? Next, in fundamental analysis you might study a company's management like a bettor would consider the jockey. Is the management experienced, and has it competed against experienced players? Lastly, you must evaluate the broad economic climate, just like a bettor will consider the weather and condition of the track.

But here's where things get even trickier. It's not good enough to find the best company, or horse, to take the metaphor a little further. After all, if all the other bettors at the track did the same work and picked the same horse that you selected, you have a problem. The odds would be adjusted so that the payout on the favorite horse will fall. Bettors know that picking a favorite horse to win doesn't pay off much. And you're also taking a chance that the favorite will lose and cost you money. Similarly, if you invest in a company that's widely considered to be a darling with other investors, your payoff is reduced for reasons you can discover in Chapter 3.

Now that you see what fundamental analysis is, broadly speaking, consider how it can be applied to investing. Fundamental analysis is used to size up investments in several key ways:

- ✓ **Analyzing the financial statements:** Fundamental analysts pore over public documents companies provide to understand how the business is performing. Many fundamental analysts' starting point is digging into a company's financial statements to see how profitable a company is, how rapidly it is growing, what kind of financial health it's in, and whether it has the ability to withstand tough economic times.

- ✓ **Getting an idea of how solid a company is:** Many fundamental analysts are *fixed-income investors.* These investors have loaned money to companies, usually by buying bonds. Bond investors give money to a company in exchange for an agreed-upon payment each month, quarter, or year. Since bond investors get a fixed amount pay, they don't care if a company is wildly successful. Bond investors, unlike stock investors, don't get a share of future earnings and growth. Bond investors just want to know the company is healthy enough so it can keep paying interest and return the money it borrowed.

- ✓ **Understanding the value of a company:** Stock investors use fundamental analysis to gauge whether a company's stock is a good deal or not. By studying financial statements, financial analysts determine whether a stock's price undervalues or overvalues the company.

- ✓ **Going beyond the financials:** Fundamental analysis goes beyond where accounting stops. While accountants wish to precisely measure business activity, fundamental analysts want to analyze it in a way to help make decisions. Using fundamental analysis, you will evaluate other factors that affect a company's prospects. Common factors you might consider include sizing up a company against its rivals, determining how skilled a company's management team is in navigating through boom and bust times, and understanding the broad economic climate.

Fundamental analysts take all the intelligence they gather to arrive at an investment decision and to take action. The most common question fundamental analysts ask themselves is whether a stock, at its current price, is cheap or expensive. The answer to that question will determine whether you choose to invest or not.

Understanding how fundamental analysis works

Fundamental analysts often dig well beyond a company's financial statements and try to unearth things. Sometimes fundamental analysts might spot a trend forming before a company's management acknowledges it. A fundamental analyst, for instance, might visit a retailer's stores and see how crowded they are to get an idea of what earnings might be in the future. Similarly, the fundamental analyst may try to get an idea of future demand by considering how busy a company's suppliers are. The goal of fundamental analysis is to measure how much a company is worth by using any shred of information possible.

The way you use fundamental analysis to understand what a company is worth gets down to the core essence of what a business is. With fundamental analysis, your goal is to monitor a company to see how it brings in money by selling goods and services to generate revenue. Next, you'll determine how much of revenue a company manages to keep after paying its expenses. What's left after paying all the bills is profit, or *earnings*.

The fact that fundamental analysts take action on their research is what separates them from accountants. Fundamental analysts compare what they think a company is worth with what other investors think. If the stock is undervalued, the fundamental analyst will buy the stock. Accountants, on the other hand, have the job of recording sales and revenue, but not trying to profit off their findings.

Investing with the stars

Since there's so much money to be made — or lost — with investing, it's not surprising just about method to pick stocks has been tried ... even astrology. In fact, during 2008, the best stock picker was Crawford Perspectives, up nearly 43% by monitoring the movement of planets to make investment calls. Unfortunately, though, you'll need more than just a clear telescope to make money on stocks. Crawford's stock picks lost 1% a year between 1998 and 2008, showing that even the heavens can be wrong.

Fundamental analysis isn't perfect. But as you'll discover in this chapter, fundamental analysis is rigorous and rooted in understanding the most basic elements of business. So even if you have no plans to be a fundamental analyst, knowing how fundamental analysis works can only boost your investment success.

Who can perform fundamental analysis?

You don't have to be a high-powered investor to use fundamental analysis. If you have an interest in finding out more deeply about how companies work, you're a candidate for learning about fundamental analysis. In fact, knowing how to read, analyze, and take action from information you glean about a company can be helpful for many users, including:

- **Stock investors:** Those looking to take an ownership stake in a company have a great financial incentive to master fundamental analysis. What they find out about companies may help them to decide when a good time to buy or sell may be.

- **Lenders:** When you give someone a loan, you want to make sure they have the ability to pay you back. If you lend money to a company, perhaps by buying bonds they issue, you're more concerned about getting your money back than about making a killing on the investment.

- **Mutual fund investors:** Even if you don't pick individual stocks or bonds to invest in, you probably own mutual funds that do. Mutual funds are investments that invest in a basket of individual securities. Using fundamental analysis, you can investigate some of the stocks your mutual funds may own. You might take a look at the top holdings of your mutual fund and question why your mutual fund owns them.

- **Employees:** Workers may be anxious about the health of their company for several reasons. Using the same techniques an investor would use, you can study your company's financial resources and roughly estimate how likely it might be to pursue aggressive cost-cutting, like layoffs. Employees who depend on a pension paid by a former employer might also want to study the health of the company.

- **Board members:** Whether you're a board member of a large company, your local museum, or your condominium association, understanding how to understand the flow of money in and out can make you more valuable. Understanding fundamental analysis will help you be a solid watchdog of the organization's management by looking at the facts, not the promises.

✔ **Donors:** Even some nonprofit charities disclose their financial standing. Fundamental analysis will help you see where donations are being spent and whether or not money is getting to those in need or being soaked up by the bureaucracy.

✔ **Consumers:** As a consumer, you might not think of yourself as investing in a company. And in most cases, you're not. Sometimes, even when you buy a product, you're forming a long-term relationship with a company. When you buy a car or an insurance product, you're probably going to be connected with the company for many years. It's a good idea to know how to analyze a company if you plan on relying on its products for a long time.

Certainly, a background in accounting can help you dig even deeper into the financial statements. And in this book, I'll show you some examples of where you might not be able to take the financial statements at face value. But thanks to advances in accounting, even beginners can get pretty comfortable extracting and massaging the information they need to perform fundamental analysis. If you want more detail on the nitty-gritty of accounting, check out *Reading Financial Reports For Dummies* (Wiley).

Fundamental analysts spend quite a bit of time looking at companies' financial statements, as you'll learn in Part II of this book. But skilled fundamental analysts do more than just pick apart financial statements. After all, if that's all it was, fundamental analysis would be synonymous with accounting. Fundamental analysts use their findings to make investment decisions.

Following the money

One of the basic rules of investigative journalism is following the money. Tracing the movement of dollars through an organization will quickly show you the motives of the leaders, availability of resources, and vulnerabilities. Regulators will often follow the movement of money to pinpoint illegal cartels, Ponzi schemes, and other frauds.

All this might sound very cloak-and-dagger. But there's something to be learned from approaching fundamental analysis with the mind of an investigator. Your job is to take available information and attempt to dig up data yourself to get a complete picture of a company and whether or not it's a suitable place for you to entrust your money. Following the way money moves through a company will tell you more about it than just about anything else.

While no two companies are the same, the basics of business are universal. That's why fundamental analysis is such a powerful tool you can apply to high-tech companies, low-tech companies, and everything in between.

Companies are merely in the business of selling things they acquire for more than what they paid. Sounds simple. But that can be easy to forget after you get mired in details like profit margins, earnings per share, and P-E ratios.

The trade cycle begins with a business idea, but more specifically when a company raises money so it can buy the equipment it needs to get started. Money might be raised by borrowing it, called *debt,* or by lining up investors willing to bet their money for a piece of future profits, called *equity.* The money raised is then used to acquire raw materials, office space, or whatever the company needs.

Next, the company tries to add value to the raw materials in some way and sell the product to customers. Typically, companies will also incur *indirect costs,* or overhead, to make all this happen. Overhead costs include everything from advertising, to research and development, to hiring skilled managers.

Now here's where fundamental analysis comes in. A few questions a fundamental analyst might ask when taking a look at a company:

- ✔ After factoring in all the costs, did the company make money?
- ✔ How much money did the company raise to get started?
- ✔ Is the company able to maintain itself without borrowing more or getting more investors?
- ✔ Can the company create new products to keep buyers coming back?
- ✔ Are competitors catching onto the idea and selling a similar product for less?

What Fundamental Analysis Isn't

Fundamental analysis is a well-known way of choosing investments. It's often the preferred method taught in business schools, largely due to its roots in things that can be measured and understood. But it's not, by any means, the only method of choosing stocks.

If you're still a little foggy on what fundamental analysis is, comparing it with other ways of evaluating investments might clear things up for you.

How fundamental analysis stacks up against index investing

If fundamental analysis seems like a lot of work, you can probably identify with *index investors*. Index investors think taking the time to pore over companies' financial statements is a whole lot of trouble for nothing. Index investors figure any information to be gleaned from company reports has already been extracted by other investors and acted upon.

For instance, if a company's stock was truly undervalued, other investors will have already recognized it and bought the stock. If enough investors buy a stock, they push the price up, and the shares are no longer undervalued. And thanks to the proliferation of electronic investing, analysts and investment firms with access to instantaneous information feeds can make such trading moves very quickly.

For that reason, index investors think trying to buy and sell stocks at just the right time, or use market timing, is impossible. In addition, index investors say that if there is an edge to fundamental analysis, it's wiped out by the cost and time consumed digging out the information. For that reason, index investors skip the fundamental analysis, and instead:

 ✔ **Diversify:** Rather than trying to pick the companies and stocks that will do best, fundamental analysts buy small stakes in as many stocks as possible. Generally, index investors will buy mutual funds that own hundreds, if not thousands, of stocks. That way, if any one company stumbles badly, the loss is very small as a percentage of the portfolio.

 ✔ **Buy index funds:** Since index investors don't think fundamental analysis gives investors an edge, they don't see any reason to pay a mutual fund manager to pick stocks for them. Instead, they buy mutual funds that own all the stocks in popular stock indexes, such as the Dow Jones industrial average or Standard & Poor's 500. The Dow mirrors the ups and downs of 30 large, well-known companies, and the S&P 500 measures the market's performance using 500 of the largest companies' shares.

 ✔ **Focus on costs:** Index investors assume the best way to make money in the stock market is by keeping costs low. Index funds generally have low expenses. And rather than spend personal time researching stocks, index investors generally buy a diversified basket of stocks and then forget about the holdings.

Comparing fundamental analysis with technical analysis

Like index investors, investors who use technical analysis shake their heads in disapproval when they see fundamental analysts poring over spreadsheets and financial statements. They, like index investors, see all the effort that goes into fundamental analysis as a waste of time and calculator batteries. That's because technical analysts assume that any information worth knowing is reflected in a stock price.

But technical analysts agree with fundamental analysts in one important way: They, too, think it's possible to beat the stock market. Unlike index investors, who think that timing the market is futile, technical analysts think stock prices move up and down in observable patterns. Knowing how to recognize patterns in stock price movements can signal a technical analyst the best times to get in, and out, of stocks. Technical analysts may not even care what a company does, since they're just looking at the price chart. To a technical analyst, buying and selling at the right time is more important than buying and selling the right stock. Technical analysts pay close attention to:

- **Stock price charts:** Technical analysts focus on stock price charts, which are graphs that plot a stock's movement over a period of time. These charts will show instantly whether a stock is rising or falling in addition to how many trades, or *volume,* are occurring.

- **Trading patterns:** Much as an astronomer sees patterns of stars in the sky, technical analysts look for stock price movements that follow a pattern. For instance, if a stock price falls to a low level, rises a bit, and sinks back down to near that same low level, technical analysts call that a *support level.* A support is considered a point where demand for a stock is strong enough to stop it from sinking much further.

- **Moving averages:** Technical analysts often pay close attention to a stock's average price over a period of time, say 200 days. When a stock falls below its 200-day moving average, or its average price over the past 200 days, that means the stock is vulnerable to fall further, technicians say. The idea is that when stocks fall below their 200-day-moving average, many investors who bought in within the past year are losing money and may be nervous and quick to sell.

Using Fundamental Analysis

If you ever see the library of a fundamental analyst, it can be a pretty intimidating sight. Inevitably, there will be a copy of *Security Analysis* (McGraw-Hill), a 766-page tome stuffed with gnarly formulas and arcane wording that makes your high-school algebra book look like a comic book. There will also be dog-eared copies of books with words like "value," "financial statements," and "ratios." You will see *Fundamental Analysis For Dummies* on the shelf as well. Shameless plug, I know.

Fundamental analysis has the rap of being for people who wouldn't be caught dead without a pen, mechanical pencil, and calculator in their shirt pocket. But even if you don't walk around carrying such instruments, you too, can benefit from fundamental analysis. With an understanding of a few terms and basic techniques, fundamental analysis is within reach if you're interested and willing to put in a bit of time.

Who knows, maybe after reading this book you'll want to dig deeper into fundamental analysis? After all, fundamental analysis is a bit like art: As you learn a little you naturally get curious and want to learn more. And financial analysis can get very detailed and precise.

How difficult is fundamental analysis?

Contrary to popular belief, you don't need to be a math wizard to use fundamental analysis. Most of the math you'll use is pretty basic arithmetic. And there's no need to memorize formulas, since I'll put most of the important ones all together for you in Chapter 8. You will need to know how to build some *financial models,* which try to forecast how much profit a company will make in the future. But to help you out, I'll point out some online tools and calculators to crunch some of the more tricky stuff for you.

Some of the more advanced techniques of fundamental analysis might require you to fire up a spreadsheet. If you want to get up to speed, Microsoft provides free help and tutorials for its Excel spreadsheet program at www.office. microsoft.com/en-us/excel. You might also take a look at *Excel 2007 For Dummies* (Wiley).

Is fundamental analysis for you?

If you're tired of trusting other people to tell you how a company is doing financially, you're a prime candidate for fundamental analysis. Most likely, you might find yourself buying investments on a hunch or whim, only to find out later the company had some serious problems you didn't know about. The whole premise of fundamental analysis is to reduce, if not eliminate, speculation and wild guesswork from investing. Fundamental analysis is rooted in the idea that you want to look at cold, hard data to make informed decisions on why an investment might be worth buying.

Above all, fundamental analysis is ideal for people who want to approach an investment fully informed of the risks and with their eyes wide open. An in-depth fundamental analysis on a stock will not only alert you to potentially troubling trends at a company, but also give you clues to whether a stock may be overvalued by investors who aren't paying attention. An overvalued company is one that commands a stock price that well exceeds any possible profit it could generate for investors.

In many ways, fundamental analysis is as much about helping you avoid poor investments as much as it about helping you find good ones.

The risks of fundamental analysis

Fundamental analysis, while it's rooted in math and objective information, isn't without its flaws. After all, if fundamental analysis was perfect, everyone would quit their day jobs, analyze stocks, and make bundles of money. That's why it's important to understand the shortcomings of fundamental analysis, which include:

- ✔ **Vulnerability to wrong data, including your assumptions:** Fundamental analysis is heavily based in fact. But if a company incorrectly reports data or you misinterpret them, you're going to have a false conclusion. Miscalculations are especially likely when making assumptions about things like a company's future growth rate, future interest rates, or profits.

- ✔ **Overreliance on past data:** Perhaps the biggest knock against fundamental analysis is how much stock it puts in a company's past performance. There is some truth to that, since numbers companies report can be a month or more old. However, true fundamental analysis uses historical numbers to make an educated guess about the future.

- ✔ **Bad timing:** Let's say you do all the homework in researching a stock. You find a stock that appears to be a screaming buy, so you buy it. Guess what? A stock can remain a screaming buy for many years or even decades until investors come to the same conclusion. Fundamental analysts often have to be wrong for a long time before making money.

- ✔ **Betting against the market:** If you buy a stock because you think it's a steal, you're in effect betting against thousands of the most sophisticated trading desks around the world with access to the same data. If you think a stock is too cheap, you're making the gamble that other investors are missing something you can see.

✔ **Concentrated positions:** If you're going to the trouble to meticulously study a company, you're going to want to make sure you're positioned to profit if you're right. Unless you have a team of analysts working for you, when you find a stock that fits your fundamental criteria, you're going to want to own a large chunk of it. As a result, investors who use fundamental analysis may have large exposure to individual companies.

This concept contradicts the idea of *diversification,* which is owning hundreds and hundreds of small pieces of many companies. With diversification, you're spreading your risk over many companies so if one has a problem, it doesn't hurt so badly. Fundamental analysts, though, think that owning just a few investments that you know inside and out is actually safer than owning everything.

Making Money with Fundamental Analysis

Face it. You're probably not reading this book because you have a deep yearning to understand how to read and analyze company information. You're looking to dig into company reports for a reason, which is most likely to make money.

Fundamental analysis can be profitable. If you're able to find hidden value in a company or its stock and buy in before other investors discover what you know, you'll cash in once the rest of Wall Street catches up to you.

Putting a price tag on a stock or bond

If you've ever wondered whether a stock is "cheap" or "pricey," fundamental analysis can be a big help. Fundamental analysis helps you understand exactly what you're getting when you buy an investment.

Here's an example to help you see what I mean. Let's say you have the opportunity to buy a tree that literally grows dollar bills. How much should you pay for the tree? You might be tempted to pay millions of dollars, especially if others have their wallets out and start bidding.

But, fundamental analysis can help you intelligently put a price tag on this amazing plant. By asking some questions and doing some due diligence, you can actually arrive at a correct price. The farmer tells you the tree grows 20 one-dollar bills every month. He also says the tree will likely die in a year and then stop growing money. Lastly, the farmer promises to pay you $20 a month if, for any reason, the tree stops growing money in less than a year.

Knowing these fundamental details, the tree can be priced. You now know the tree is expected to generate about $240. So, is the tree worth $240? Not so far. Remember, the tree won't grow the $240 right away. You have to wait a year to get the whole wad of cash. Because you have to wait a year to get the $240, the tree is worth less than $240. So if there's a bidding war for the tree that drives the price over $240, you know to walk away based on your fundamental research.

Being profitable by being a "contrarian"

Being a successful fundamental analyst can be pretty lonely. If you're trying to make money from studying a company and determine the company is worth more than its stock price, you're betting that other investors bidding for the stock are wrong.

Fundamental analysis, therefore, is at odds with the *efficient market theory*. Efficient market theory says that trying to beat the market by picking winning stocks is futile. The *strong form* of the efficient market theory says that all information that's knowable about a company is reflected in a company's stock price. So, let's say that after reading this book you dig through a company's financial statements and find that a company has great prospects. Efficient market theory would suggest that you're not the first person to discover this, and that other investors have already bid the stock up with the same information.

But before you throw your hands up and give up on fundamental analysis, there are some caveats to the efficient market theory worth noting. Most importantly, while stocks may reflect all information over the long term, there can be short-term periods when prices might excessively rise or fall due to extreme and fleeting optimism or pessimism. For instance, many high-technology stocks skyrocketed during the late 1990s, as investors bid up share prices on the idea that they'd be worth a fortune in the future. Fundamental analysts, looking at the fact many of the companies didn't make money and never would, avoided the dot-com bubble. Eventually, the fundamentals caught up to them and many of the stocks collapsed 90% or more. In some cases, the companies completely failed.

To profit from fundamental analysis, you have to be comfortable going against the crowd — or in Wall Street parlance — being a contrarian. When other investors are overly enthusiastic about a stock, they bid the price so high that it's practically impossible for anyone to make money.

The Fundamental Analysis Toolbox

One of the great things about fundamental analysis is that you don't really need much to get started. If you have a computer and calculator, you're pretty much set.

Unlike technical analysis, which may require sophisticated and costly stock chart services, most of the data you need for fundamental analysis is provided free from nearly every company. Plus, many free online services offer increasingly detailed access to company financial data, making it easy for you to download and analyze. There are three key financial documents that are the cornerstone of financial analysis: the income statement, balance sheet, and statement of cash flows.

Introducing the income statement

Want to know how much a company made or lost during a year or a quarter? The income statement is for you. This financial statement steps you through all the money a company brought in and how much it spent to make that money. If you've ever read news stories about how much a company earned during a quarter, for instance, the information was taken off the company's income statement.

The income statement is the financial statement containing data you probably hear the most about, including revenue, net income, and earnings per share. You can find out more about reading this important document in Chapter 5.

Balance-sheet basics

Want to know how much money a company has or how much it owes to others? That's where the balance sheet comes in. This financial statement spells out all the cash a company has in addition to its debt. The difference between what a company owns (its *assets*) and what it owes (its *liabilities*) is its *equity*. Expressed slightly differently, the basic formula that applies to the balance sheet is:

Assets = Liabilities + Equity

Sometimes it's helpful to understand corporate-finance jargon by putting it in personal-finance terms. If you've ever calculated your personal net worth by subtracting all your loans from all your savings, you've essentially created a balance sheet.

Getting the mojo of cash flows

One of the first things fundamental analysts need to understand is that earnings aren't necessarily cash. Accounting rules, for instance, allow companies to include in their earnings sales from products they haven't actually collected from customers yet. Yes, you read that right. A company might say it earned $100 million, even though it hasn't collected a dime from customers. This method of accounting, called *accrual accounting,* is done for a good reason. Accrual accounting lets analysts see more accurately how much it cost a company to generate sales.

But accrual accounting makes it critical for investors to monitor not just a company's earnings, but how much cash it brings in. The statement of cash flows holds a company's feet to the fire and requires it to disclose how much cold hard cash is coming into the company. The statement of cash flows lets you see how much cash a company generated from its primary business operations. The statement, though, also lets you see how much cash a company brought in from lenders and investors.

Familiarizing yourself with financial ratios (including the P-E)

While the financial statements are enormously valuable to financial analysts, they only go so far. Not only do companies tend to only give the information they're required to, the data can only tell you so much. You didn't expect companies to do everything for you, right? That's how financial ratios can be very important.

Financial ratios take different numbers from the income statement, balance sheet and statement of cash flows, and compare them with each other. You'll be amazed at what you can find out about a company by mixing numbers from different statements. Financial ratios can provide great insight when applied to analysis.

There are dozens of helpful financial ratios, which you can read about in more detail in Chapter 8. But at this point, you'll just want to know the basic flavors and ratios and what they tell you, including:

✔ **Valuation:** If you've ever heard of the price-to-earnings ratio, or P-E, you've used a financial ratio. The P-E is one of many *valuation ratios.* Valuation ratios help fundamental analysts find out if a stock is cheap or expensive by comparing the stock price to a basic piece of data about a company. For instance, the P-E ratio compares a stock's price to its earnings. The higher the P-E, the more richly valued a stock is.

✔ **Financial health:** If a company is no longer a going concern and isn't functioning, it's not a great idea to invest in it. Some ratios, called *liquidity ratios,* measure how easily a company is able to keep up with its bills. Fundamental analysts will look for red flags that a company might be about to face some tough times.

✔ **Return on investment:** If you're going to give your money to a company, either as a loan or investment, you want to make sure you're getting something in return. Return on investment ratios help you determine how well the company is putting your money to work.

✔ **Operating performance:** The more a company can increase its sales, while at the same time lower costs, the more profitable it is. This balancing act is the essence of business. And the stakes for investors are huge, since the more profit a company generates, the bigger piece of the pie that's left for investors. Operating performance ratios let you quickly see how well a company is managing its costs and increasing sales.

Chapter 3

Gaining an Upper Hand on Wall Street: Why Fundamental Analysis Gives Investors an Edge

• •

In This Chapter

▶ Finding out how fundamental analysis can turn you into a better investor

▶ Discovering how some of the best investors put fundamental analysis to use

▶ Uncovering clues on when to buy or sell a stock

▶ Applying fundamental analysis to buy-and-hold investment strategies

• •

*F*undamental analysis isn't the easiest way to invest. There's a bit of math involved. You'll need to learn some terms. And to perform fundamental analysis, you need to ferret out and analyze somewhat arcane pieces of financial information.

Why go to all this trouble? That's the question you'll find the answer to in this chapter. You'll discover why the rigors of fundamental analysis, and the ultimate goal of not overpaying for stocks and finding cheap stocks to buy, can help you obtain better long-term success in investing. Meanwhile, you'll see how some basic fundamental analysis can help you avoid making mistakes that will be difficult to recover from.

Of course, no discussion of fundamental analysis is complete without exploring its best-known master: Warren Buffett. Buffett is a hero in investing, thanks to his discipline and long-term ability to find and hold companies with attractive fundamental characteristics.

Finally, in this chapter, you get a general taste of how fundamental analysis can give you cues on when you might consider buying or selling stocks. No method will work 100 percent all the time, but fundamental analysis can at least provide a guide and keep you from getting caught up in stock manias and bubbles.

Better Investing with Fundamentals

One of the biggest strengths of fundamental analysis is the fact it attempts to help you keep the emotion out of investing. While *momentum investors* chase after the hottest stocks hoping they'll go higher, and *day traders* buy and sell every few minutes looking for a quick buck, fundamental analysis is more of a data-driven discipline.

Fundamental analysts analyze investments by examining the business that's behind a stock or bond. Even if you're just looking to buy a few shares of a company, you approach the analysis with the same level of research, or *due diligence,* as if you're thinking about buying the whole company. Fundamental analysis lets you approach a stock as an investor, not a speculator.

Investors look to buy a stock because they believe the underlying company will generate profits in the future that exceed the price they're paying. Speculators look to make money on an investment by simply finding someone else to sell it to for a higher price.

The careful consideration of a company's fundamentals, such as revenue and earnings, is a key distinction of this approach from other methods of choosing investments. The name fundamental analysis really says it all, as the approach gets down to the most basic aspects of a business, including the trade cycle, which is discussed in Chapter 2.

Fundamental analysis is generally connected with *value investors.* Value investors tend to buy stocks they think are *undervalued,* or have stock prices below what they think the company is actually worth. But fundamental analysis can help you no matter how you invest. Perhaps you're a *technical analyst,* who studies stock charts to find stocks to buy. Maybe you're an *index investor,* who buys all the stocks in a broad stock market index, such as the Standard & Poor's 500. No matter what kind of investing you prefer, fundamental analysis can help you find suitable stocks and investments.

Picking stocks for fundamental reasons

Value investors are often drawn to the idea that they can get an edge on other investors by doing their homework and studying a company's financial statements. These investors believe if they put in the time to understand a company's business, accurately forecast its future, and pay the right price, they can achieve greater upside and less downside than the market as a whole.

There's some truth to this. Academic studies have shown that stocks that are cheap, or value priced, tend to have strong long-term performance.

Fundamental analysis can also help you protect yourself from your own speculative juices. By studying the cold hard numbers of a company's business, you can get a strong dose of reality while other investors get caught up in the hype surrounding a particular stock. Since fundamental analysis is based in the laws of business, it can give you a greater perspective on how much an investment is worth.

Many investors puzzle over how the price of a stock is determined. Knowing this is a key to seeing how fundamental analysis can help you.

A stock's price is determined by an auction, very similar to how the price on a Pez dispenser is set on eBay. Investors buy and sell stocks every trading day, pushing the price up and down based on how optimistic or pessimistic they are about a company's future potential. Just as you can see a bidding war erupt over a Pez dispenser and push its value to extreme highs, the same can occur for a stock if many investors are willing to buy it.

A great example of how fundamental analysis can help you spot a frenzy over a stock, causing its price to get out of line, occurred in March 2000. Shares of Palm Computing, a maker of the popular Palm electronic organizer (remember those?), soared 150% in their first day of trading to more than $95 a share. At that price, investors put a total price tag of $54.3 billion on the company and its 23 million shares.

Just a little bit of fundamental sleuthing could have protected investors from the coming brutal collapse in the stock. Here's how. Palm Computing was 95% owned by its parent company, 3Com, at the time. And the entire value of 3Com, including its 95% stock in Palm Computing, was just $28 billion. So why would investors be willing to pay nearly twice as much for a piece of 3Com? It's kind of like paying $20 for a slice of pie when you can buy the whole pie for $10. Fundamental analysts knew something was a little off. And they were right. The stock lost more than 70% of its value in just seven months.

Uses for the index investor

Index investors don't try to pick individual stocks or time the market. Index investors buy a broad basket of investments and hold it for a long period of time (see Chapter 2 for more on index investors). Many index investors think trying to choose stocks that will outperform the broad market is extremely difficult, if not impossible. As a result, index investors buy small stakes of hundreds of companies, so that trouble at any one firm won't hurt much.

Why the "three factors" matter

It's rare that academic research can make you money. But one of the most influential pieces of academic research ever written about investing is certainly worth your time.

Professors Eugene Fama and Kenneth French found that nearly 95 percent of stock price movements are explained by just three things, two of which are determined by a company's fundamentals. The three factors that move stocks are:

- **Market risk:** Movements of the broad economy have a large sway on how individual stocks perform.

- **Size:** Shares of smaller companies measured by *market value* tend to beat the stock market, in part, because they are riskier and less established. Market value, also called market capitalization or market cap, measures the total price Wall Street assigns to a company by multiplying a stock price by the total number of its shares outstanding. You can find out more about market capitalization later in this chapter.

- **Price or value:** The lower a stock's price, relative to its book value, the better it tends to do relative to the rest of the stock market. Book value is a key aspect of fundamental analysis, as you'll read about in Chapter 8.

Index investors may often say fundamental analysis is a waste of time. Even so, many index investors apply some aspects of fundamental analysis. For instance, index investors routinely choose to invest in baskets of either *value* stocks or *growth* stocks. Value stocks are those that are largely ignored by investors and command low stock prices relative to their fundamentals, such as profits or asset values. Growth stocks, on the other hand, are the darlings of Wall Street and demand huge stock prices compared to their fundamentals.

In addition, index investors regularly parcel money between shares of large companies and small companies. These measures of size, again, are rooted in fundamental analysis.

You'll notice that even an index investor might boost returns by paying attention to fundamental factors. If you want to measure a company's market value, you'll need its number of shares outstanding, which comes from the balance sheet. Likewise, a stock's book value comes from its balance sheet.

Assisting technical analysts

Like fundamental analysts, technical analysts think they can beat the stock market by picking the right stocks at the right time. But unlike fundamental analysis, technical analysis calls for a close study of stock price movements over time.

Still, technical analysts can benefit from fundamental analysis, too. For instance, some technical analysts might look for companies that are increasing their revenue or earnings growth each quarter. This information is found on a company's income statement. Similarly, technical analysts might look for the best company in an industry by looking for companies with the most attractive financial ratios.

Dooming your portfolio by paying too much

No matter what type of investor you are, there are several absolutes. Here's one of them: If you overpay for a stock, you're accepting a sentence of poor returns in the future. Your return on a stock is a function of how much you pay for it. By definition, the more you pay for an investment, the lower your return will be.

Imagine you have the opportunity to buy a Laundromat. The Laundromat has been open for 30 years, and in each of those years, it generates a profit of $100,000. Since the Laundromat is in a strip mall that will close in five years, you figure the business will generate $500,000 in profit over the years and then will be shut down.

To keep this example simple, forget about the role of *inflation,* or the decreasing value of money each year, at this point. Also assume that your estimate was correct, and the Laundromat generated $100,000 a year in profit.

Just imagine what would happen if you offered to buy this Laundromat for $200,000. Your gain would be 150%. You know this because your profit is $300,000 because that's the difference between the Laundromat's earnings ($500,000) and what you paid ($200,000). Your return is your profit of $300,000 divided by the price you paid, $200,000.

Now, what if you got into a bidding war with another person interested in buying the Laundromat? In the heat of the moment, you offered to buy the business for $400,000 instead of $200,000. Your return will take a big hit, now equaling 25%. Nothing changed with the Laundromat. It will function the same whether you paid $400,000 or $200,000. But your return is now the profit of $100,000 divided by your purchase price of $400,000.

The same goes for investments, including stocks and bonds. If you increase the amount you pay for a share of stock, for instance, you eat into your return.

Overpaying for a stock is even more dangerous than increasing your offer for the Laundromat. If a company you invest in suffers a slowdown and its earnings are smaller than expected, you'll find your return to be very small, or you may not get back what you invested.

Sitting through short-term volatility

Sometimes the excitement of daily market activity can get intoxicating. Ticker symbols scrolling at the bottom of the TV screen during financial shows can make you feel as if the markets are constantly moving and changing. And that's true; markets are constantly moving as investors trade shares back and forth and push stock prices up and down.

But a fundamental analysis can help you block out a great deal of this noise and be a better investor as a result. An example is perhaps with your house. Imagine buying a home for $200,000, which you know is worth that much. After having an appraiser look at the condition of the roof, remodeled kitchen and bath as well as looking at the prices of identical homes in the area, you have a pretty good idea of what the house is worth.

With this in mind, would you panic if you were sitting on the patio while a person walking by randomly offered you $100,000 for the home? Probably not. After all, you know the home is worth more than $100,000. Besides, you're not in the market to sell anyway.

Still, that's what stock investors commonly do when they pay too much attention to day-to-day movements in stock prices. They may have felt great about buying a stock for $10 a share, but if the stock falls to $8 a month later, they panic and wonder if they should sell.

One of the mantras of fundamental analysis comes from Benjamin Graham, the pioneer of the methods and mentor to Warren Buffett. Fundamental analysts will often say the market is a voting machine in the short term, but a weighing machine in the long run. In other words, stock prices can be kicked dramatically higher or lower in the short term. But over the longer term, the underlying value of a company will prevail, and its true heft will be recognized.

Fundamental analysis helps you focus on a investment's true value, or weight, using Benjamin Graham's analogy. If you know you correctly analyzed a company and assigned the correct value to it, then you don't need to be as concerned about whether or not a company is popular or not in any given day, month, or year. Having a fundamental grasp of a company gives you the peace of mind to hold an investment for a long period of time and resist the urge to sell at the wrong time.

Relying on the Basic Info the Pros Use

It's natural to think successful fundamental analysts have some kind of secret that's beyond the reach of regular investors. Looking at the long-term success of Warren Buffett, for instance, makes you think perhaps he has a super-computer that's able to forecast the future. Similarly, many analysts who study companies have deep insights about their businesses, which might lead you to think they have access to data you don't.

But here's the truth. Fundamental analysts, with a few exceptions, are using all the same financial statements you have access to. Even the professionals are looking at all the same things I'll show you in this book such as:

- ✓ **The financial statements:** The income statement, balance sheet, statement of cash flows and ratios are the cornerstone of the analysis done by most fundamental analysts.

- ✓ **The financial ratios:** These seemingly simple calculations put the numbers in the financial statements into perspective. That perspective helps you determine if stocks are cheap or expensive.

- ✓ **Industry analysis:** Understanding the dynamics of the industry a company is in can help you do a better job investing.

- ✓ **Economic analysis:** Investments can swing in value based largely on how the broad economy is doing. The influence of the economy became clear in 2008, when shares of companies having nothing to do with sub-prime loans were dragged down with the financial debacle.

Clearly, the pros do have distinct advantages. The large firms may employ armies of research experts to pore over the financial statements, allowing them to trade while you're still downloading the results. And some of the professional systems make fundamental analysis easier by automatically calculating growth trends and the financial ratios. Finally, experience can be a big help in helping a fundamental analyst spot things that a beginner might miss.

What is the "Warren Buffett Way"?

For many fundamental analysts, Warren Buffett is the ultimate role model. And there's no denying his success. For instance, shares of Buffett's Berkshire Hathaway rose from $70,000 a share to $96,600 in the ten years ending December 2008 — an impressive 38% gain. During that same time period, the Russell 3000 index, which measures the performance of the stock market in general, lost 0.8% in value including dividends, according to Russell Investments. His longer-term record is strong, too. No wonder Buffett is called the Oracle of Omaha.

Trying to figure out Buffett's secret is the investment world's equivalent of the search for the Holy Grail. Scores of investors make the pilgrimage to Berkshire Hathaway shareholder meetings in Omaha each year, trying to figure out how Buffett does it. Hour-long lunches with Buffett auction off on eBay for hundreds of thousands of dollars. And there are countless books on Buffett, most notably *The Warren Buffett Way* (Wiley).

Interestingly, though, Buffett doesn't make much of a secret of his techniques. Every year, in his letter to shareholders and also in Berkshire Hathaway's "Owner's Manual" he paints a picture of his approach. And much of his approach is based in key elements of fundamental analysis, including:

- **Invest as an owner, not a trader.** Buffett is very clear that he looks at an investment not as a short-term trade, but a long-term relationship. Berkshire Hathaway will often invest in a company and hold it for a very long time, perhaps never selling the position. "Regardless of price, we have no interest at all in selling any good businesses that Berkshire owns," according to Berkshire's Owner's Manual.

- **Consider carefully a company's intrinsic value.** Buffet repeatedly discusses *intrinsic value,* which is a measure of what a company is truly worth. Intrinsic value is how much cash a company is expected to generate over its lifetime, which is a good measure of what it's worth. Buying a stock for less than its intrinsic value gives you a bit of a margin of safety. You'll find out how to calculate a company's intrinsic value in Chapter 11.

- **Analyze management.** Buffett routinely says even a seemingly ho-hum company can generate dazzling returns with a good management team at the helm. For that reason, Buffett will often leave the top officers and directors of a company in place, even after buying a company.

- **Stick with businesses you understand.** The better you grasp how a company makes its money and operates, the more informed you'll be after reviewing its financial statements. You'll also know better what to look for, since every industry and company has unique financial traits.

- **Find businesses that have a real advantage.** In capitalism, if a company has a good idea, other firms will try to copy it and steal away market share. Buffett combats that by investing in businesses with a strong brand or unique product, such as Coca-Cola.

Investors who want to ride Buffett's coattails could just invest in Berkshire Hathaway. But given his successful long-term investing record, it's not surprising there's an industry out of helping investors mimic him. There are more than 4,000 books with Buffett's name in the title, according to Amazon.com.

Others try to mimic what Buffett does. There's a mutual fund called the Wisdom Fund, which attempts to mirror Buffett's investments. Still others try to figure out what Buffett is investing in by reading Berkshire Hathaway's *annual report,* a document that discloses all the firm's large holdings.

It's never a good idea to blindly buy stocks just because another investor did. Still, reviewing the stocks that pass Buffett's fundamental analysis might be a good place to start. The list of Berkshire Hathaway's holdings in publicly traded companies can be found at www.buffettsecrets.com.

Blindly following moves of top investors isn't an instant route to riches. That's especially the case when trying to take cues from Buffett. Buffett constantly reminds his shareholders that he plans to hold investments for a long time. And his holdings can also suffer large losses. For instance, had you bought Tesco at the beginning of 2008 after seeing it was a top holding at the end of 2007, you would have suffered a 75% loss.

Checking in on Graham and Dodd

As much as Buffett is revered and admired, he, too was a student of fundamental analysis. Buffett has utilized and perfected the tools of professors Benjamin Graham and David Dodd, who are discussed at more length below. Graham and Dodd, whose names are synonymous with a method of investing called value investing, trace their roots to Columbia University, which Buffett attended.

The origins of value investing

Value investing, along with the work of Graham and Dodd, is usually central to the work of fundamental analysis. Graham and Dodd explained that a stock is really a claim on the cash a company is expected to generate in the future, or its intrinsic value, as referred to above. Just know that if a stock is trading for:

- Less than the cash it will generate, then it's *undervalued* and may be bought.

- More than the value of cash a company is expected to churn out, it's *overvalued.*

Using fundamentals to see when a stock is priced right

But Graham and Dodd took things a bit further than just weighing whether stocks were over or undervalued. Other lessons from Graham and Dodd worth noting include:

- **Protecting yourself.** Buy stocks well below what they are worth, or their intrinsic value. This extra cushion gives you a *margin of safety* in case the business runs into trouble and the stock price falls further.

- **Investing isn't necessarily speculating.** While it's tempting to think of Wall Street as a giant casino, Graham and Dodd explained that wasn't necessarily the case. If you're buying stocks with little information about the companies' business, then yes, you're betting or speculating. When you speculate, you bet you can sell the stock to someone else for more. But with fundamental analysis, you can become more of an investor by understanding what you paid and what you can expect to receive in exchange.

- **Being cautious of companies with excessive debt.** Companies that borrow heavily to finance their operations may face onerous debt payments during difficult economies.

Figuring Out When to Buy or Sell a Stock

Most investors are frustrated by the difficulty of getting the timing just right. Even professional investors complain that while it's hard enough trying to find the right investment and buy it at a good price, it's even harder to know when to sell. Fundamental analysis can help you with this because you'll learn how to estimate what a company is worth. As discussed above, knowing what a company is worth is very helpful, since you'll know whether the current stock price is higher or lower than what you think the company's value is.

On the flip side, the discipline of fundamental analysis can help you evaluate when you might want to sell a stock. If a stock price is well below what you think the stock is worth, why would you sell at that price unless you had to?

Looking beyond the per-share price

Many investors get obsessed with the per-share price of a stock. It's easy to understand why. When you buy a slice of pizza, for instance, you might not think to calculate how much, based on the per-slice price, how much you're paying for the entire pie.

But one of the basic premises of fundamental investing is just that. You want to know how much you're paying for your slice of a company, and how that compares to what it's really worth. And if there's one aspect of fundamental analysis you can use immediately from this chapter, it's that the per-share price of a stock, by itself, doesn't tell you much.

Just looking at a company's per-share price can lead you to make incorrect judgments. Some investors, for instance, have puzzled over how shares of Visa could trade for less than $60 a share while rival MasterCard commands a price of more than $160 a share, since Visa processes more credit card transactions than MasterCard does. You might assume Visa is a better value than MasterCard, especially since MasterCard is a smaller company than Visa in terms of revenue. You will learn more about using revenue to compare the sizes of companies in Chapter 6.

Fundamental analysis, though, will show you that Visa's lower per-share price doesn't mean it's a screaming buy. And that's due to the use of market value, perhaps the most basic thing fundamental analysts consider. Market value tells you how much investors are paying for an entire company based on the price of the single share of stock. Using the pizza metaphor, market value tells you what the price of the whole pizza is, based on the price of one slice. You can apply this information immediately to stocks, by using this formula:

Market value = share price × number of shares outstanding

The key parts of market value are:

- ✔ **Share price:** How much investors are willing to pay for a slice of ownership in a company. You can get a company's share price from many sources, ranging from your online brokerage firm, investing Web sites or in the business section of your newspaper.

- ✔ **Number of shares outstanding:** The number of slices, or shares, a company's value is cut into. The number of shares outstanding is available in a company's balance sheet, as described more fully in Chapter 6.

Applying market value to Visa and MasterCard reveals much more than simply looking at their share prices does. The analysis shows that despite its lower per-share price, Visa is actually the company with the bigger total value. You figure this out by:

Calculating market value of Visa:

$60 a share price × 846 million shares = $50.8 billion

Calculating market value of MasterCard:

$160 a share price × 129.2 million shares = $20.7 billion

You can see that investors are in fact paying a greater amount for Visa than MasterCard. Whether or not they're paying too much is another question and something you can explore in more detail in Chapter 8. But at this point, it's important to understand how fundamental analysis goes well beyond just taking a look at a company's share price.

Seeing how a company's fundamentals and its price may get out of alignment

You don't need a long memory to remember how fundamental analysis could have helped your investing. During the tech-stock boom of the late 1990s, investors were so enamored with dot-coms, they were willing to pay boundless amounts for them. And just a few years later, in the mid-2000s, a housing boom drove up shares of homebuilders' stocks. What's remarkable is that there were two massive bubbles in just one decade. Fundamental analysis could have helped you sidestep the intense pain after both these bubbles inevitably burst.

Academics argue over why bubbles and manias occur with investing. And you can leave that heady discussion to them. Just know that sometimes, over-enthusiasm for stocks can drive their prices, albeit temporarily, to levels that aren't justified by their underlying businesses. Fundamental analysis is one way to try to see when a bubble is forming and try to profit from it.

 Even masters of fundamental analysis have difficulty timing bubbles just right. Many analysts had warned that tech-stocks were overvalued in 1998, for instance. These investors had to bear being wrong and missing out on huge gains as tech stocks continued to soar in 1999 and early 2000.

Investors who pay attention to company fundamentals are often able to at least recognize when a bubble is forming. Weak fundamentals, for instance, were the tip-off for the dot-com bubble. More than a third of the 109 Internet companies that failed had business models that didn't bring in enough revenue or had costs too high to ever make a profit, according to Boston Consulting.

Fundamental analysis can help you recognize when stocks are rising too much, well beyond what's justified by their businesses. Investors will often become charmed by *story stocks*, or companies that seem to have boundless potential. Consider the rise of satellite radio. Like many investment ideas based on promise, the story was irresistible. Subscribers fed up with commercial-filled FM radio were rushing to sign up for monthly subscriptions that gave them thousands of crystal-clear radio stations from satellites. Even automakers were installing satellite radio players in cars. The growth of satellite radio companies looked unstoppable in 2000.

And most investors certainly took the bait. Sirius Satellite Radio's stock soared, racing to the point where it had a market value of $1.9 billion in 2000. While the company was losing money, it told investors customers were signing up at a rapid clip and that subscription fees would roll in. Meanwhile, the company continued to heavily spend on costly items, including paying personality Howard Stern $100 million a year for five years, plus issuing him nearly $200 million in stock. Investors continued to buy in.

But eventually, the investors who took the time to read the company's financial statements with horror were proven right. Eventually, Sirius bought rival XM Satellite in 2008, for form Sirius XM Radio, with hopes that it could gain an advantage through being larger. Still, fundamental analysts spotted two signs they routinely look for, including:

- **Lack of profit:** Even as the company grew, it continued to lose more and more money. Losses at the company continued to surge, swelling from $226 million in 2003 to $5.2 billion during the twelve months ended September 2008.

- **Large debt burden:** As of 2009, the company faced the prospect of a $1 billion pile of debt coming due. That's the corporate equivalent of your mortgage lender telling you that you have to pay your entire mortgage balance back next year.

Despite the glowing promises of the company, investors ended up suffering as those promises didn't pan out. The company's stock price collapsed 99% from the high in 2000 to less than 20 cents a share in February, as Sirius XM flirted with bankruptcy until receiving a costly bailout from Liberty Media. Fundamental analysis proved correct.

Using buy-and-hold strategies with fundamental analysis

You might be thinking that fundamental analysis sounds like a good idea, but fear that doing so might cause you to constantly change your opinion on a stock. After all, companies report their earnings each quarter, and the new data, in theory, could cause you to change your opinion on the stock.

But fundamental analysis doesn't require you to constantly buy and sell stocks. In fact, many investors tend to do their homework, buy a stock, and hold on. They realize that constantly buying and selling stocks can be hazardous for your portfolio because it may hurt you with:

✔ **Mounting trading costs:** Every time you buy or sell a stock, it costs you something. Certainly, you can reduce commissions by opening an account with a deep-discount online brokerage, as described in *Investing Online For Dummies* (Wiley). But the costs are still a factor, including ones you might not notice.

There are two prices for stocks, the *bid price* and the *ask price.* The ask is the price you must pay when you buy a stock. The bid is the price you get when you sell. The ask is always higher than the bid, just like the price you get for trading in a car to a dealer, the bid, is less than the price the dealer will resell the car for, or the ask. When you buy a stock, you're paying a hidden fee, which is the difference between the bid and ask, or the *spread.*

✔ **Unnecessary taxes:** Flipping in and out of stocks can end up making Uncle Sam rich. If you sell a stock for a profit before you've owned it at least a year, it's a *short-term capital gain.* Short-term capital gains are taxed at your ordinary income-tax rates, which can be up to 35%. On the other hand, if you hold onto a stock for more than a year and sell it, the highest tax rate you pay is 15%. By just holding on a little longer, you can save a bundle on taxes.

✔ **Mistakes:** It's tempting to think that you're never wrong. And after reading this book and applying fundamental analysis, you'll be more informed than many other investors. Still, it's easy to make a mistake if you sell too early.

Looking to the long term

While it's not always the case, investors who rely on fundamental analysis are often resigned to being patient. After all, when you're counting on the fact that the stock market and its scores of traders, portfolio managers, and other investors are wrong, you can't expect them to arrive at your way of thinking overnight.

Fundamental analysis often works best when paired with a *passive investing* strategy. With passive investing, you do all your homework, pick your stock, and then wait. The stock might fall further. But it's up to you to have the courage to trust your research and wait until other investors see what attracted you to the stock.

And because making money with fundamental analysis requires you to go against the crowd, you'll often need to buy the stock when you think others are wrong. A few of the times where stock prices might, temporarily, under-value a company include:

- **The wake of an accounting scandal:** When investors can no longer trust a management team because the financial statements have been falsi-fied, they might sell the stock indiscriminately. If the stock is adequately beaten down to a point where you feel the company's not being properly appreciated, there could be opportunity.

  Trying to buy a stock after it's been "cooking the books" is extremely dif-ficult. Since fundamental analysis is based on accurate financial account-ing, making a decision based on false information is complicated and beyond the scope of this book.

- **Amid pending litigation or liability claims:** Stocks will often trade at discounts, or below their true value, when investors are worried a com-pany might face massive claims. This has happened with companies involved in tobacco and asbestos.

- **Slowing growth:** When a company matures, it may see the rate of increase in revenue and earnings slow. When that happens, *growth investors,* who buy growth stocks, may dump the stock so they can move on to the new darling.

- **Industry shifts:** When there's a major disruption to an industry, the stocks in the group might get seriously punished. Following the credit crunch, for instance, stocks in the financial sector lost 58% of their value as a group in 2008. Certainly, not all banks and financial firms deserved to be punished that badly.

Being willing to step up and invest in a company others want nothing to do with can be lucrative. Beaten-down stocks that get rediscovered by investors can rally strongly.

For instance, investors had to be brave and confident enough to buy stock in Tyco in June 2002. The diversified industrial supply company was mired in a scandal pertaining to alleged accesses by its CEO, Dennis Kozlowski. But by the end of 2002, the value of the investment soared more than 250% as inves-tors figured they overestimated the trouble the company was in.

Patience isn't always a virtue

According to classic value investing, if you've done your fundamental analysis, you can practically buy your stocks and forget about them. Unless there's a

major change that warrants changing your opinion, which you can find out
about in Chapter 10, value investors hang on and wait for the market to wake
up. But the danger is, sometimes investors were right to dump the stock.

Overconfidence in fundamental analysis can turn a bad decision into a devastating one. The brutal decline suffered by Lucent shareholders is a classic
example. Lucent was born out of the technology arm of AT&T, which was
known for innovative patents for telecommunication and computing. Lucent,
considered a blue chip by many investors, routinely showed up on lists of the
most popular stocks with individual investors.

But the stock's downfall remains an example of the dangers of hanging on too
long. The stock hit its all-time high of $85 a share in 1999 amid the technology
boom. Many investors looking at the stock's falling market value figured the
company would come back. They kept thinking that as the stock fell to $75,
$65, and $55. But it didn't come back. The stock collapsed to $2.34, the price
at which rival Alcatel offered to buy it in 2006.

Chapter 4

Getting Your Hands on Fundamental Data

In This Chapter

▶ Understanding what information companies must provide to investors

▶ Getting a grasp on some basic accounting and math for fundamental analysis

▶ Discovering how to access fundamental data right when they are released by companies

▶ Getting familiar with databases that allow you to access financial information

*Y*ou might have your financial calculator or spreadsheet fired up and ready to start analyzing fundamental data. There's just one little problem: You need to get the data first.

Luckily, when it comes to getting your hands on data, there's never been a better time to be a fundamental analyst. You're able to get data faster, at less cost, and with less technical expertise than ever before. The ability to obtain financial data almost immediately from companies allows fundamental analysts to closely monitor how a company is doing.

This chapter will show you what types of fundamental data companies provide to investors, what form they come in, and when you can expect to get them. You'll also get a quick refresher on accounting basics you'll need in order to understand what's contained in the reports when they land. Finally, this chapter will show you how to obtain financial data, including a detailed look at the treasure trove of fundamental data provided by the nation's top financial cop, the Securities and Exchange Commission, or SEC.

Getting In Sync with the Fundamental Calendar

Companies you can invest in don't get to decide whether or not to give you their financial information. And that's a relief. Just imagine how haphazard it would be if companies could choose. What if they just weren't in the mood to report their revenue or earnings in a quarter? If a retailer had a bad holiday selling season, for instance, it could tell investors, "Sorry, we're not going to tell you how we did." Such *selective disclosure* would be the corporate version of letting your kids only bring report cards home if they got all A's.

In reality, publicly traded companies agree to be somewhat *transparent.* Transparency is a popular buzzword in business, but it's a noble goal. To be transparent, companies must adhere to strict rules about what financial information they disclose, and must even meet deadlines. And this goes for nearly all publicly traded companies, or those that sell ownership stakes of themselves to the general public who buy the shares. Similarly, when companies borrow money from the public, they too, must disclose their financial results to the public.

By taking the public's money, companies agree to give investors quarterly updates on their financial progress. Access to current and accurate fundamental data is one of your most basic rights when you either invest in or lend money to a company.

Which companies must report their financials to the public?

Just about any company you can invest in must follow financial reporting rules. That includes companies that are publicly traded, as explained above. But even some private companies, which haven't sold stock, must provide some financial information if they have $10 million or more in assets and have 500 or more owners.

Most major stock market exchanges, including the New York Stock Exchange and NASDAQ, require their listed companies to provide quarterly and annual financial reports to investors. That includes foreign companies with shares of stock that trade on either exchange.

Some private companies offering generous stock option programs to employees often find themselves eventually having to start filing financial reports. Internet search company Google, for instance, was private for roughly six years after it was founded in 1998. The company quickly hit the $10 million threshold for total assets, meaning it was required to provide financial statements. At that time, Google decided it might as well become publicly traded and sell shares to investors in an IPO since it was going to have to report its financial statements. Google launched its IPO in August 2004.

Kicking it all off: Earnings season

Sports fans wait all year for the beginning of football, basketball, or baseball season. And children can't help but anticipate the holiday season. But it's *earnings season* that fundamental analysts look forward to.

Four times a year, shortly after the end of the quarter, companies will begin to report their financial results to investors. Since most companies are on a calendar year, the results generally start trickling out two weeks after the quarter ends. Four times a year, usually in January, April, July, and October, thousands of companies report their financial results en masse. These times of year are called earnings season.

Aluminum maker Alcoa earned the unofficial designation as the company to kick off earnings season. The company's advanced accounting system allows it to close its books very rapidly following the end of the quarter. Alcoa is the first stock that's a member of the Dow Jones industrial average to report its earnings each quarter.

No data is bad data

If a company claims to be publicly traded but doesn't provide financial information, be highly skeptical. The lack of financial information is especially critical when dealing with stocks that trade on the largely unregulated markets known as the *Pink Sheets* or *OTC Bulletin Board*.

Unlike regulated exchanges, like the NYSE and NASDAQ, stocks that trade on the Pink Sheets and OTC Bulletin Board are not required to provide any financial information to investors. You read that right. These companies may even have ticker symbols, but never disclose how much they made or even how much revenue they generated. Most of the stocks on these markets are lightly regulated, if at all.

And the lack of financial information is a huge reason why investors, especially those who rely on fundamental analysis, are often best served by avoiding stocks that trade on the OTC Bulletin Board or Pink Sheets. These markets are infamous hangouts for so-called *penny stocks*. These stocks, which generally trade for a few pennies, are often just a name and little else. Sometimes penny-stock companies claim to have products and a management team, but don't actually generate any money to speak of. Penny stocks are popular with speculators, who like to talk up a shell company's prospects, get investors excited enough to buy in, and then dump the shares for a quick profit.

Not all companies follow a calendar year. For instance, retailers generally bring in a vast majority of their sales each year during December. For that reason, many retailers close their books at the end of January, to give them time to tally up their performance in December and give a full report for the year. When a company ends its year, for accounting purposes in a month other than December, it's called a fiscal year.

Getting the earnings press release

You don't have to be a newspaper reporter to appreciate the *earnings press release*. Contrary to its name, the earnings press release is for all investors, not just the media. After the end of a quarter, companies will publicly announce their financial results by distributing the press release. The press release is usually, but not always, accompanied by a conference call for investors and analysts. During the call, the management team will go over the quarter or year, describe the information in the earnings press release, and answer questions from the analysts who cover the company's stock for research firms.

When you read or hear a company reported its financial results, the information almost always comes from the company's earnings press release. While earnings press releases are technically unofficial and preliminary, they're usually accurate enough for investors, analysts, and the news media to use the numbers immediately. It's important to remember, though, that the earnings press release is not reviewed by an accountant or auditor.

When companies issue an earnings press release, they will often notify the regulators by filing a form *8-K*. The 8-K filing is the official way to signal to the world that the company has released critical information.

Regulators do not directly stipulate what companies must say in earnings press releases. But generally, earnings press releases contain several key parts:

- ✔ **Summary of the results:** Most earnings press releases will give the numbers investors want most right at the top, maybe even in the headline. That includes the revenue and earnings the company generated during the quarter and how much it grew (or shrunk) from the same quarter last year.

  Be leery when a company brags about a quarter being a "record" quarter. Even if a company's revenue rose to a record amount, its costs may have also run out of control and eaten into its earnings.

- ✔ **Management comment:** A member of the management team will usually opine on how the quarter went. As you might imagine, these statements are generally very carefully crafted, overly optimistic, and not particularly useful.

- ✔ **Description of major business events during the year:** Companies might break down — and even provide succinct bullet points — of the major accomplishments during the period.

✔ **Guidance for the future:** Most companies will often provide *earnings guidance,* or an estimate on how much the company might earn in the upcoming year. This guidance is important since it lets you know what the company expects in the near future.

✔ **Financial statements:** The earnings press release is the first glimpse investors will get of the company's income statement and balance sheet. These statements are among the most critical documents for fundamental data you'll get.

It's a good idea, when reading an earnings press release, to bypass most everything except the financial statements. While earnings press releases are intended to be honest representations of a company's performance, companies use the first parts of the earnings press release to put their performance in the best light. In contrast, the financial statements are the purest and least-biased parts of the press release.

Bracing for the 10-Q

Following the earnings press release, the next document to trickle from the company is the *10-Q.* The 10-Q is the official financial report submitted by a company to summarize its performance during the quarter.

Most companies have 40 days from the end of each fiscal quarter to produce and provide the 10-Q to investors. Generally, companies file the 10-Q a week or two after they provide the earnings press release.

Both the earnings press release and 10-Q serve the same basic purpose: They tell investors how the company did, financially, during the quarter. But since the 10-Q is written primarily to satisfy regulatory requirements, it's usually much more straightforward and contains less spin.

The 10-Q must be filed with the chief regulator of the financial markets, the SEC. As a result, companies are careful to include the following key components:

✔ **Financial statements:** Companies don't waste any time getting straight to the point with the 10-Q. The key financial statements are presented right at the top, while they're usually at the bottom of earnings press releases.

Don't make the mistake of assuming since you read the earnings press release, you don't need to bother with the 10-Q. A vast majority of companies don't include a statement of cash flows in the earnings press release. The statement of cash flows, however, must be included in the 10-Q. As you'll discover in Chapter 7, the statement of cash flows is an extremely important document used in financial analysis.

✔ **Footnotes:** Just as some books just don't fit correctly in your bookshelf, some financial information doesn't slip nicely into the financial statements. Unusual or noteworthy financial events might require more description than will fit into the financial statements, and those are available in the footnotes.

Never skip the footnotes. Companies will often throw items in the footnotes, hoping you'll miss them as an investor. Enron, for instance, stuffed much of the information about its cryptic partnerships in the footnotes.

✔ **Management's discussion and analysis of financial condition:** This section of the 10-Q is usually called the MD&A. In the MD&A, management steps investors through its financial results for the quarter. The narrative is usually stripped down and, well, straightforward since executives know the SEC will review it. So they don't want to say anything that may haunt them later.

✔ **Controls and procedures:** The company will let investors know if they found any problems in the way they monitor their accounting and present the information to investors. Following the accounting scandal at Enron, new rules from the *Sarbanes-Oxley Act of 2002* forced companies to make sure they had adequate controls in place over their accounting.

✔ **Other information:** Here, companies can throw in other material that might be of note to investors. This may include any pending litigation or whether the company sold additional stock, or is having trouble paying interest on its debt.

Many investors don't realize a company's 10-Q is not officially audited by a third-party accounting firm. That doesn't mean you can't necessarily trust the numbers; just know a little more skepticism isn't a bad idea.

Running through the 10-K

If you've ever run a 10-K race, you know that it can be pretty grueling if you haven't trained properly. The same goes for companies looking to report their annual financial performance in the form called the 10-K. This document is a monster, and producing it is one of the biggest financial chores a company faces. It's also the most comprehensive piece of fundamental data you'll get as an investor. Most companies are required to release their 10-K filings within 75 days from the end of their fiscal year. Some smaller companies, though, have 90 days to comply with the rules.

Due to the complexity of producing a 10-K, there can be a significant delay between the end of the calendar year and the time the report gets released.

The 10-K is kind of like a company's annual review. The level of detail of the 10-K is exhaustive, and unless you know what you're looking for, it's easy to get lost in the hundreds of pages of tables and text.

That's why fundamental analysts rarely curl up with a 10-K and read it from start to finish like a novel. They just know how to skip around in a 10-K and look for these key elements:

- ✔ **Everything in the 10-Q, just for the whole year:** All the data you get in the 10-Q for the quarter, you get for the year in the 10-K. That includes the financial statements and legal proceedings, but also, a more expanded MD&A where the management team explains more fully how the year progressed. The controls and procedures section may also be more fleshed out, since the 10-K has been checked over by the auditors.

- ✔ **Changes in accounting and disagreements with accountants:** You might not expect to see conflict and intrigue in a company's financial report, but sometimes you can find it here. Companies and their accountants will state in this section whether or not they didn't see eye to eye on financial reporting matters.

- ✔ **Long-term financial data:** Companies give you the financial results for the year that just ended. But you'll also find data for the past three, five, or even ten years. These data are very useful when looking for *trends,* or changes in fundamentals like revenue and earnings.

- ✔ **Business summary:** Here, the company lays out the nitty-gritty of what it does for a living. The company may break down its major business units and even, in some cases, tell you which parts of the business are the most profitable. You'll find out how to study the profitability of a company's units in Chapter 5.

- ✔ **Risk factors:** Imagine showing up to pick up a date, but before you leave for the movies, he or she sits you down with a huge list of everything that's wrong with themselves. That's what companies must do in their 10-Ks. If there's a known factor that could impair a company's fundamentals, it is required to tell you about it here.

- ✔ **Auditor's opinion:** Close to the bottom of the 10-K, the accountants will need to sign off on the books to indicate they reasonably reflect the financial condition of the firm.

When reviewing a 10-K, always read the auditor's opinion. The statement from the auditor can be telling. While an auditor may not wave a red flag and tell you not to buy stock, you can read between the lines. For instance, if you see the word *qualified,* watch out. That means the auditor has some issues with the way the books are kept, so you should too. Also, be careful when an auditor says a company may not be able to remain a *going concern.* That's accounting talk for, "This company might not make it."

Annual reports: A corporate beauty contest

Some companies go to great expense creating visually stunning annual reports. Some truly are wonders of publishing, putting some magazines to shame. Surfwear maker Quiksilver, for instance, produces annual reports containing full-color photos of surfers, exotic beaches, and colorful surfboards. By contrast, Warren Buffett's Berkshire Hathaway's is a boring-looking document with no photos, but packed with wisdom and worth a read even if you don't own the stock.

Yet other companies try to make a statement with their annual reports. Starbucks, for instance, in 2007 only put out a six-page full-color annual report that was then bundled with a black-and-white printout of its 10-K. It said its sparse annual report was an effort to reduce paper waste. In fact, thinning annual reports is a growing trend as companies look to cut costs. Companies may produce just a few colorful pages, and slip the 10-K inside. This trend, which really began in 2006, will likely continue as more investors prefer to download companies' financial information electronically.

Flipping through the annual report

If you visit a CEO's office, you'll surely see the annual report sitting on the coffee table. And to be sure, many companies' annual reports are gorgeous, well, as much as financial documents can be. The annual report is essentially the 10-K, magazine-style. There are lovely photos of smiling executives, employees, and customers. Even the financial statements are given a face-lift, usually printed on luxurious paper using an elegant font. The annual report is usually released several months after the 10-K is published, often landing around the time companies have their shareholders' meetings.

Unlike the 10-Q and 10-K, which you can download directly from the SEC's Web site, the annual report is a paper-based document. If you call a company, most times it will be happy to mail you a copy. You can also usually view an electronic form of the paper annual report by downloading it from the company's Web site.

The annual report is the glossy and slick version of the 10-K. Companies produce the annual report mainly to hand out to employees and customers while courting them.

The annual report is the management team's opportunity to put its spin on how the year went. Most annual reports, for instance, begin with a letter to shareholders that is generally very hopeful, even after a dismal year.

There's no proxy like the proxy statement

If you're looking for the most salacious statement released by companies, that must be the *proxy statement*. The proxy statement is a document the SEC requires companies to distribute to shareholders ahead of the annual shareholder meeting. It's kind of like the absentee ballot you might get prior to a presidential election.

Shareholder meetings happen every year as companies gather shareholders, usually in the spring, to go over their initiatives and goals. The proxy is sometimes known by its regulatory name, 14A, named after the portion of the SEC rules that stipulate what it must contain.

The proxy statement is fascinating reading because it lays out all the most sensitive information most companies have to offer, including:

- ✔ **Executive compensation:** Not only are the annual salaries of the top executives spelled out, but the amounts of their bonuses, too.

- ✔ **Corporate matters subject to a vote:** Companies' proxies contain a section that looks almost like a ballot. There will be a number of measures that require shareholder approval. Usually, the items up for a vote include the selection of the auditing firm, and the board members standing for reelection on the board.

- ✔ **Shareholder proposals:** If a company has any ill will with shareholders, it will become very clear in the proxy. Dissident shareholders may offer proposals to replace the management team. Other investors might lobby for the company to adopt more environmentally friendly manufacturing.

- ✔ **Related-party transactions:** This is one of my favorite parts of the proxy. It shows whether any of the company's officers or directors have business relationships with it. Individuals that have business relationships with the company, in theory, may have trouble being impartial since there's a potential conflict of interest.

The proxy is so important to fundamental analysis that you can explore it more fully in Chapter 9.

Getting up to Speed with the Basic Accounting and Math

Even if you hated math in high school and avoided accounting in college, you can still put fundamental analysis to use. In fact, the more you dig into the financials of companies and see how math and accounting can help you, who knows, maybe you'll get curious to learn more. And if that's the case, you might look into *Business Math For Dummies* (Wiley) or *Accounting For Dummies* (Wiley).

But here, in this section, I'll give you the basics of what you need to know about the concept of accounting. You'll see that accounting is really just a way to condense millions of individual business transactions down to a form that makes it possible for you to analyze.

When you're studying financial statements, just remember there are three primary functions of business you're trying to analyze: operating activities, investing activities, and financing activities.

Finding smooth operators

A company's operations get the most attention. Typically, when you hear a company is or is not "doing well," that is a reference to the firm's operating activities.

Simply stated, a company's operations are the process of converting raw materials into products that are, hopefully, sold to customers for a profit. Many elements go into operations, including effective new product development, which generates revenue, in addition to cost control, marketing, and manufacturing. The income statement, explored more in Chapter 5, lets you see how well a company is operating.

You have to spend money to make money

Unless they've found a goose that lays platinum eggs, all companies, at some point, must put money back into their business. Equipment used to make products wears out and needs to be replaced. Companies outgrow their headquarters and must acquire a bigger building. And it's common for companies to overhaul their computer systems to keep up with tracking their business.

When companies spend money to make more money, they're *investing* in their future. And while investing is a necessary part of doing business, it can also be done poorly. Companies might spend too much for equipment they didn't need. Or worse, they might over expand, resulting in a glut of their product, which hurts their profits. You can read more about profit margins in Chapter 5. There are two key things for a fundamental analyst to monitor when it comes to investment:

✔ **Is the return on the investment adequate?** If a company is spending money to expand, and revenue and profit aren't growing too, you might be throwing your money down the drain as an investor.

✔ **Is the company using the equipment it has bought?** In business, having too much capacity is not a good idea. You don't want to spend money renting a warehouse, for instance, if it's usually empty.

Getting in tune with high finance

So, you can understand how a company operates and how much it's spending on itself. But who's going to pay for all this stuff? That's the final and critical element that accounting helps you with.

Generally speaking, companies can *finance,* or fund their operations, in two ways. They can either rustle up investors, or they can borrow money. Investors provide money, called *equity capital,* to companies in exchange for a piece of the company. If all goes well, the company operates extremely well, profits soar, and investors are very happy since their share of the company will be worth more. When you buy stock in a company, you are an investor.

Some beginning investors incorrectly think money they use when buying a stock goes directly to the company. That's not usually the case. Companies sell their stock to the public once, in a process called an initial public offering, or IPO. When those shares sell for that first time, the companies get that money. But after the IPO, the company doesn't get additional cash. The shares and money are trading hands between other investors in the *secondary market.*

When it comes to financing itself, a company may also look to borrow money. Companies may borrow money from a local bank or sell IOUs, called *bonds,* to the public. Investors who lend money to a company just want to get their money back, plus an amount of interest agreed upon ahead of time.

If a company fails, investors and lenders are treated very differently. And the difference has a big influence on whether or not you decide to buy a company's stock or bond.

If a company is unable to keep paying interest to its lenders, the company goes into *default.* Typically, at that point, the bondholders take control of the company. In the worst-case scenario, when a company cannot be saved, bondholders get repaid first. So, let's say a company defaulted and had a giant garage sale to sell its desks and chairs. The money would be used to pay back debt holders before stock investors see a penny. That means, as stock investors, you're accepting the possibility that you can lose your entire investment.

Learning a key fundamental math skill: Percentage changes

If you've noticed so far, I've tried to spare you from much ugly math in the first couple of pages. And hoping not to scare you off, I try to introduce math topics in this book gently and only when it's relevant.

But there's one math skill that you'll encounter so frequently in fundamental analysis, you might as well tackle it now. And that's the concept of *percentage change*. Because fundamental analysis is infatuated with looking at increases and decreases in business factors, such as sales and revenues, the percentage change is a way to put gains and declines into context. For instance, if I told you that the price of a sweater rose $50 this year, that doesn't tell you much. But if I told you the price was $50 before, then you know that the price doubled to $100.

You calculate a percentage change this way:

$$((\text{New number} - \text{old number}) \div \text{old number}) \times 100$$

Going back to the sweater example, the new price is $100 and the old price was $50, so:

$$((100 - 50) \div 50) \times 100 = 100\%$$

 If a value rises by 100%, then it has doubled. Similarly, if a number rises by 200%, it has tripled and 300%, quadrupled. Some make the mistake, for instance, of seeing the 2 in the 200% and saying it has doubled when it has in fact, tripled.

How to Get the Fundamental Data You Need

You might have the fastest car in the neighborhood, but if you don't have any gas, you're not going to get far. So goes fundamental analysis. You might build the fanciest financial spreadsheet, but it's not going to do you any good if you don't have the raw financial numbers to put in it.

Until the dawn of the Internet, getting fundamental data could be a real hassle. You would have to call or write a company and ask it to mail — yes, mail — its 10-K, 10-Q and annual report to you.

Thankfully, the days of having to deal strictly with paper financial statements are over. But the skills of the fundamental analyst must keep up with the electronic age. In this section, you'll find out how to quickly, and for no cost, get your hands on the fundamental data you'll need to complete your analysis.

Getting acquainted with the SEC's database

You can spend thousands of dollars for access to Web sites that provide fundamental data. But really, to get started, you don't have to spend a dime.

The SEC's website at `www.sec.gov` is a treasure trove for fundamental analysis. You'll find all the financial forms discussed above in this chapter, and then some. All the fundamental data are stored in the SEC's *Interactive Data Electronic Applications,* or IDEA, database. You can use IDEA to look up any public company's filings and even download the financial statements to your computer so you can do further analysis.

You might hear or read references to the SEC's EDGAR database. EDGAR was the SEC's primary financial-form database prior to IDEA. EDGAR is still available on the SEC's site, but it's not worth the time. IDEA can do everything EDGAR could and adds additional information.

Step-by-step directions on accessing company fundamentals using IDEA

Now that you know how powerful IDEA is, it's time to dive in and discover how to get what you need from it. For the example below, I'll show you how to get the 10-Q, 10-K and proxy statement for General Electric. Just follow these steps:

1. **Log into the SEC's Web site at `www.sec.gov`.**

2. **Click the "Search" link on the upper right-hand corner of the page.**

3. **Enter the name of the company in the Company name blank.**

   It's the first blank in the top of the blue-shaded box. Type in general electric for this example.

4. **Scroll down and click the Find Companies button.**

5. **Choose the company name.**

   Because General Electric has separate business units, you'll see companies like General Electric Capital Assurance Co. But you want the main company, so click on the red numbers to the left of where it says General Electric Co.

6. **Click on the form you want.**

   If you want GE's 10-Q, scroll down until you see the form 10-Q listed and click on the "Documents" button. If you want the 10-K, choose 10-K, and the proxy is marked as 14-A.

7. **Click on the red code under the document in the first line.**

   This line should have the form under the "Type" head, which in this case is the 10-Q. When you're downloading the 10-K, the line should read 10-Q.

When you're scrolling down through the list of forms, you might notice that some have a blue button that says "Voluntary Interactive Data." These forms are presented in a special format that computers can read, called *eXtensive Business Reporting Language* or XBRL. Financial statements available in XBRL can be easily processed and downloaded. If you click on the Voluntary Interactive Data button, you'll be moved to an area of the SEC's Web site that lets you view financial reports using XBRL. You can easily skip between the income statement and balance sheet without scrolling, for instance. XBRL also lets you easily download the financial statements to a spreadsheet. Since it's not required to file using XBRL, only a handful of companies do. But that's changing.

Most of the major Web portals, such as Yahoo, at `finance.yahoo.com`, and MSN, at `money.msn.com`, provide summaries of companies' primary financial statements. MSN Money also lets you access all the regulatory forms. Most companies, too, put their financial data on their Web sites. But as a fundamental analyst, it's important to know how to get the data direct from the source: The SEC's IDEA database.

Pulling fundamental data from Web sites into spreadsheets

Sometimes reading a company's financial statements using the SEC's IDEA isn't enough. If you want to perform the analysis you'll find out about in the next part of this book, you'll likely need to download the data into a spreadsheet.

If the company you're analyzing provides XBRL data, it's easy to download into a spreadsheet.

Luckily, there's a handy trick using Microsoft Excel all fundamental analysts should know about. While it's possible to cut-and-paste the financial data from a company filing into a spreadsheet, the results can be a disorganized mess. Instead, use an Excel function that's built to order. Here's how:

1. **Open the filing.**

   Find the filing you're interested in downloading using the steps above. Copy the Web address from the address bar in your browser by high-lighting the address and holding the Control button and the C key.

2. **Open Microsoft Excel.**

3. **Instruct Excel to find the filing.**

   Choose Excel's "Data" pull-down menu, and then select Import External Data and then New Web Query.

4. **Provide the Web address of the filing.**

   Paste the filing's address by holding down the Control button and choose the V key, in the address bar at the top.

5. **Import the filing.**

   Click the Import button at the bottom of the page.

6. **Select the relevant financial data.**

   Scroll down until you see the financial data you would like to download. Click the small yellow arrow next to the data.

After you follow these steps, the financial information you want, such as the company's income statement or balance sheet, will automatically appear in a spreadsheet. This will be a handy skill that can help you with the analysis you'd do later in the book.

Finding stocks' dividend histories

Dividends are periodic cash payments some companies make to their share-holders. The dividends are paid out of the company's cash as a way of return-ing profits to the shareholders. Dividends are a very important piece of your total return on an investment.

Don't ignore dividends. These cash payments, over time, account for about one-third of the total return investors make on the market, according to Standard & Poor's. The remaining two-thirds of total return come from the stock price rising.

Dividends are also important ways to help value a company, as you will discover in Chapter 8. Companies that pay dividends generally pay them quarterly.

The best way to look up a dividend history is on the company's Web site. Going back to the GE example, go to www.ge.com and click on the investor relations link at the top of the page. Next, click on the Stock Information link on the left-hand side. You'll see a link for Dividend History, which listed GE's dividend payments going back for nearly a decade.

Getting stock-split information

When a company's stock price rises dramatically and begins to approach $50 a share or more, the executives might decide to split the shares. The theory goes that some naïve investors, who read too much into a stock's per-share price, might assume a stock trading for $50 or more is too expensive.

In a stock split, the company cuts its share price, say in half, by cutting the shares into multiple shares. For instance, let's say you own 100 shares in a stock trading for $60 a share. If the company has a 2-for-1 split, you will suddenly have 200 shares, but they'll be worth $30 apiece. Management feels some investors are more likely to buy stock in a company for $30 a share than $60.

Some investors assume that a stock split is a major boon since they suddenly have more shares. But, as discussed in Chapter 3, the per-share price of a stock doesn't tell you much. The value of your shares is still $6,000, whether you own 100 shares at $60 or 200 shares at $30 a share. The company's market value also stays the same.

Understanding when stock splits occur is important for fundamental analysis, though, since it can affect the number of shares outstanding, which is described in Chapter 3. You'll need an accurate count of shares outstanding to do some of the fundamental analysis later in the book.

Fortunately, many companies provide stock-split histories on their Web sites. For instance, if you follow the instructions above to get GE's dividends, you'll notice stock splits are listed on the same page.

MSN Money also helps you look up if, and when, a company split its shares. Here's how:

1. **Log into www.live.com.**

2. **Enter "quote:" in the search box followed by the stock's symbol.**

   For GE, for instance, enter quote:GE and click the green icon that looks like a magnifying glass.

3. **Click on the small stock chart that appears in the search results.**

   This will take you to MSN's Charting feature.

4. **Click on the Download MSN Money Investment Toolbox link that appears in the chart.**

   This will download a small piece of software that will let you get advanced charts. You only need to follow this step once.

5. **Observe the chart.**

   If the stock has been split, you'll see a small box that's half white and half red. For instance, the chart tells you that GE last split its stock, by 3 for 1, on May 8, 2000.

Part II
How to Perform Fundamental Analysis

The 5th Wave   By Rich Tennant

"This company's statement shows a 13 percent increase in the good, a 4 percent decrease in the bad, but a whole lot of ugly left in inventory."

In this part . . .

You may already know what fundamental analysis is, but you may not be clear on how to use this important technique to evaluate investments. I've designed this part to step you through how to thoroughly analyze a company and dig into its key financial statements, including the income statement, the balance sheet, and the statement of cash flow. I also show you how financial ratios can help you get quick and insightful information about companies. Lastly, you can discover how to unearth some of the more sensitive items about a company's management by using the proxy statement.

Chapter 5

Analyzing a Company's Profitability Using the Income Statement

*I*n everything from sports to school, you've probably been trained to measure results. At the end of the game or class semester, you either get a score or grade that determines how well or poorly you did, and how you measured up to expectations and ranked against your peers.

When you measure the success of a company, you really don't do anything differently than when you gauge the results of last night's basketball game. Fundamental analysts carefully evaluate a company's income statement to see how well the company did, examining how much money it brought in, how much it spent to operate, and the final amount of profit it generated.

Companies lay out all of their critical information for you in their income statement. In this chapter, you dig into the parts of the income statement necessary for fundamental analysis. Better yet, this chapter gives you the tools to know how to *read* those parts, which is critical when you want to determine whether a company's stock is cheap or expensive (see Chapters 10 and 11 for more on determining a stock's worth). Don't let the cryptic appearance of the income statement scare you. The pointers in this chapter prepare you to get everything you need out of the income statement.

Digging Deep Into the Income Statement

When you invest in a company by buying its stock, you're probably not doing it to be charitable. By buying shares of stock, you're claiming a piece of the company's future revenue and profits. If all goes well, the company will grow and your stake will become more valuable.

The trick, though, is knowing how to make sure the company is keeping its end of the bargain by making money. That's where the income statement comes in. Companies that have issued stock on a stock market exchange such as the New York Stock Exchange or Nasdaq, or borrow money from the public, are required to issue an income statement. The income statement spells out in gory detail how the company did during each quarter and year. Fundamental analysis requires you to pay close attention to the income statement for any sign the company isn't progressing as it should or, conversely, doing better than many thought it could.

Cutting through to the key parts

Luckily for investors, the accountants have somewhat standardized the way companies must prepare the income statement. No two income statements look identical, and subtle differences can make comparing one company's income statement with other companies' problematic, (you can read about making comparisons more in Chapter 16). Income statements can also vary a bit depending on what line of business a company is in. Still, income statements tend to follow the same basic structure.

You can dedicate a great deal of time obsessing over every nuance of financial statements, including the income statement. If that's of interest to you, check out *Reading Financial Reports For Dummies* (Wiley), which gets into the nitty-gritty of financial reporting. In this book, though, you'll get a look at the basic layout of the income statement and what you'll need to do some serious fundamental analysis.

The basic structure of an income statement includes these items:

- **Revenue:** This is how much money the company brought in by selling goods and services. Revenue is often called the "top line."

- **Cost of goods sold:** It takes money to make money. Cost of goods measures what a company must spend to actually create the good or service sold. These are *direct costs*, meaning they are costs for items that may literally go into the products. Cost of goods sold, for many manufacturing companies, is the largest single cost of doing business. For instance, with an automaker, the cost of goods sold might include the cost of steel used to build the cars.

✔ **Operating expenses:** *Indirect expenses* are incurred by companies as they conduct business, but may not go directly into the product. These costs are usually necessary or important, but peripheral. These indirect costs are called *operating expenses* or better known as *overhead*. Operating expenses may include:

- **Marketing expenses:** Include advertising and other promotional expenses.

- **Research and development:** What a company spends to cook up new products or services to sell to customers.

- **Administrative expenses:** Expenses connected with support staff, such as legal, human resources, and other functions that are directly tied to manufacturing the product.

✔ **Other income:** Companies sometimes bring in money for things other than selling products and services. This income is recorded as other income. For instance, a company might win a legal settlement or sell a factory.

✔ **Other expenses.** Similarly to how other income doesn't qualify as revenue, other expenses do not qualify as normal operating expenses. Other expenses might include the cost to restructure a unit of the company, paying severance to lay off employees, or depreciation — accounting for wear and tear (see the sidebar, "Appreciating depreciation").

✔ **Earnings before interest and taxes.** After you subtract cost of goods sold, operating expenses, and other expenses from revenue, what you're left with is earnings before interest and taxes.

✔ **Interest expense.** Most companies borrow money to fund their operations or to buy inventory. Here, the company discloses how much it's paying to borrow money.

✔ **Taxes.** Companies must pay taxes too. Here, companies disclose how much they they paid to Uncle Sam.

✔ **Net income.** Finally, after paying all these costs and expenses, what's left is the profit, or net income. This is how much the company earned during the period, based on accounting rules or *GAAP*.

Ever hear a company say it used GAAP? No I don't mean that they used expense accounts to buy khakis and collared shirts at a popular clothing store. Instead, I'm talking about GAAP — Generally Accepted Accounting Principles — painstakingly detailed rules that instruct companies on the right way to report results.

Appreciating depreciation

Accountants normally classify depreciation as an other expense. This can sometimes be a tough thing for nonaccountants to understand. *Depreciation* is an accounting method of recording wear and tear on things like factories or equipment. Think of it this way. If you buy a car for $15,000, in a year's time that car might only be worth $13,000. But while you're out $2,000 in value, you didn't actually have to write a check for $2,000 to anyone. The same applies to a machine a company might use to make products. The erosion of value of the machine is an expense that goes into the cost of making the product being sold.

Taking in the Top Line: Revenue

For a fundamental analyst reading an income statement, revenue is a critical item because it tells you how:

- ✔ **Rapidly the company is growing (or shrinking):** Comparing revenue generated during a year or quarter with revenue reported in the same period a year ago can be very telling. This simple comparison tells you whether the company's growth is on an uptrend or downtrend.

- ✔ **Strong demand is for a company's products:** Companies love to brag about how popular their products are. But revenue is where hype can be quantified. Strong demand for a product will show up in the revenue line, even if the company's expenses are out of line and still losing money.

- ✔ **A company ranks in sheer size next to its rivals:** While there are many ways to measure a company's size, such as number of employees, revenue is as good a benchmark as any other. If you want to find out which company is the biggest in a competitive field, you should always check out revenue first.

Fundamental analysts pay close attention to revenue for the reasons listed above, but there's also reason to be skeptical. Accounting rules give companies a great deal of leeway in how and when they record or "recognize" revenue. The most classic distortion may occur when a company books revenue before the product is actually bought or received by a customer. Regulators, for this reason, warned companies to be more conservative when booking revenue. The General Accounting Office, a unit of the government charged to study waste in both the private and public sectors, found that improper *revenue recognition* was to blame for more than a third of misstated financial statements. Always be skeptical of revenue.

Breaking down a company's revenue

Most companies will provide several revenue figures. Generally, there will be a total revenue line that totals up the money the company brought in from all its business units. But if the company is complex, it might break total revenue down into its component parts so you can see which units are performing best.

Due to its large size and wide array of technology businesses, International Business Machines is a great example of how you can use the revenue line to peer deeply into a company's operations. Below, in Table 5-1, is a breakdown of IBM's 2008 results, to give you an idea of how digging into what makes up total revenue can be revealing about a business:

Table 5-1	IBM's Total Revenue Breakdown in 2008
Source of revenue	*Revenue (in billions)*
Global technology services	$39.3
Global business services	$19.6
Systems and technology	$19.3
Software	$22.1
Global financing	$2.6
Other	$0.8
Total revenue	$103.6

Source: IBM (www.ibm.com/investor/4q08/press.phtml)

As you can see above, had you just looked at total revenue you would have missed a helpful breakdown in IBM's business. Dissecting IBM's revenue into units gives you several key findings, including a:

✔ **Sense of a company's business diversification.** While IBM is best known for making large corporate computer systems, in reality the company gets its revenue from a swath of technology businesses. No single line of business accounts for more than 38% of total revenue. As a fundamental analyst, this is important information because it tells you whether IBM is overly concentrated in an area of technology you're not optimistic about. Similarly, this analysis will tell you if the company exposes you to the area of technology you want to invest in. For instance, if you want to invest in technology hardware, IBM probably isn't the best for you.

✔ **Indication of the most important business at the company.** Investors may not realize it, but IBM is more of a technology services firm than anything else. It got 38% of its revenue from services in 2008.

✔ **Clue of reliance on noncore businesses.** Over the years, it's common for large companies to branch into businesses that are outside their core business. Several large companies, like General Electric and General Motors, have practically spawned banks as they extend credit to customers buying their products. Straying from a core business is something you, as a fundamental analyst, need to pay close attention to. With IBM, you can see the company has a financing business that provides loans to customers. However, the financing business is a very small portion of its total operation at about 3% of revenue.

If you want to figure out how large a unit of a company is, divide the unit's revenue by total revenue and multiply the result by 100. Using IBM's financing unit as an example, divide the unit's revenue of $2.6 billion by IBM's total revenue of $103.6 to arrive at 0.025. Multiply 0.025 by 100 to convert the result into a percentage of 2.5%.

Keeping tabs on a company's growth

If there's one thing many investors will agree on, it's the importance for a company to keep growing. As the prices of raw materials rise, it's critical for companies to keep up by increasing revenue either by raising prices or creating new products with higher price tags. Even if you're investing in a mature industry, just looking for a stable return, you still want to see revenue increasing over time so the company's earnings keep up with inflation.

Finding out how rapidly a company is growing is simple if you know your way around the income statement. Here's what you need to know:

1. **Download the historical revenue data.**

   You'll first need to get your hands on the revenue data. The best way to do this is by downloading the income statement from an online source. You can review how to do this in Chapter 4.

2. **Pull out the revenue line item for several years.**

   In most cases, one of the very first lines in the income statement is total revenue. Pull out total revenue from the income statement and place it in a spreadsheet or write it down so you can do further analysis.

   Again using IBM as an example, Table 5-2 show you how to put IBM's total revenue into a format you can further analyze.

3. Calculate the year-to-year percentage change.

Now that you have each year's total revenue in one place, you can calculate the company's revenue growth from year to year. Calculating percentage changes is covered in more depth in Chapter 4. But the way I like to remember this is that you subtract the "old" number from the "new" number, then divide by the "old" number and multiply by 100.

Consider an example calculating IBM's 2008 revenue growth:

$103.6 (2008 revenue, the "new" number) – $98.8 (2007 revenue, the "old" number) / $98.8 (2007 revenue, the "old number") = 0.049.

Then multiply 0.049 by 100 to convert the number into a percentage, which is 4.9%. This analysis show you IBM's total revenue grew by 4.9% in 2008.

4. Repeat step 3 for each year so you can see a multiyear trend.

One year's revenue change doesn't really tell you much. The fact that IBM's revenue grew 4.9% is of limited value unless you compare it with something else. You may compare IBM's growth to its competitors' growth, as you will read more about in Chapter 16. But for now, you will want to see how 2008 revenue growth compares with growth in past years. I'll save you the trouble by calculating the percentage changes and presenting them in Table 5-3.

Now that you have each year's revenue growth, you can see just how rocky revenue can be, even at a large company like IBM. You'll notice revenue grew by as much as 9.7% in 2003, and shrunk by up to 5.4% in 2005. Understanding just how uneven revenue growth can be from year to year, is critical to the work of fundamental analysis because you can see if a firm is *cyclical*. A cyclical company is one that experiences large swings in revenue based on the health of the overall economy. As an investor, you might not be willing to pay as much for shares of a cyclical company if the economy is about to enter into a period of slower growth.

Resist the temptation to take simple averages of revenue growth and assume that average growth will continue forever. For instance, if you averaged IBM's growth between 2001 and 2008 by adding up the growth numbers and dividing by the total number of years, you'd find the company grew, on average, by 2.6% a year. But fundamental analysts dig deeper and study year-to-year changes, to see how revenue ebbs and flows.

Don't forget to also calculate the percentage changes of growth in the different business units. Taking the time to see how rapidly different parts of the business are growing can give you a peek into the company's direction. At IBM in 2008, for instance, the software unit grew the most rapidly by rising 10.5% over 2007, while the systems and technology unit shrunk by 9.5%. As a fundamental analyst, you might look into IBM's software unit further for more explanation.

Table 5-2	IBM's Annual Revenue
Year	Total revenue ($ billions)
2008	$103.6
2007	$98.8
2006	$91.4
2005	$91.1
2004	$96.3
2003	$89.1
2002	$81.2
2001	$83.1
2000	$85.1

Table 5-3	IBM's Annual Revenue Growth
Year	Total revenue growth
2008	4.9%
2007	8.1%
2006	0.3%
2005	−5.4%
2004	8.1%
2003	9.7%
2002	−2.3%
2001	−2.3%

What are the company's costs?

With very few exceptions, companies don't keep all the money they collect from customers. A good portion of the revenue goes out to pay direct costs, such as raw materials, and indirect costs like overhead and advertising. All these costs are recorded in the income statement so investors may see how much a company spent to generate revenue.

Is a company an international player?

As companies find themselves competing globally, fundamental analysts need to understand how important sales outside the U.S. are to a company. Analyzing revenue will give you great detail on a company's global footprint.

Most companies will break out what percentage of their revenue came from different parts of the world, if not in the income statement, in the notes of an earnings press release issued to shareholders or in the regulatory filings. You can read more about where to get these documents in Chapter 4.

Digging into costs

If you're beginning to notice a trend here, one of the biggest skills in fundamental analysis is the ability to tear apart the numbers and see what comprises them. Analyzing a company's costs is a great example. While some investors just look at total expenses, or maybe consider cost of goods sold and operating expenses, there's much intelligence to be had by digging deeper.

To show you what I mean, let's crack open the financial can on Campbell Soup. The income statement shows you how much it costs to make a can of soup, among the other products the company manufacturers, as you can see in Table 5-4.

Table 5-4	Breakdown of Campbell Soup's 2008 Costs	
	2008, in millions (fiscal year ended Aug. 3, 2008)	*2007, in millions (fiscal year ended July 29, 2007)*
Revenue	$7,998	$7,385
Cost of goods sold	$4,827	$4,384
Marketing and selling expenses	$1,162	$1,106
Administrative expenses	$608	$571
Research and development expenses	$115	$111
Other expenses or income	$13	($30)
Restructuring charges	$175	

Source: Campbell Soup (investor.shareholder.com/Campbell/releasedetail.cfm?ReleaseID=333834)

Again, don't let the table of numbers overwhelm you. Fundamental analysts rely on two simple but powerful techniques to convert a pile of numbers into meaningful data. With just a little math, you'll be able to analyze the data and paint a picture that tells you a great deal about Campbell Soup.

First, common-size the costs and expenses. Again, just looking at Campbell Soup's costs and expenses don't tell you much at first. You want to put them into perspective by comparing them with something. One of the best tricks used in fundamental analysis is *common-sizing*. Common-sizing is simply taking lines on financial statements and quantifying their size by comparing them to a total. When common-sizing is applied to the income statement, you compare each expense to revenue. That way, you can easily see whether the company's expenses are growing at an alarming pace compared with the growth of the business.

Best of all, common-sizing is simple. All you need to do is divide each cost and expense by total revenue and multiply by 100 to convert the number into a percentage. Start with Campbell Soup's cost of goods sold in 2008. Divide the cost of goods sold of $4,827 by the company's total revenue of $7,998 and multiply by 100. You should get 60.4%. In other words, the cost of making soup and other products cost 60.4 cents of every dollar of revenue. Next, follow the same directions for all the costs on Campbell Soup's income statement. Table 5-5 shows you what you'll find when you're done.

Table 5-5	Common-Sized Campbell Soup	
	2008, Expenses as a % of Revenue	*2007, Expenses as a % of Revenue*
Cost of goods sold	60.4%	59.4%
Marketing and selling expenses	14.5%	15.0%
Administrative expenses	7.6%	7.7%
Research and development expenses	1.4%	1.5%
Other expenses or income	0.2%	-0.4%
Restructuring charges	2.2%	0%

Looking at the numbers above, you'll probably notice that the percentages haven't changed much from 2007 to 2008. That is likely a sign that the company is doing a good job keeping the growth of expenses in check and moving at pace with the business. The one very slight exception is the cost of goods sold. In 2007, the company spent 59.4% of revenue on costs to produce products. That went up very slightly in 2008. It's a minor change, but points to an issue that's worth digging further into. Perhaps the company's raw materials costs rose slightly, or more customers are buying goods that cost slightly more to make.

When you common-size an income statement, it's often best to use several years of data so you can see the trends from year to year. If a company's research and development budget is soaring, for instance, you'll spot the trend. Often an unusual blip on the common-sizing will clue you into something worth looking further into.

Next, measure the growth of costs and expenses. It's also important to keep tabs on how rapidly costs and expenses are growing from year to year. Measure the growth of costs and expenses in the same way as measuring the growth in revenue above.

What is the company's bottom line?

After paying all the bills, including all the direct costs, operating expenses and taxes, what's left is the company's net profit.

The basic formula is as follows:

> Revenue – cost of goods sold – operating expenses + other income – other expenses – interest expense – taxes = Net Income

Net income is the end-all be-all for many investors. It's the number that is used to see how a company did compared with the past and versus expectations investors had. You will want to see how rapidly net income grew or shrunk compared with previous years.

If you notice that a company's net income is growing more slowly than revenue, that's a quick tip-off that its expenses might be running amuck.

An efficient way to see how net income is faring next to revenue is to calculate the year-over-year percentage changes for revenue and for net income. By placing the growth of revenue and net income side-by-side, you'll see, very quickly, how well the company is controlling costs as demand for its products rises and falls.

Calculating Profit Margins and Finding Out What They Mean

If you hear that a company made $400 million last year, you recognize that sounds like quite a bit of money. But, fundamental analysis requires taking things a step farther. Fundamental analysis gives you the tools to put net income into perspective and understand what it means for you as an investor.

Differences between the types of profit margins

One of the best ways to size up a company's profit is by studying *profit margins*. At its most basic level, a profit margin is how much a company has left after paying for its expenses. However, there are several ways to measure profit margins, all of which are instructive in fundamental analysis. There are three main types of profit margins fundamental analysts should be aware of, including:

Gross profit margin

A company's *gross profit* is one of the simplest ways to look at profitability. Gross profit is what's left of revenue after subtracting direct costs, also known as cost of goods sold. Gross margin measures how much the company makes after paying costs directly connected with producing the product.

The *gross profit margin* takes things a bit further by comparing gross profit with a company's revenue. In other words, the gross profit margin tells you how much of revenue is kept, after paying direct costs, relative to sales.

Here's an example: Caterpillar. The maker of earthmoving and construction equipment reported revenue of $51.3 billion in 2008, and its cost of goods sold reached $39.6 billion. By subtracting $39.6 billion from $51.3 billion, you find Caterpillar's gross profit was $11.70 billion. That's great, but doesn't tell you much. Here's where fundamental analysis comes in. Divide the company's $11.70 billion gross profit by its total revenue of $51.3 billion and multiply by 100. This quick division tells you Caterpillar had a gross margin of 22.8%.

What's that mean in plain English? After paying for direct costs, such as steel and laborers' time on the assembly line, Caterpillar kept nearly 23 cents of every dollar in revenue. Just to give you an idea what gross margins typically are, among the 500 companies in the Standard & Poor's 500 index, the average gross margin is about 45.1, says Thomson Reuters. The fact Caterpillar's gross margin is lower shows just how much of the firm's costs are concentrated in raw materials and other direct costs.

Gross profit margin is not as useful when studying software and Internet companies. A vast majority of the cost of producing software is overhead, and not direct costs. That's one reason why Microsoft has very large gross profit margins. For instance, Microsoft kept 81 cents of every dollar of sales after paying direct costs during its fiscal 2008 year, which ended June 30, 2008. But its operating margin, which reflects a more accurate picture of the cost to create software, is much lower, as we'll discuss next.

Operating profit margin

A company's *operating profit* is one step more sophisticated than the gross margin. Operating profit not only factors in a company's direct costs, but indirect costs, too. Operating profit is what's left of revenue after subtracting overhead costs.

Taking things a step further is the *operating profit margin.* The operating profit margin is calculated by dividing operating profit by revenue. It tells you how much the company keeps of revenue after paying direct costs and overhead. Operating profit margins are critical indicators for fundamental analysis, since they give a good idea of how profitable a firm is with respect to its core business.

Going back to Microsoft shows clearly why for some businesses, the operating profit margin is more meaningful than gross profit margin. The operating margin includes the costs of research and development and advertising, for instance, which are important to generating successful software products. Table 5-6 shows you how operating profit margin is calculated.

Here you can see why Microsoft is considered to be such a profitable company, with its enviable 36.9% operating profit margin. This operating profit margin is about double the average 18% operating profit margin of companies in the Standard & Poor's 500, says Thomson Reuters.

Some fundamental analysts take issue with operating profit, because it includes some expenses that are not actual costs. For instance, operating profit subtracts depreciation from revenue, even though depreciation isn't an actual bill the company must pay. For this reason, some fundamental analysts recommend ignoring some of these intangible expenses when understanding how much a company is worth, as will be discussed further in Chapter 11.

Table 5-6	Figuring Microsoft's Operating Profit Margin
Fiscal 2008 result	*$ millions*
Total revenue	$60,420
Minus cost of goods sold	–$11,598
Minus research and development expenses	–$8,164
Minus sales and marketing expenses	–$13,260
Minus general and administrative expenses	–$5,127
Equals operating profit	$22,271
Operating profit margin	36.9%

Source: Microsoft www.microsoft.com/msft/financial/default.mspx

Net profit margin

A company's *net profit* or *net income* is the most comprehensive measure of profitability. Net profit tells you how many dollars the company kept after paying all its costs and expenses. The *net profit margin*, which is net profit divided by total revenue, tells you how much of every dollar in sales the company keeps after paying all costs and expenses.

Companies can lose money, too. When that happens, it's called a *net loss*.

At its simplest level, net profit is operating profit minus everything else.

Finding out about earnings per share

You might be wondering by now, "Okay great, the company made millions of dollars. Wonderful. So, what's in it for me?"

That's exactly what earnings per share is all about. Usually, one of the last items listed on a company's income statement is *earnings per share*, most commonly known as *EPS*. If net income tells you how large a pie is, EPS tells you, the fundamental analyst, how big your slice is.

EPS is calculated by dividing net income by the number of *shares outstanding* at the company. A company's number of shares outstanding is the total number of shares that are owned by members of the public as well as *restricted shares* held by officers and directors of the company. Restricted stock shares are given to individuals with close connections to the company, such as the executive team of a company that was acquired. Restricted stock comes with strings attached, which may bar the owners from selling for a certain amount of time. The number of shares a company has outstanding is available on the balance sheet, to be discussed more fully in Chapter 6.

Everything you really need to know, though, is right on the income statement, including:

- ✔ **Basic earnings per share:** This measure tells you how much of a slice of the company's net profit you're entitled to as a shareholder. The formula in its simplest form is:

  Net income / number of shares outstanding

  Some companies have special classes of stock, called preferred stock. These dividends, if paid, should be subtracted from net income in the formula above when calculating basic earnings per share.

- ✔ **Diluted earnings per share:** When you read in the newspaper about how much a company earned, you're most likely reading about diluted earnings per share. Diluted EPS measures how much the company earned based on each share of stock. If you think of net income as a pizza, diluted EPS tells you how big of a slice you're entitled to. Diluted EPS is commonly used because it's the most conservative. It divides net income by the total number of shares that could possibly be outstanding, including the impact of employees converting their stock options into real shares.

Never underestimate the danger of employee stock options on the value of your claim to a company's earnings. When employees are given options, and those options become valuable either because the employee works at the company for a set period of time or the stock rises, those shares can be converted into real shares. The avalanche of shares can water down, or dilute, how much of a claim you have on the company's earnings. This is called dilution, and is a big reason why you need to carefully compare basic EPS with diluted EPS. If diluted EPS is dramatically less than basic EPS, that's a signal employees might be holding large baskets of options.

Comparing a Company's Profit to Expectations

Ever notice how a company's stock price falls, even after the company posts a huge increase in earnings? You can learn more about how to use information from the income statement to determine stock prices in Chapter 10. But it's critical to realize that profits and earnings don't always move in lockstep with stock prices.

It's true that over time, a company with rising revenue and earnings will likely see its stock price rise, too. And as discussed in Chapter 3, correctly forecasting how to determine how much a company will earn and how much it will be worth in the future can be great for long-term success. Fundamental analysts can help you determine whether a stock is cheap or expensive relative to the company's revenue and earnings.

But in the short term, stock prices and earnings can seemingly have nothing to do with each other. And that's where the skill, and a bit of luck, comes in when you try to match fundamental analysis with stock prices. The fact is that in the short term, stocks rise and fall largely based on how a company's earnings compare with what's expected.

The importance of investors' expectations

Remember, when you're studying a company's income statement, you're not alone. There are hundreds, if not thousands of other investors looking at the same numbers and trying to place a price on the stock. They then buy and sell based on their fundamental analysis, to establish the current price.

If the company's revenue and earnings match what most people were expecting, that means the current stock price was likely correctly set. Only if the other investors were way off will the stock move much higher or lower after a company releases its income statement. You will discover more on this topic later in the book. But the role of expectations for earnings is important to discuss now since it shows that just because you master the income statement doesn't mean you'll necessarily be a successful investor.

Comparing actual financial results with expectations

Even before a company puts out its income statement, analysts and other investors have had a chance to guess what they think the company will earn. These *earnings estimates* are usually based on diluted earnings per share.

These estimates are available online at many places, but below are instructions on how to find them at MSN Money.

1. **Log into MSN Money at moneycentral.msn.com/investor.**

2. **Enter the symbol of the stock you're interested in the box in the upper left-hand corner of the screen and click the "Get Quote" button.**

3. **Click on the "Earnings Estimates" option listed in the navigation bar on the left-hand side of the screen.**

4. **Find the earnings number in the "Average Estimate" row under the quarter you're interested in. That's the earnings estimate.**

Once the company reports its earnings, you can then compare the actual earnings with the estimate.

It can be tricky to get an apples-to-apples comparison between the analysts' EPS estimate and the actual reported EPS from the company. While analysts will usually forecast operating earnings, companies may sometimes include unusual and nonrecurring items that make comparison with the estimate problematic. For that reason, many companies attempt to help investors by offering *pro forma earnings*. Pro forma earnings don't follow GAAP. Instead, adjustments are made by the company to make the reported EPS match the estimate.

Pro forma earnings can be helpful when you're trying to see if a company's earnings beat, matched or missed earnings estimates. But pro forma earnings can also be abused by companies. By not following GAAP, companies have great leeway in adding certain one-time gains and ignoring charges they'd rather you not see. The Securities and Exchange Commission in 2002, for instance, said Trump Hotels & Casino Resorts departed from accounting rules and gave a misleading impression the company beat estimates when it reported quarterly results in October 1999. While the company told investors it was leaving out a one-time $81.4 million charge, it didn't disclose it also added a one-time gain of $17.2 million to its results. Investors assumed the company beat estimates due to strong performance, the SEC said, when in fact, Trump's numbers were lifted by the gain.

Chapter 6

Measuring A Company's Staying Power with the Balance Sheet

In This Chapter

▶ Calculating the size of a company's financial resources using the balance sheet

▶ Discerning the difference between a company that is financed by debt or stock

▶ Realizing the importance of watching a company's working capital

▶ Gaining awareness of companies' ability to water down your holding with dilution

For many investors, following how companies are doing each quarter is almost a sport. Some investors may read about companies' earnings and revenue, just as sports fans follow the track records of their favorite teams.

And certainly, knowing how well a company is doing, or how strong its business is operating, is an important part of fundamental analysis. But knowing about earnings and revenue is just the tip of the fundamental analysis iceberg. Fundamental analysts not only know how a company is doing, but what kind of financial shape it's in.

And that's why it's important for you to understand how to dig into a company's *balance sheet*. The balance sheet is a financial statement that tells you if a company is financially healthy. A strong balance sheet, or one that's rich in cash and low on debt, can help a company endure a severe but temporary downturn in its business.

In this chapter, you'll take a tour of the balance sheet and gain an understanding of how this financial statement can help improve the results of your fundamental analysis.

Familiarizing Yourself with the Balance Sheet

If you've ever calculated your personal net worth, you already have a pretty good understanding of what a company's balance sheet is. When you tally up your net worth, you generally perform a quick calculation that might look something like this:

Value of things you own – value of things you owe = net worth

Consider this simple personal finance situation: You bought a $200,000 house, put 20% down ($40,000) and borrowed the rest ($160,000). Meanwhile, you have $20,000 in your savings account. You would calculate your net worth like this:

$200,000 (home value) + $20,000 (savings) – $160,000 (loan amount) = $60,000 net worth

Keep this example in mind as you learn about how a company measures its assets, liabilities, and equity, as explained next.

Separating your assets from your liabilities

Just as biologists classify living creatures by placing them in a genus and species, accountants attempt to put everything companies own and owe into three buckets. Those buckets are:

- ✔ **Assets:** Things a company owns. These might include *tangible assets*, such as physical manufacturing plants or raw materials sitting in a warehouse. Assets, too, might be *intangible*. Intangible assets are things like patents and trademarks, which have value even though you can't touch them.

- ✔ **Liabilities:** Things a company owes. Usually, liabilities include debt the company is on the hook for.

- ✔ **Shareholders' equity (or just equity):** What's left of a company's assets after accounting for its liabilities. Technically, equity represents all the money put into the company by investors and the portion of the profits the company has held onto. When companies hold onto earnings, rather than returning them to shareholders (often in the form a dividend), they are called *retained earnings*. It's the equivalent to your own net worth.

The most basic equation of business

Once accountants place a company's assets and liabilities into the proper buckets, it's possible to apply some basic math. And the calculation you use to measure your net worth is practically identical to how companies measure their shareholders' equity. The formula companies use is just rearranged a bit and the terms are different.

Companies don't necessarily refer to net worth. Net worth is more of a term used in personal finance. Instead, the difference between what companies own and what they owe is called shareholders' equity.

So, here's the most basic formula used in business and the fundamental building block behind the balance sheet:

Assets = Liabilities + Equity

As you can see, this formula states a company's assets must equal the sum of what it owes and what the shareholders own (shareholders' equity). At all times, a company's assets must equal the sum of its liabilities and equity. The fact that both sides of this equation must be equal, or balance, is where the balance sheet gets its name. Clever, I know.

Some investors have an easier time understanding the fundamental formula used on the balance sheet by picturing it visually. For you right-brained readers out there, below in Table 6-1 is a diagram that's often scribbled on the blackboard in Accounting 101 classes.

Understanding the Parts of the Balance Sheet

Now that you understand the basic structure of the balance sheet, it's time to start picking it apart. To do this, first know assets, liabilities, and equity can each be broken down further into smaller, more telling components. Deconstructing a company's assets, liabilities and equity can be extremely useful in understanding how a company funds itself and keeps paying the bills by managing its ready-and-available cash, called *working capital*.

When you dissect a balance sheet, you begin to gain deeper knowledge about all the moving parts that make up a company. The balance sheet tells you what a company owns, what it's borrowing, and where it gets the money to keep itself in operation.

Table 6-1	Visual Take on the Balance Sheet
Assets	Liabilities
	+
	Equity

Covering your bases with assets

The best place to start exploring a company's balance sheet is its list of assets. The portion of the balance sheet that records a company's assets typically has the following parts:

- **Current assets:** A company's current assets are things it owns that could theoretically be sold for cash within a year. These assets, also called *short-term assets*, are those the company can tap reasonable quickly to meet immediate cash obligations. Current assets can be further broken down into:

  - **Cash:** This is the easiest asset to understand. Companies have savings accounts, too, and keep cash handy to pay bills.

  - **Cash equivalents:** Companies will sometimes invest cash that's stockpiled in short-term and high-quality investments that can be quickly sold. These investments give companies liquidity, or access to cash, but allow them to earn a slightly higher return that just holding cash.

    When many fundamental analysts refer to a company's cash, they are usually including cash equivalents in addition to cold-hard cash.

  - **Marketable securities:** Sometimes companies have cash available that they don't need immediately, but expect they might need within a year. They might invest this cash in high-quality debt that matures in a quarter or two. These investments are relatively safe, but not as readily accessible as actual cash or cash equivalents.

  - **Accounts receivable:** When companies sell a product, they often don't collect the cash right away. If you buy a book, for instance, you might use your credit card and the merchant isn't paid immediately. These short-term IOUs are called accounts receivable.

  - **Inventories:** Companies must spend money to accumulate the things they plan to sell. Nearly all manufacturing companies, for instance, must buy raw materials to make their products. The value of these assets show up in the inventories line.

  - **Prepaid expenses.** If a company pays a bill ahead of time, it has a credit with the supplier or merchant. That credit is an asset, since it reduces what the company must spend in the future.

✔ **Long-term liabilities:**

- **Property, plant and equipment.** Assets that cannot be turned into cash in a year are called long-term assets. One of the biggest groups of long-term assets include a company's *property, plant and equipment*, nicknamed *PP&E*. These assets include buildings and other machinery and computers a company might own. For an oil company, for instance, PP&E might be oil rigs used to pull crude out of the earth.

- **Goodwill.** Goodwill is an asset you can't feel or touch, making it intangible. Goodwill usually appears on a company's balance sheet after it buys another company. Goodwill is the amount paid for another company, above that company's actual value according to accounting rules. The extra amount paid is considered an asset on the acquiring company's balance sheet.

- **Other intangibles.** Goodwill isn't the only asset a company might have that can't be touched or seen. Patents, brands and trademarks, for instance, have value even though they're not physical items.

- **Total assets.** All of the assets are added up to create a grand total of everything the company owns. This is called total assets and will be a number that's used frequently in analysis, especially with financial ratios discussed in Chapter 8.

Total assets is an important number on the balance sheet. It must, and will, match the total of the company's liabilities and equity.

Just to give you an idea of what to expect when perusing the asset section of a balance sheet, Figure 6-1 shows you the top section of Hershey Food's 2007 balance sheet.

Getting in touch with a company's liabilities

Just like it seems there's always a bill in your mailbox when you open it, the same goes for companies. During the normal course of business, companies have hungry suppliers and service providers who demand to be paid for their products or services. But bills are just one form of liabilities companies have. The liabilities section of a balance sheet breaks down everything companies owe into these parts:

✔ **Current liabilities:** If a company has bills that are due within a year's time, they're considered to be *current liabilities*. Not paying these bills usually means trouble for a company. Current liabilities come in several flavors fundamental analysts need to be aware of:

- **Accounts payable:** Companies don't typically have to pay right away for things they buy. Suppliers will usually extend *trade credit* to companies, giving them at least 30 days or even longer to pay for certain supplies, raw materials or services.

- **Short-term debt:** This is the amount of debt the company must pay back within a year.

- **Current portion of long-term debt:** Typically companies arrange to borrow money for many years. A portion of that *long-term debt*, though, is generally due within a year and is called the current portion of long-term debt.

- **Other current liabilities.** Here's the catch-all bucket for liabilities that don't quite fit anywhere else.

✔ **Long-term liabilities:**

- **Long-term debt:** The costs of starting and maintaining a business can be massive. As a result, some companies turn to lenders to borrow money from, and if they're lucky, they can line up long-term debt that doesn't have to be paid for more than a year or longer.

  Keeping an eye on a company's long-term debt load is critical. While only the current portion is due within a year, the year of debt may come due shortly. If the company is unable to pay the debt or refinance it by borrowing from someone else, the company may *default*. When a company defaults, the lenders may threaten to take control of the company.

- **Other long-term liabilities:** This includes liabilities, due in more than a year, that don't fit in any of the other categories. A company will break down liabilities that are in here in the *footnotes* to the financial statements. The footnotes, typically available in a company's *10-Q* or *10-K*, provide a more detailed breakdown of liabilities.

- **Deferred income taxes:** Companies must keep two sets of financial statements. There's the version you see, which is presented in this book, and a version for tax purposes for the IRS. Sometimes the accounting for taxes can be quite different in the two sets of books. Deferred income taxes help reconcile the differences. If a company has deferred income taxes, that means it may owe taxes in the future.

The liabilities section of the balance sheet might often look like Figure 6-2, which is from Hershey's 2007 *10-K*.

Hershey's Assets on 2007 Balance Sheet		
Current assets		In $ thousands
	Cash and cash equivalents	$129,198
	Accounts receivable	487,285
	Inventories	600,185
	Prepaid expenses and other	209,906
	Total current assets	1,426,574
Long-term assets		
	Property, plant and equipment	1,539,715
	Goodwill	584,713
	Other intangibles	155,862
	Other assets	540,249
Total assets		4,247,113

Figure 6-1: Hershey's assets on the balance sheet in 2007.

Hershey's Liabilities on the Balance Sheet in 2007		
Current liabilities		In $ thousands
	Accounts payable	$223,019
	Short-term debt	850,288
	Current portion of long-term debt	6,104
	Other current liabilities	539,359
	Total current liabilities	1,618,770
Long-term liabilities		
	Long-term debt	1,279,965
	Other long-term liabilities	544,106
	Deferred income taxes	180,842
Total liabilities		3,623,593

Figure 6-2: Hershey's liabilities on the balance sheet in 2007.

Taking stock in a company's equity

Shareholders' equity represents the total claim investors have on a company's assets, free-and-clear of debt. That includes money investors injected into a company, in addition to profits that the company has held back, or retained. The equity section of many companies' balance sheets include the following sections:

- **Preferred stock:** Companies may issue ownership stakes that are kind of a blend between debt and equity. Like debt, *preferred stock* pays a cash payment that's arranged ahead of time. However, as with common stock dividends, companies may suspend these preferred stock payments at any time.

- **Common stock:** When you're looking to buy a stake of a company, typically these are the shares you're buying. When you look up a stock quote, most of the time you're getting the price of a share of a company's common stock.

- **Retained earnings:** It's up to a company whether or not to return its profits to shareholders in the form of dividends. If the company keeps earnings, it records the sum here.

- **Treasury stock:** Sometimes not all of a company's shares are available to bought or sold. A company might buy back its stock when it thinks it's cheap, and put it aside. A company might also authorize to issue stock, but not actually issue it. Either way, the pool of unused shares are called treasury stock.

- **Total shareholders equity:** The shareholders equity line of the balance sheet measures the value of shareholders' stake in the company.

A summary of the equity section of Hershey's balance sheet appears below in Table 6-2.

Table 6-2	Hershey's Equity on the Balance Sheet
	$ thousands
Preferred stock	N/A
Common stock	$299,095
Retained earnings	$3,927,306
Treasury stock	−$4,001,562
Total shareholders' equity	$592,922
Total liabilities and stockholders' equity	$4,247,113

Analyzing the Balance Sheet

Now that you understand the pieces and parts that make up the balance sheet, it's time to start applying fundamental analysis. Just as you dug more deeply into the income statement in Chapter 5, in this section you'll develop tools to glean insight from the balance sheet.

Sizing up the balance sheet with common sizing

If you noticed while looking at Hershey's balance sheet above, just looking at the numbers in isolation isn't particularly useful. It's helpful to put the assets, liabilities, and equity into perspective by comparing them with something. That's why *common sizing*, a fundamental analysis tool applied with the income statement in Chapter 5, can be equally helpful when analyzing the balance sheet.

When common sizing a balance sheet, you are attempting to show how significant a company's different assets, liabilities and forms of equity are to the entire firm. You only need three formulas to common size the entire balance sheet:

- ✔ **Assets:** Divide each type of asset by the company's total assets.
- ✔ **Liabilities:** Divide each type of liability by the company's total liabilities and stockholder's equity.
- ✔ **Equity:** Divide each category of equity by the company's total liabilities and stockholders' equity.

Multiply the results of the three items above by 100 to convert the figures into a percentage.

Imagine if you wanted to see how much Hershey relies on borrowed money, versus money raised from stock investors, to fund itself. That's a perfect reason to common size the liabilities portion of Hershey's balance sheet.

To do this, you start with Hershey's accounts payable ($223,019) and divide it by total liabilities and stockholders' equity ($4,247,113). The result is 5.3%, and I'll explain what that means in a bit. First, you might want to finish common sizing the whole statement. Table 6-3 shows you the results of common sizing the key parts of the liabilities and equity portion of Hershey's balance sheet.

Table 6-3	Common-Size Analysis of Hershey
	% of liabilities and shareholders' equity
Accounts payable	5.3%
Short-term debt	20%
Current portion of long-term debt	0.1%
Total current liabilities	38.1%
Long-term debt	30.1%
Total shareholders' equity	14%

Common sizing a company's liabilities gives you an instant view of where Hershey gets the money to keep itself going, or its *capital structure*. Understanding a company's capital structure is key to understanding how well it's positioned to withstand an economic downturn or how profitable it will be during strong economic growth.

Just by doing a few multiplication problems, you get a very unique fundamental look into Hershey. You can see Hershey receives its financing from a balanced number of sources, but leans toward relying more on debt. Hershey gets 20% of its financing from short-term loans, more than 30% from long-term loans and 14% from equity.

When companies rely on borrowed money to pay for their operations, it's called *leverage*. Leverage can greatly enhance a company's returns for stock holders as long as the company can comfortably keep up with its interest payments. Interest on debt is largely fixed, much like a monthly payment on a 30-year fixed mortgage is static. Interest also has a tax benefit of being deductible. The question, though, is whether or not a company has borrowed too much. You can find out if a company is overleveraged by analyzing working capital, later in this chapter, and financial ratios in Chapter 8.

Looking for trends using index-number analysis

While balance sheets take a snapshot of a company's assets, liabilities and equity at a set time of the year, the parts inside are constantly changing. When interest rates are low, for instance, a company may decide to leverage itself by borrowing more. Similarly, when stock prices are lofty, a company may choose to raise equity by selling stock.

Because assets, liabilities and equity are evolving, it's important in fundamental analysis to pay attention to trends and changes between quarters and years.

The index-number trend method is a great way to help you spot changes in a company's capital structure over time. You can do an index-number analysis by choosing a year to be your starting point and then compare all assets, liabilities and equity to that point.

For instance, if you want to start your analysis of Coca-Cola since 2005, you would first download the balance-sheet items for 2007, 2006, and 2005. In Table 6-4 you can see what some of the key parts of Coke's balance sheet were in those years.

Table 6-4	Coca-Cola's Balance Sheet Since 2005		
$ in millions	*2007*	*2006*	*2005*
Cash and cash equivalents	$4,308	$2,590	4,767
Property, plant and equipment	8,493	6,903	5,831
Long-term debt	3,277	1,314	1,154
Shareowners equity	21,744	16,920	16,355

Certainly, you could eyeball the numbers above to get a general idea of the trends in the company's assets and liabilities. But the index-number analysis is easy and will make the changes pop out. To create an index-number table, divide each line in the balance sheet by the corresponding value for the base year and then multiply by 100.

For instance, to calculate the index-number value for Coke's cash and cash equivalents in 2006, divide its cash and cash equivalents in 2006 ($2,590) by cash and cash equivalents in 2005 ($4,767) and then multiply by 100. The result is 54.3. If you complete the analysis of Coke's balance sheet, you get something that looks like Table 6-5.

The index-number value of the base year, 2005 in Table 6-5, will be 100. 100 is the baseline of our analysis.

Table 6-5   Index-Number Analysis of Coca-Cola's Balance Sheet

$ in millions	*2007*	*2006*	*2005*
Cash and cash equivalents	90	54	100
Property, plant and equipment	146	118	100
Long-term debt	284	114	100
Shareowners' equity	133	103	100

After completing the index-number analysis of Coke, you can quickly see what's going on with the company's capital structure. The first thing that jumps out is the fact Coke started increasing its level of debt in 2006 and really ramped it up in 2007. In its 10-K, Coke acknowledged a greater use of leverage, primarily to pay for acquisitions such as Vitamin Water maker Glaceau and energy drink Fuze. As a fundamental analyst, you note this. After all, the company has been trying to broaden its lineup of beverages beyond Coke. That diversification, though, is coming with the expense of greater financial risk as the company must pay higher interest expense.

Appreciating working capital

When it comes to fundamental analysis, a key consideration is how prepared a company is to meet its short-term obligations.

A company may have a very bright long-term future ahead of it, but if it can't meet payroll and pay its bills in the next month, it might not survive long enough to reach its potential.

Just as you would certainly pay your heating bill before putting money in a 401(k), companies, too, must make sure they have enough cash to satisfy short-term obligations.

How do you determine whether a company can handle its short-term bills? Analyzing *working capital* is one of fundamental analysts' favorite tools to access a company's immediate financial situation. Working capital tells you whether a company can access cash needed to pay its most pressing bills over the coming year. It's a measure of *short-term liquidity*.

Working capital will be discussed more in Chapter 8, along with the other financial ratios. But it's important enough to start thinking about along with the balance sheet. The formula for working capital is:

Working capital = Current assets – current liabilities

If a company has positive working capital and more current assets than current liabilities, that gives a fundamental analyst a bit of comfort. However, if current assets are less than current liabilities — that means if a company's business hits a snag — it may be forced to extreme measures to meet its bills, including selling off manufacturing plans or equipment in a fire sale.

Analyzing here and now: The current ratio

Closely related to working capital, and perhaps of even more value in fundamental analysis, is a concept called the *current ratio*. The current ratio attempts to put a company's current assets into perspective by comparing them with current liabilities. The formula is:

Current ratio = Current assets / current liabilities

The higher a company's current ratio, the better prepared it is to pay for liabilities due within the year. Companies with high current ratios have a greater safety cushion in case business drops off.

As a very general rule of thumb, fundamental analysts like to see at least a current ratio of 1, or even 1.5. The typical company in the Standard & Poor's 500 index had a current ratio of even more than that, 1.72 as of 2008.

But because different businesses require different levels of short-term liquidity, you should always compare a company's current ratio to its industry. You can see what the typical current ratios for several industry sectors are by checking out www.reuters.com.

The Danger of Dilution

Just as it's possible for a company to borrow too much, it's also possible for it to sell too much of itself to shareholders. Remember, shares of stock are like slices of a pizza. If you have a large pizza that's cut into eight slices, everyone gets a decent amount of food. However, if you cut that same pizza into 16 slivers, then you're likely to start hearing complaints.

When companies issue too many shares, they are in effect slicing their profits into smaller and smaller slices. This process of bringing in more investors is known as *dilution*. And since dilution can seriously water down the value of your investment, it's something worth being aware of as a fundamental analyst.

Paying for peanut butter with jelly

Many mergers have bad endings. But in what may be one of the most logical mergers since peanut butter and jelly first came together to create PB&J, was the J.M. Smucker acquisition of Jif peanut butter from Procter & Gamble in June 2002. Since it paid for the roughly $800 million deal using stock, J.M. Smucker's number of shares outstanding roughly doubled to nearly 50 million shares. Was the deal successful, even though it cut the company's profits into twice as many slices? After the deal was done, J.M. Smucker's profits more than doubled in the year after the deal.

You want to keep a close eye on company's number of *shares outstanding*. This number tells you how much of a company's profit you, as a shareholder, are entitled to by owning a share of stock. Most companies disclose their number of shares outstanding on the balance sheet. The more shares outstanding, the smaller the slice of profits you're entitled to.

How stock can be watered down

Dilution occurs when a company's number of shares outstanding increases. A company may increase its number of shares outstanding for a number of reasons, including to:

- **Acquire another company using its stock.** When a company's stock price is high, relative to competitors', it may use its shares as a currency for acquisitions. A company may issue new shares and use them to buy another firm. Stock deals can be popular with companies, since they don't consume precious cash, and investors like them because they may be tax-free events.

- **Pay *stock options* to employees.** Hoping to make the workforce feel like and act like owners, some companies may issue shares to employees and executives. Stock options allow employees to buy shares of stock at discounted prices, as long as the company's stock rises.

- **Reduce leverage.** Companies that have borrowed too much in the past and have a life-threatening brush with bankruptcy, may try to clean up their balance sheet by issuing stock and paying down debt.

Knowing how stock options can contribute to dilution

When companies dole out stock options to employees, that value of your stock can be seriously threatened. Stock options, a form of compensation for employees, are tied to the company's stock price. If the company's stock rises, employees may cash in the options in exchange for company stock, forcing the company to sell additional shares to meet the demand for new shares.

Dot-com companies handed out stock options so freely in the late 1990s that investors faced seeing the value of their shares shrivel up by 24%, according to a story in USA TODAY. The risk of dilution is why fundamental analysts should pay close attention to a company's diluted earnings per share, which accounts for the potential dilution, as explained in Chapter 6.

Some companies periodically attempt to reduce the danger of dilution and make their shares more valuable by buying back shares. In a buyback, companies use their cash to take shares off the market. Stock buybacks, in theory, make each share more valuable because a company's profits are sliced into fewer pieces. Some companies may buy back stock even if they haven't issued options, if they think the shares are cheap.

Stocks will often rally after a company announces a stock buyback. But fundamental analysts know better than to fall for this trap. For one thing, companies might buy back stock with borrowed money, which increases their interest costs and risk. Many companies also say they will buy back stock and never actually do. Other firms end up issuing more new shares than they bought back, all but erasing any benefit of the buyback.

Chapter 7

Tracking Cash with the Statement of Cash Flow

. . . .

. . . .

"**S**how me the money!" Those words screamed out by Cuba Gooding's character, a fictitious Arizona Cardinals wide receiver in the 1996 comedy "Jerry Maguire," captured one football player's desire for cold hard cash. And that same line could just as easily apply to fundamental analysis and the statement of cash flows.

Accounting rules can become so convoluted it's hard to just see how much cash a company is bringing in. You might read through a company's income statement and balance sheet and feel as if you have a pretty decent understanding of how the company is doing and what it owns. But revenue and profit are just numbers on a financial statement. It's cash that really matters. It's cash that pays the bills.

The *statement of cash flows*, or *cash-flow statement*, is all about showing you the money. The statement meticulously tracks the flow of cold hard cash in and out of a company. There's nothing more reassuring than knowing a company is bringing in cash.

Fundamental analysts relish in the brutal honesty of the cash-flow statement. And while the statement has its limitations, in this chapter you'll find how tracking the cash flowing in and out of a company can take your analysis skills to the next level.

Looking at the Cash-Flow Statement As a Fundamental Analyst

To understand why a company's cash flow can be more revealing about a company's performance, consider this simple example. Imagine your daughter has borrowed $10 from you to start a lemonade stand. The only stipulation for the loan is that she reports back to you on how the business is going.

Excited about being an entrepreneur, your daughter quickly spends the $10 you lent her to get up and running. She buys lemons, sugar, cups, and stirring spoons. It's a hot summer day, so it looks like a winning business idea.

At the end of the day, you ask your daughter how she did. Hardly able to contain her smile, she beams that business was great and she completely sold out of lemonade. She estimates she sold 50 cups of lemonade at 50 cents a cup. You do the math quickly and determine her profit was $15. Constructing an income statement in your head, as explored in Chapter 5, you calculate she brought in revenue of $25 (50 cups of lemonade at 50 cents) and spent $10 to make the product. That's a net income of $15.

But when you extend your hand to ask for your $10 back, thinking you'd let her keep the $5 profit, she reports that she doesn't have any cash at all. It turns out that she accepted IOUs for all the lemonade she sold. Suddenly the business isn't necessarily looking so good, since there's no cash flow.

This example is a gross simplification. But it gets to the point of why cash flow is critical to analysis.

Accounting rules, even if properly followed, may give the impression a company is doing better than it really is. Profit, as measured by rules made by accountants, are subject to dozens of estimates, approximations and hunches. But cash is cash. You either have it or you don't.

Getting into the flow with cash flow

You might be wondering why you need to even bother with the statement of cash flows. After all, the income statement, explored in Chapter 5, tells you how profitable the company is. And the balance sheet, discussed in Chapter 6, tells you how solid a company's financial resources are.

The statement of cash flows, though, deserves a spot in your fundamental analysis routine. The statement can provide valuable information when evaluating a company because it:

✔ **Cuts through the optics of accounting.** As you learned in Chapter 5, measuring a company's profit is a pretty convoluted process. There are even more machinations going on behind the scenes, as accountants classify expenses and revenue. In contrast, cash is cash. You either make cash profits or you don't.

✔ **Links the different financial statements together.** The income statement and balance sheet are somewhat independent of each other, since they're measuring different aspects of a business. The statement of cash flows, though, draws upon information from both the income statement and balance sheet to give you one, complete view of the company.

✔ **Highlights cash generated from actually doing business.** The statement of cash flows makes it very clear how much of the cash coming into a business is the result of the company actually selling its products and services. It's a helpful way to look past some one-time gains a company might receive, say, by selling assets.

Accounting standards were tightened in the early 2000s following the implosion of Enron. Even so, the income statement is to be regarded with some healthy skepticism. The statement of cash flows can let you intelligently look for potential red flags in a company's accounting, which is one of the hallmarks of fundamental analysis.

Consider the example of a company that offers customers, who agree to buy products or services now, a very lenient repayment schedule. Doing so would allow the company to book revenue now, boosting net income. The trouble, though, is that the company is essentially stealing net income from a future period. When companies do this, it's referred to as *channel stuffing,* because the company is pushing product into the hands of customers prematurely to book sales now. The statement of cash flows, however, makes channel stuffing easy to spot, since the company didn't receive cash.

Breaking the cash-flow statement into its key parts

The way the statement of cash flows is organized tells you a great deal about a company. The statement is divided into three main sections. Cash coming into or going out of a company is placed into one of three categories, including:

✔ **Cash flows from operating activities.** Here, investors can get a good idea of how much cash a company brings in, or uses, during its normal course of business. It counts cash coming in from customers as well as cash used to pay suppliers for materials, to the government for taxes, and to pay workers' salaries.

✓ **Cash flows from investing activities.** Companies keep careful track of money they've spent upgrading, or investing in, themselves. This section, for instance, counts the cash consumed buying new assets such as equipment or facilities.

✓ **Cash flows from financing activities.** While companies are generally hoping to become self-sufficient and support their operations with the cash they generate from their business, sometimes they need cash injections. This section of the balance sheet tallies up how much cash is plowed into a company by *lenders* and *investors*. And on the flip side, this section accounts for cash used to pay cash dividends to investors or to pay down debts.

Unfortunately, many companies aren't as forthright with their statements of cash flows as they are with the balance sheet and income statement. When companies report their earnings using *earnings press releases*, a vast majority do not provide a statement of cash flows. You can read more about what's contained in the earnings press release in Chapter 4. You may need to wait for weeks after a company reports its earnings before getting the statement of cash flows. Companies are required to include the statement in their 10-Q or 10-K filings.

A few companies including Amazon.com, though, have started providing a statement of cash flows with their earnings press release. That's a positive trend for fundamental analysts that other companies will hopefully follow.

Examining a company's cash flow from operations

Typically, the first section of a company's statement of cash flows deals with measuring how much cash a company brings in during its normal course of business. This key section, the first in the cash-flow statement, measures *cash from operations*, or formally called *cash provided by / (used in) operating activities*. The section tells you how much cash the company generated, or used, in the course of doing business. Table 7-2 shows you how much Kraft Foods generated in cash from its operations.

Reading the statement of cash flows can get complicated because there are many lines in the statement. Adding to the confusion is the fact some of the lines are positive and some are negative. Don't stress. Just remember that the statement of cash flows is really just converting a company's net income into a number that represents a company's cash flow. Secondly, just remember when a number in the cash-flow statement is positive, that means the activity brought cash into the company. Similarly, when the number is negative, the item consumed cash. If you're more of a visual person, Table 7-1 shows you how to think of these adjustments.

Table 7-1	Generating or Consuming Cash
If an Item on the cash flow statement is . . .	*It . . .*
Negative	Uses cash
Positive	Generates cash

A few of those adjustments made to net income to arrive at a company's cash from operations are described in the following sections.

Depreciation and amortization

Usually, the biggest adjustment to net income to convert it into cash from operations is *depreciation* and *amortization*. Depreciation is an expense companies are required to include on their income statement, that doesn't actually cost a company cash. Depreciation tallies the expense of the wear and tear on its equipment. Amortization, on the other hand, is the erosion of value of intangible assets, like patents or trademarks.

Depreciation can be a somewhat difficult item for investors to understand. Think of it this way. Every year, the value of your car falls due to age, and wear and tear. It's a real expense, since it is technically costing you money. But when your car depreciates, you don't get a bill for it. You don't have to write a check, and it doesn't cost you cash immediately. As a result, depreciation is added back to net income when measuring a company's cash flow from operations.

Tax adjustments

Companies keep two sets of books. There's one set for investors, which measures earnings according to the accounting rules. Then there's a set required by the Internal Revenue Service for taxes. The different sets of books have different rules. As a result, a company may pay taxes to the IRS before the tax expense is recorded in the books monitored by accountants. Confused yet? Don't worry. Just know that when a company actually writes a check and pays taxes, which aren't recorded on the income statement, it must subtract the amount from net income. It's subtracted since paying the taxes ate up some of the company's cash.

Gains on divestitures

When a company sells a unit, it may add the profit on the sale to its net income. But remember, that profit didn't result from the company selling products or services. Since the sale didn't generate sales from operations, the amount is subtracted from net income.

Asset impairments or losses on sales of discontinued operations

Believe it or not, companies sometimes make poor business decisions. They might try a new business concept, which flops spectacularly, or realize an asset they bought has lost its value. When companies are hit with these charges, accountants consider them to be costs and require the companies to take a hit to the income statement. However, savvy fundamental analysts know many of these flops don't actually cost companies cash. And that's why many of these charges are added back to net income to arrive at cash from operations.

Accounts receivable

If you're worried about a company claiming it's doing better than it really is, this section of the cash flow statement is critical. As you discovered in Chapter 6, a company's *accounts receivable* is a tally of how much its customers owe for products they've bought. If you see accounts receivable soar, that means customers are mostly buying on credit instead of paying cash. The increase in accounts receivable eats into a company's cash because the company is essentially giving customers a credit card.

If you're worried a company might be stuffing the channel, pay close attention to the change in accounts receivable. A big jump in accounts receivable compared to the increase of a companies' revenue can be a tip-off.

Accounts payable

When you buy something using a credit card, you get the asset without using cash. It's the same concept with companies, who may buy supplies or materials on credit. They're able to get their hands on the things they need to conduct business, without using cash. When a company's accounts payable increases, it's considered a boost to cash and added to net income.

If you notice accounts payable is rising relative to a company's *cost of goods sold* (discussed in Chapter 6), watch out. It might mean the company isn't paying its bills on time, which may inflate its cash.

Inventories

If you've ever read about just-in-time manufacturing, you understand why companies go to great lengths to keep inventories low. Buying piles of materials needed for business consumes precious cash. So by keeping *inventory* levels down, companies can hang onto cash. You'll see this immediately on the statement of cash flow. If inventories rise, the increase is subtracted from net income to measure a company's cash from operations. Likewise, if a company uses up inventory, it's a boost to its cash levels.

Net cash (used in) / provided by operating activities

Here's the end-all-be-all when it comes to measuring a company's cash flow from its operations. After making all the painstaking adjustments to net income, to add back items that didn't use cash and subtract those that did, you get a company's cash from operations or net cash (used in) / provided by operating activities (see Table 7-2).

When net cash (used in) / provided by operating activities is positive, that means the company generated cash from its normal line of business. If the number is negative, that means the company burned cash. Some companies will put the negative number in parentheses while others make the number red in the financial statements.

Table 7-2	Kraft's Cash From Operations in 2007
Item	*In $ millions*
Net income	$2,590
Depreciation and amortization	886
Deferred income tax benefit	(416)
Gains on divestitures	(15)
Asset impairment	209
Accounts receivable	(268)
Inventories	(191)
Accounts payable	241
Income taxes	124
Other	411
Net cash provided by operating activities	3,571

Source: Kraft Foods' 2007 10-K

Considering a company's cash from investments

When you buy a company's stock, you want to make sure it's making adequate investments in itself to keep things in working order. That's where the section of the cash-flow statement, called the *cash from investing* or *cash provided by / (used in) investing activities* comes in.

This part of the cash-flow statement lets you see how much cash the company is using to keep its factories humming or stores looking presentable. Generally, investments companies make in themselves can consume large amounts of cash for things including:

- **Updating stores to remain relevant.** A retailer, for instance, may need to periodically remodel stores to keep them interesting to shoppers.

- **Enhancing capacity.** A manufacturer that's running full tilt may need to add warehouse space to handle increased demand.

- **Upgrading equipment.** A hospital may be able to improve patient satisfaction and reduce wait times by buying a state-of-the-art device that works faster or is more effective.

- **Acquisitions.** Companies might decide it's cheaper to buy a rival that's already in an area of business, instead of trying to launch its own business.

- **Divestitures.** When companies sell off a unit, they typically receive cash. That cash received isn't from operations. It's from investing; at least that's what the accountants say. Even if a company technically lost money on a unit that's sold off, if it gets at least some cash, that's still considered a positive cash flow.

For simplicity, companies will often lump all their investments in improving, enhancing or updating their facilities into a single item on the cash-flow statement called *capital expenditures,* or *cap ex* for short. If you're interested in digging more deeply into what capital expenditures a company made, the details will be provided in the footnotes in the 10-K.

Below in Table 7-3 you can take a look at the investments Kraft Foods made to its business in 2007. Notice the huge drain of cash from acquisitions. Kraft Foods bought the global biscuit business of Groupe Danone for $7.6 billion on November 30, 2007.

Table 7-3	Kraft's Cash From Investing Activities in 2007
Item	*In $ millions*
Capital expenditures	($1,241)
Acquisitions	(7,437)
Proceeds from divestitures	216
Other	46
Net cash (used in) investing activities	(8,416)

Getting into a company's cash from financing activities

Companies are often like politicians: They seem to be constantly raising money. Instead of trying to line up financing for their campaigns, though, companies need funding to keep themselves going.

A classic example would be a young retail company. The company may not have enough cash to buy all the shirts, pants, and shoes it needs to put into its store. The retailer, then, might borrow money to buy the merchandise, and plan to pay it back after the goods are sold. The money borrowed is considered a positive cash flow from financing activities.

A company's financing activities may bring in or use up cash in a variety of primary ways. Generally, cash is brought in by borrowing money or selling stock to investors. All this is summarized right in the *cash from financing activities* section of the statement of cash flows. Table 7-4 shows an example using Kraft. The biggest uses or generators of cash from financing activities include:

- ✔ **Increasing or decreasing the company's debt load:** As you discovered while reading about the balance sheet in Chapter 6, companies can finance themselves by using their profits, by borrowing or by selling stock to shareholders. Each of these forms has its advantages and disadvantages.

  Here, in this section of the statement of cash flows, you can see whether or not a company is generating cash by borrowing or using cash by paying back debt. If a company decides it has borrowed too much, for instance, it may choose to use cash to pay down its debt.

  Kraft's cash-flow statement, in Table 7-3, distinguishes between its *short-term debt* and *long-term debt*. Short-term debt is most pressing, as it's due within a year, while long-term debt matures in more than a year. Kraft in 2007 issued more than $12 billion in new long- and short-term debt.

- ✔ **Buying back the company's stock:** From time to time, companies might choose to buy their own stock. When they do this, they use cash to take shares out of the hands of the public by buying them. This reduces the number of slices a company's profits are cut into, potentially making each share more valuable.

- ✔ **Paying out dividends to shareholders:** Some companies, usually those in mature businesses with stable cash flow, might generate more cash than they need to run themselves. These companies generally will return cash to shareholders by issuing dividends. These payments consume cash.

✔ **Net cash provided by / (used in) financing activities:** After accounting for all the cash brought in by borrowing and issuing stock, and cash used by extinguishing debt, buying back stock and paying dividends, you get the final result. *Net cash provided by / (used in) financing activities*, or cash from financing activities, shows you whether the company was a net gainer or user of cash after considering all money-raising events.

Table 7-4	Kraft's Cash From Financing Activities in 2007
Item	*In $ millions*
Net issuance (repayment) of short-term borrowings	$5,649
Long-term debt proceeds	6,495
Long-term debt repaid	(1,472)
Repurchase of common stock	(3,708)
Dividends paid	(1,638)
Other	(205)
Net cash (used in) investing activities	5,121

How Investors May Be Fooled by Earnings, But Not Cash Flow

Investors often pay very close attention to a company's revenue and profits. Too much attention, probably. Every quarter, during so-called *earnings season*, investors look at what companies said they earned, compare those results with their expectations, and either buy or sell the stock.

The fact investors pay such close attention to earnings is not missed by companies' managements. There's a huge incentive for companies to never miss *earnings expectations*, or how much investors think the company will make, since doing so can cause a stock price to fall precipitously. Adding to the incentive to not disappoint: Many executives' pay packages are closely tied to the companies' stock price. If earnings disappoint and the stock falls, there goes the Hawaiian vacation for the CEO.

Meanwhile, due to the flexibility of accounting rules, there are ways for management to *manage earnings*. The term "manage earnings" describes a whole host of things management can do to even out net income and earnings each quarter, and reduce the chances of disappointing investors.

Management's ability to manage earnings largely stems from the way the income statement is constructed. Generally, financial transactions use *accrual accounting*. Accrual accounting records revenue when sales are made, and costs when they're incurred. That is very different from cash accounting, which records revenue when sales are *collected* and costs are *paid*.

When a company's profit is widely different from the cash it's bringing in, that's something of great importance to a fundamental analyst. I'll show you how fundamental analysts watch for this potentially disturbing trend later in this chapter.

Companies can also inflate the cash. The most common way would be to avoid paying their bills. Eventually, though, this tactics will catch up with a company when its suppliers or other creditors threaten legal action or stop shipping supplies and raw materials.

A quick-and-dirty way to monitor a company's cash flow

You can spend hours analyzing the statement of cash flows. And later in the book, I'll share with you some financial ratios and other things you can do to analyze the cash coming into and out of a company.

But here, I want to share with you one of the fastest and most effective fundamental ways to analyze a statement of cash flows. It's such a simple form of analysis, it's not a bad idea to do with any company you invest in or have an interest in.

If you recall, profits certainly are important. But cash flow is king. You could have a company making giant profits according to the income statement, but without bringing in much cash. Remember the lemonade stand discussed earlier in the chapter? The answer: Compare a company's net income with its cash from operations. It's very simple fundamental analysis to do. All you need is the company's statement of cash flows.

If a company is generating as much cash as it's reporting in net income, that can be a good indication it has *high-quality earnings*. High-quality earnings are those that are backed up by cold hard cash, not just smoke and mirrors made possible from accounting rules.

If this analysis seems confusing, keep reading. Once you follow the steps below and practice a few times, you'll be surprised at how easy it is to compare a company's net income with its cash from operations.

Don't assume the tightening of accounting standards in the early 2000s stomped out low-quality earnings. Certainly, many companies cleaned up their accounting in 2002 and 2003 in the wake of Enron. Even so, the number of firms with lower-quality earnings have been creeping up again. Table 7-5 shows the number of companies in the Standard & Poor's 500 that reported net income that was greater than their cash from operations.

Table 7-5	Earnings Quality Rises and Falls
Year	**Number of companies in S&P 500 with higher net income than cash flow from operations**
2007	72
2006	84
2005	73
2004	53
2003	42

Source: Standard & Poor's Capital IQ. Based on members of S&P 500 as of 2008, cash flow from operations in 2007 and net income in 2007

Below I'll show you how to perform this form of cash-based earnings-quality analysis on Kraft, with the following steps:

1. **Look up the company's net income.** As you learned in Chapter 5, a company's net income is available on the income statement. But you can also take it from the very top line of the statement of cash flows. For Kraft, net income was $2.6 billion in 2007.

2. **Look up the company's cash flow from operations.** Cash flow from operations is how much the company generated from its business. It's kind of like the cash version of net income. If you recall, Kraft's cash flow from operations was $3.6 billion in 2007.

3. **Compare net income with cash flow from operations.** You'll want to see cash flow from operations be at least equal to, if not larger, than net income. That tells you that the company is generating as much cash as it purports to generate in earnings. Table 7-6 summarizes what you need to know.

   For instance, at Kraft, the company brought in $1 billion in cash above its reported earnings in 2007, giving you decent confidence the company has high-quality earnings.

Table 7-6	Sizing Up a Company's Earnings Quality
If cash from operations is . . .	**It means the company . . .**
Greater than net income	Generates more cash than it reports to shareholders as earnings. It has high-quality earnings.
Less than net income	Generates less cash than it reports to shareholders as earnings. It has low-quality earnings

Just because a company's net income is less than its cash flow from operations doesn't mean it's committing fraud. It just means a substantial portion of the profit it's reporting isn't materializing in cash. This might happen, for instance, when a fast-growing company sells goods so rapidly it must book profits before it can collect cash from customers. Still, when you see cash flow from operations that's less than net income, it's a reason to be concerned and dig further to determine the cause.

Understanding the Fundamentals of Free Cash Flow

Face it. Earnings may impress investors, but cash flow pays the bills. Even if a company posts remarkable revenue growth, if it can't get money into the doors fast enough to pay its own bills, it's toast. That's where free cash flow comes in. Free cash flow tells you how much cash a company generates (or uses) during the normal course of doing business, including the cost of upgrading and maintaining its equipment and facilities.

That's a mouthful, I know. Just remember free cash flow is a relatively easy fundamental analysis tool that can tell you a great deal about a company's generation or burning up of cash. Watching a company's free cash flow is kind of like watching the fuel gauge when you're driving. Just as you want to know when fuel is running low, you want to know when cash is drying up.

There are many ways to analyze cash flow. Some analysts attempt to determine how much cash a company is throwing off by studying *earnings before interest, taxes, depreciation and amortization*, or *EBITDA*. EBITDA adjusts a company's net income by adding back interest, taxes, depreciation, and amortization. EBITDA can be another way to study how profitable a company is and offers a rough idea of how able a company is to pay its interest costs. But don't make the mistake of assuming EBITDA is a company's cash flow, even though many analysts do. EBITDA doesn't factor in the cash eaten up by inventory, extending credit to customers or used to buy new equipment. Trust me on this one. When you want to know how much cash a company is using up, rely on free cash flow as described in the section below.

Enron's lack of earnings quality

The implosion of Enron left many investors flabbergasted. But for fundamental analysts who know how to measure a company's earnings quality, there were some huge red flags to warn them. When Enron's stock price was still relatively lofty at $63 a share, the company's financial statements showed shockingly low earnings quality. When the company published its earnings press release, it wowed investors with a better-than-expected profit of $425 million for the quarter. But fundamental analysts knew better. An examination of the company's cash-flow statement showed Enron burned $464 million in cash during the same quarter it reported spectacular earnings. That was a huge warning signal, and a big reason how a fundamental analyst would have known to avoid this disastrous stock that ended up losing nearly its entire value.

Calculating free cash flow

The term free cash flow might sound pretty complex and academic. But you might be surprised at how easy it is to calculate a company's free cash flow. Everything you need to measure free cash flow is available on the statement of cash flows.

In fact, if you've followed the calculation of a company's cash from operations in that part of the chapter above, you're more than halfway to arriving at free cash flow. The formula for free cash flow looks like this:

Free cash flow = Cash from operations – Capital expenditures

Again picking on Kraft as an example, you can calculate the company's free cash flow by subtracting its capital expenditures of $1.241 billion from its cash from operations of $3.571 billion, to arrive at free cash flow of $2.3 billion. Kraft is generating cash. But that's not always the case. In the next section of this chapter, I'll show you how to analyze a company that's burning through cash and find out how long it'll take before it burns through its entire wad.

Some beginning fundamental analysts are uncertain why capital expenditures should be subtracted from cash flow from operations to arrive at free cash flow. The idea is a company cannot continue very long without reinvesting and upgrading its infrastructure. The example of a manufacturing company is especially helpful. After a certain period of time, machinery that's left with no maintenance will break down or not work properly. Putting money into keeping up equipment is critical if a company is to remain in business.

Measuring a company's cash-burn rate

One of the great reliefs of reality shows is that eventually, the contestants with no talent finally get the boot. Whether it's the singer with the horrible voice in "American Idol" or the clumsy player in "Survivor," eventually those that don't belong are eliminated.

The same brutal and harsh reality applies in the business world. Companies that run out of cash are often history (unless they're able to get a bail-out). And as a fundamental analyst, it's important to understand how this Darwinism works.

When a company relies on borrowed money, the death toll occurs when a company misses interest payments on its debt. At that point, lenders can take over the company and force it to restructure itself. But what if a company hasn't borrowed? For these companies, the music stops when they run out of cash.

And at this point, you have all the basic skills you need to measure when a company will run out of cash, or its cash burn. When you do a cash-burn analysis, you measure how long a company's cash pile will last if it continues to consume cash at its current rate.

Some of the best examples of cash burn occurred during the dot-com boom. Several Internet companies raised gobs of money during the boom. But after the Internet bubble burst, many were unable to either sell stock or borrow. That meant they only had the cash they'd saved to survive on.

Since many Internet companies were losing money and burning cash at such a rapid pace, they stood to run out of cash before they could ever make a dime for investors. In April 2000, USA TODAY found that three of the 14 largest online retailers would burn through their cash piles in less than 12 months. All three ended up either filing for bankruptcy protection or being acquired by rivals for pennies a share, all but wiping out investors.

Fundamental analysis can help you steer clear of these situations. Here's the formula you need:

Year's supply of cash = Cash and cash equivalents / free cash flow

If the company burned cash, it will have a negative free cash flow. Convert it into a positive number before using the formula above.

An example is Value America, an online retailer that was a darling on Wall Street during the Internet boom. During 1999, the company burned $109.9 million in cash from operations. Value America spent an additional $16.3

million for capital expenditures. Adding the two numbers together, Value America's free cash flow was a negative $126.2 million. Meanwhile, the company ended 1999 with cash and cash equivalents of $52.1 million.

So, using the formula:

$$52.1 / 126.2 = 0.4$$

Think of yourself as a doctor telling a patient how many months they have to live. To convert the 0.4 into a time frame, multiply 0.4 by 12 to see how many months the cash will last. The result? Value America had just enough cash to survive just shy of five months. And guess what? The company filed for bankruptcy protection in 2000. Fundamental analysts pay close attention to companies' cash-burn rates for this reason, since it's critical for companies to generate enough cash to become sustainable.

Chapter 8

Using Financial Ratios to Pinpoint Investments

In This Chapter

▶ Finding out how financial ratios let you quickly apply fundamental analysis

▶ Discovering what the critical financial ratios are and how to calculate them

▶ Uncovering how to interpret the P-E ratio to make investment decisions

▶ Digging into how to measure and read how pricey the stock market is using its P-E

*T*he financial statements, by design, give off an aura of orderliness. All the items are neatly arranged in rows and columns, giving the impression that finding everything you need to know is just a matter of flipping to the correct page and reading the number. If only it was that easy.

While accountants do a great job of recording a company's financials in a tidy way, extracting the information you need for fundamental analysis gets a little messy. Reading the financial statements from top to bottom only tells you so much. To really take your fundamental analysis to the next level, you'll need to learn how to put items on financial statements into perspective. And that means taking a number from one financial statement and comparing it with another. *Financial ratios* are one of the best ways to do this. Ratios compare one financial measure with another to give you real insight into what the numbers mean.

In this chapter, I'll show you some of the most critical ratios of the financial statements and how to apply them. Because it's such an important ratio, I describe the price-to-earnings ratio in the most depth.

Using Financial Ratios to Find Out What's Really Going on at a Company

You might not realize it, but you're probably already using ratios in your daily life. For instance, the fact you put 12 gallons of gasoline in your car doesn't tell you anything about the vehicle's efficiency. But if you look at how many miles you drove on those 12 gallons and examine miles per gallon, you can find out if your car is a gas-guzzler or not. Similarly, when remodeling your home, you may figure out which carpet or tile is the best buy by comparing the price per square foot, which is also a ratio.

Financial ratios work the exact same way as these everyday ratios. By comparing a piece of data from one financial statement to another piece of data, often from another financial statement, you get fundamental insight into the company that neither number alone would provide. Financial ratios are helpful in fundamental analysis because they allow you to:

- ✔ **Compare several companies' financials against each other.** Financial ratios give you a relatively common basis in which to rank companies, usually in the same industry, against each other.

- ✔ **Draw conclusions from all the financial statements.** By pulling numbers from the *income statement* and *balance sheet*, you can glean insights you'd never get by reading just one of the statements.

- ✔ **Get quick insights.** With just a few division problems, you can get a pretty good idea at how skilled a management team is and how well the business is operated.

Some ratios allow you to compare two numbers you might not think would have anything to do with each other. One of my favorite examples is one ratio that measures employee productivity. Just divide a company's total revenue by its number of employees and you find out, on average, how much business each employee brings in. The higher the number, the more productive each worker is. You can then compare the company's productivity to rivals in the same industry, as shown in Table 8-1.

ExxonMobil, for instance, reported total revenue of $477.4 billion in 2008. The oil company started 2008 with 107,100 employees. When you divide revenue by the number of employees, you find out that every employee, on average, generated $4.5 million in revenue. If you work at ExxonMobil, maybe it's time to ask for a raise?

When analyzing financial ratios, it's most useful to compare a company with its competitors. For instance, ExxonMobil and energy companies generate high revenue per employee since their businesses are so *capital intensive*. Capital-intensive businesses rely on machinery to generate a large portion of their revenue, which makes the employees look like productivity superheroes.

Table 8-1	Squeezing Revenue Out of Workers
Industry sector	*Revenue per employee in $ thousands*
Energy	$4,507
Utilities	$1,290
Communications	$780
Basic materials	$716
Health care	$655
Consumer staples (including food)	$574
Technology	$538
Financial	$472

Source: Thomson Reuters

Which financial ratios you should know and how to use them

Financial ratios are kind of like vegetables. There are countless veggies, including some you may not have even heard of. And just to push this analogy even further, while some people love broccoli, others can't even stand the sight of the stuff. The same goes with financial ratios. You could create an entire book just dedicated to financial ratios. Some fundamental analysts love some, like return on equity, while others find them to be misleading. I'll give you my opinion on the ratios, but it's up to you as a fundamental analyst to decide which ones are the best.

There are hundreds of financial ratios because they're just division problems, and there's nothing to stop you from comparing just about anything on the financial statements with something else. The question, though, is whether or not the ratio is valuable.

That's why in this section, I'm going to step you through the greatest hits of financial ratios. These are the ratios you're most likely to encounter, and those that are believed to have some value.

Generally, financial ratios fall into one of five categories, including:

✔ **Profitability:** These ratios allow you to put the profit, or loss, generated by a company into perspective. These ratios are typically called *profit margins*. But there are several kinds of profit margins, including *gross*, *operating* and *net*. These ratios are covered in detail in Chapter 5, so I won't go through them again here.

✔ **Management effectiveness:** Ever wonder if a CEO is doing a good or bad job? Many investors just look at the stock price to make that judgment. But that's somewhat unfair since the CEO can't control the minds of investors. However, ratios like return on assets, return on equity and return on invested capital are affected by CEOs' decisions.

✔ **Efficiency:** When you invest or lend money to a company, you want to know your cash is being put to good use. And that's the goal of the *efficiency ratios*, to indicate how wisely the company is managing its resources.

✔ **Financial condition:** When you invest in a company, you want to know it has the resources it needs to endure. The *current ratio*, discussed in Chapter 6, introduced you to the idea of using ratios to check a company's staying power. But there are more such tools at the fundamental analysts' disposal.

✔ **Valuation:** A stock's per-share price, while the fixation of most investors, doesn't tell you much about how expensive the stock is. It's the stock's valuation, or how much you're paying for a company's earnings, that matters.

Using ratios to grade management

There's something refreshing about the way the performance of athletes is measured. Runs, goals and baskets are all meticulously counted as part of keeping score. But in sports, individual's performances are tracked even more closely, as everything from errors to misses and fumbles get tallied up. At the end of a game, there's no doubt over how a player did.

Fundamental analysis brings that same rigor to measuring companies' leaders, including the CEOs. CEOs, hoping to hang onto their jobs, are infamous for putting the best face possible on their companies' results. But fundamental analysis lets you, the investor, look past the promises and spin to see how management actually did. Using Cisco Systems' financials, I'll step you through how to calculate the main ratios you'll need to size up the management. To save you time, I've pulled all the raw data you'll need and put it all in Table 8-2.

All the lines you see in the table above come from the income statement or balance sheet. If any of these look unfamiliar, flip back to Chapter 5 and Chapter 6 to refresh your memory.

Return on equity

For many investors, the key ratio to pay attention to is *return on equity*, or *ROE*. This measure tells you how much profit the company is generating from money entrusted to it from investors. The formula is:

Return on equity = Net income / average shareholders' equity

Table 8-2	Financial Summary for Cisco Systems	
Line Item	*$s millions fiscal 2008*	*$s millions fiscal 2007*
Net sales	$39,540	$34,922
Cost of goods sold	$14,056	$12,586
SG&A	$10,387	
R&D	$5,153	
Depreciation and amortization	$499	
Net income	$8,052	$7,333
Diluted earnings per share	$1.31	$1.17
Total assets	$58,734	$53,340
Cash and cash equivalents	$5,191	$3,728
Short-term investments	$21,044	$18,538
Accounts receivable	$3,821	$3,989
Inventories	$1,235	$1,322
Accounts payable	$869	$786
Interest expense	$319	$377
Current liabilities	$13,858	$13,358
Current portion of long-term debt	$500	0
Long-term debt	$6,393	$6,408
Number of shares outstanding	6,163	6,265
Shareholders' equity	$34,353	$31,480

Source: Cisco Systems

To measure Cisco Systems' return on equity, you first need to calculate average shareholders' equity. That's shareholder equity from one year plus the previous year, divided by two. For Cisco, that's $34,353 plus $31,480, divided by 2.

Next, you divide the company's net income ($8,052) by the average shareholders' equity ($32,917). The answer for Cisco is a very strong 24.5%. If you do the same analysis for other companies in the tech sector, you'd find an average ROE of about 20%. And to put this into perspective, companies in the S&P 500 generated an average ROE of 21% in the mid-2000s.

Don't assume that just because a company has a higher ROE than another, it's a better company. A company's ROE may be depressed because it has a large investment in assets. Those assets might give the company an edge over rivals in the long run. That's why it's best to compare one company's ROE to another's, in the same industry.

Return on invested capital

For savvy fundamental analysts, return on invested capital, or ROIC, is the ultimate gauge of a company's profitability. It tells you how much money the company makes on all the money, including both debt and equity, that's been entrusted to it.

Calculating ROIC is very worthwhile, even though it takes a little math. To keep it simple, I've broken down the calculation into steps below.

There are many variations on how to calculate ROIC; some are overly simplistic and others are mind-numbingly complex. You're essentially dividing a company's cash income by its total debt and equity. Below, I give you the steps that will work for most fundamental analysis:

1. **Calculate the company's *earnings before interest and taxes, or EBIT*.** This is a rough measure of the company's cash profit, excluding the cost of paying interest expense and taxes. It's a very rough estimate of how much profit the company has available to pay interest with. The formula looks like this:

   (Revenue - cost of goods sold - SG&A - R&D - depreciation and amortization)

   For Cisco, that's:

   ($39,540 – $14,056 – $10,387 – $5,153 – $499) = $9,445

2. **Adjust EBIT for taxes.** Multiply the answer from step 1 by (1 – tax rate). This adjusts EBIT for taxes.

   For Cisco, that's:

   $9,445 * (1–0.375) = $5,903. That's Cisco's tax-adjusted EBIT.

3. **Calculate the total capital possessed by the company for the most recent year.** This measure tells you how much money, including *debt* and *equity* from shareholders, the company has at its disposal. If you need a refresher on the difference between debt and equity, review Chapter 6.

   (Total common equity + current portion of long-term debt + long-term debt)

   For Cisco, that's:

   ($34,353 + $500 + $6,393) = $41,246 for 2008

4. **Calculate the total capital for the previous year.** For Cisco, that's:

   ($31,480 + 0 + $6,408) = $37,888 for 2007

5. **Take the average total capital.** Add the two years together and divide by 2.

   For Cisco, that's:

   $$\$39{,}567 = (\$41{,}246 + \$37{,}888)/2$$

6. **Calculate ROIC.** Divide the answer from step 2 by the answer from step 5.

   For Cisco, that's:

   $$\$5{,}903/\$39{,}567 = 0.149$$

7. **Convert ROIC into a percentage.** Multiply the answer from step 6 by 100. For Cisco, that's 0.149 * 100, or 14.9%.

For an ROIC, 14.9% is very strong. That means the company is generating a nearly 15% return on all the cash that's entrusted to it. The average ROIC of S&P 500 companies was about 13 in the mid-2000s. But again, it's best to compare a company's ROIC with other firms in the industry, and since the industry average is 15, Cisco is right in line.

When ROIC is lower than return on shareholders' equity, that tells you part of the company's returns are the result of the use of borrowed money, or *leverage*. Borrowed money can boost a company's returns when things are good, but sting when business slows. Meanwhile, during a credit crisis, if borrowing costs rise, a highly leveraged company will see its ROIC fall.

Checking up on a company's efficiency

When you invest in a company, you want to know it's running a tight ship. You don't want the company taking its time collecting money from customers or letting inventory sit in the warehouse. There are many ratios that can help you figure out how well a company is managing its affairs.

Accounts receivable turnover

This ratio tells you how quickly a company is collecting its bills from customers. It's helpful for many investors to convert this into the number of days it takes to collect the bills. Here's how:

1. **Calculate the average accounts receivable.** Add the first year's accounts receivable to the second and divide by 2. For Cisco, that's:

   $$\$3{,}905 = \$3{,}821 + \$3{,}989 / 2$$

2. **Divide the answer in step 1 by revenue.** For Cisco, that's:

   0.099 = $3,905 / $39,540

3. **Convert step 2 to days by multiplying by 365.** For Cisco, that's:

   $0.099 \times 365 = 36$

So for Cisco, the number above means it takes, on average, 36 days for the company to collect its bills from customers. You'll want to compare this with the industry to see how it compares.

It's valuable to compare a company's accounts receivable turnover and see if it's getting larger over time. That can be a warning sign that the company is having trouble collecting from customers.

Inventory turnover

Inventory turnover tells you how long its takes the company to clear out the goods sitting in the warehouse. The good news is calculating the formula works the same as *accounts receivable turnover*, except you substitute average inventories with average accounts receivable and cost of goods sold with revenue.

The formula looks like this:

Average inventory / cost of goods sold * 365

For Cisco, that's:

33.2 = Average inventory ($1,278.50) / cost of goods sold ($14,056) * 365

To get average inventory, add inventory from one year to the previous year, and divide by 2.

So, it takes Cisco 33.2 days to clear inventory from its warehouses. That's pretty standard. You'll want to be careful of companies if the days to clear inventory is rising at a rapid clip or stretches well above 40 days.

It takes longer to clear inventory in some industries than others. For instance, a shipbuilding company may hold inventory for a longer time before it's sold. That's why it's important to track the company over time to see if the number of days to clear inventory is rising.

Accounts payable turnover

With this measure, accounts payable turnover, you can find out how long a company is taking to pay its bills. You don't want to invest in a deadbeat company that's not paying its bills, since it might find itself getting cut off from suppliers. Here's how to calculate accounts payable turnover, converted into days:

1. **Calculate the average accounts payable.** Add the first year's accounts payable to the second year's, and divide by 2.

   For Cisco, that's $827.5 = $869+$786 / 2

2. **Calculate the increase, or decrease, in inventory.** Subtract the previous year's inventory by the first year's to see if the company added or removed from its stockpiles. For Cisco, that's: $1,235 – $1322 = –$87. That means Cisco drew down its inventory.

3. **Add the answer from step 2 to the company's cost of goods sold.** For Cisco, that's $13,969 = -87 + $14,056

4. **Divide the answer from step 1 by the answer of step 3.** For Cisco, that's 0.059 = 827.5 / 13,969

5. **Multiply the answer from step 4 by 365 to convert to days.** For Cisco, that's 21.6.

So it looks like Cisco is a prompt payer of its bills. You should get worried if you see the number of days rising over time and heading considerably over 35 days.

A rapid accounts payable turnover ratio may indicate the company is comfortable with its short-term cash flows. If you see this slow down, it could be a sign the company is trying to bolster its short-term cash.

Evaluating companies' financial condition

No one wants to give money to a deadbeat. If your neighbor hits you up for money, you probably have no idea if you'll ever get it back. But with a company, there are very concrete ratios that can indicate how able a company is to repay you. Some of those include the following.

Debt to equity

The debt-to-equity ratio is one of the most basic measures of a company's debt load. It tells you, at a glance, how a company's pile of debt compares with the amount of money it has raised from stock investors. The higher the number, the more loaded it is with debt relative to stock. The formula is:

Current portion of long-term debt + long-term debt / total equity $\times$ 100

For Cisco, that's 20.1 = ($500 + $6,393) / $34,353 $\times$ 100

So for every $20 that the company has borrowed, it has raised $100 from equity investors. That's a very low level of debt, especially if you consider that during the mid-2000s, companies in the S&P 500 had borrowed $75 for every $100 raised from investors. Generally, you don't want to see companies borrowing much more than $100 for every $100 raised from investors.

Quick ratio

When you want to size up how well-equipped a company is to handle its short-term cash obligations, the current ratio does a great job. You can re-read how to calculate the current ratio in Chapter 6.

But some might think the current ratio is too lenient. After all, it includes the value of inventory. Some fundamental analysts think including inventory isn't a great idea, since you can't exactly sell off raw materials very easily to pay bills. That's where the quick ratio comes in. It disregards inventory to help you really see how able a company is at meeting short-term obligations. The formula is:

Cash and cash equivalents + investments + accounts receivable / current liabilities

For Cisco, that's:

2.2 = $5,191+ $21,044 + $3821 / $13,858

That means that the company has $2.20 in assets that are already cash or can be easily turned into cash to handle liabilities due in a year. That is a very strong position, given that in the mid-2000s, companies in the S&P 500 had $1.21 in very close-to-cash assets for every $1 in liabilities coming due in a year. You want to see this ratio be at least 1, and preferably higher.

Interest coverage ratio

The interest coverage ratio helps you figure out how well a company is able to afford its interest payments.

This ratio can be calculated in many ways. Generally, you compare the company's profits before interest costs and taxes to its interest expense, to see how able it is to pay its bills. It's similar to how you're supposed to compare your monthly gross pay with your monthly mortgage bill to see if you can afford the house. Too bad more people didn't do this ahead of the financial crisis, but I digress.

Just divide EBIT by the company's interest expense. For Cisco, that's:

29.6 = $9,445 / 319

Reflecting the fact it has very low debt, Cisco has a very high interest coverage ratio. It generates nearly $30 in available cash profits to pay for every $1 in interest due. Most companies, on average, only generated about $15 in available cash profits to pay their interest. The higher the ratio, the better.

Some companies, including Cisco, list their interest expense as a footnote in their 10-K. After opening the 10-K, using the instructions in Chapter 4, just search for the words "interest expense" and you'll turn up the amount.

Getting a handle on a company's valuation

When you hear investors talk about whether or not a company is cheap, often times they're referring to a stock's valuation. There are dozens of valuation ratios, sometimes called *multiples*, to help you figure out how pricey a stock is.

More often than not, the ratio used to measure a stock's valuation is the price-to-earnings ratio, or P-E. The P-E is so important, I dedicate the next section to it. But for now, below are some descriptions of valuation ratios other than the P-E.

Price-to-book ratio

Many serious fundamental analysts pay closest attention to the price-to-book ratio. This ratio compares a company's stock price to its book value, or value of everything the company owes, free and clear of debt. The formula for price-to-book is:

Price-to-book = Company's stock price / (shareholders' equity / number of shares outstanding)

To practice, let's take the day that Cisco reported its fiscal 2008 results on July 28, 2008. The stock price closed at $21.98. So its price-to-book ratio was:

3.94 = $21.98 / ($34,353 / 6,163)

The higher the price-to-book ratio, the more investors are paying up for the companies' assets. The ratio will rise and fall as investors get more confident or less confident about the company and the stock market.

How do you know if a stock's price-to-book is high or low? One easy way is comparing it with the price-to-book of stocks inside exchange-traded funds, or ETFs, which are baskets of stocks. iShares, for instance, has an ETF that tracks stocks with high, average and low price-to-book ratios. Stocks with low price-to-book ratios are called *value stocks*. And stocks with high price-to-book ratios are called *growth stocks*. There's no set definition of what defines a high or low book value, and it changes over time.

You can look up the average price-to-book ratios of large value stocks by entering IVV in the Ticker or Keyword blank at ishares.com. And you can see the average price-to-book ratios of large growth stocks by entering IVW. In early 2000, stocks in the S&P 500 had an average price-to-book of 3.1, while stocks with high price-to-book ratios averaged 3.66. I'll give you more pointers on how to do this in Chapter 10.

Dividend yield

The dividend yield tells you how much the company is paying out in cash dividends relative to the stock price. You can calculate a dividend yield by dividing the amount of dividends a company pays out in a year by its stock price, and then multiplying by 100. So if a company pays $1 a year in dividends and has a stock price of $25 a share, it has a dividend yield of 4%. To put this dividend into perspective, remember large companies have paid an average dividend yield of 3.8% since December 1936, says S&P.

In theory, the dividend yield is the cash payout you receive by holding onto a stock. Some investors are tempted to automatically buy stocks that pay large dividend yields. However, dividends can be cut with little notice. In fact, companies with large dividend yields are often those under the most distress.

Earnings yield

A company's *earnings yield* tells you how much, as a percentage of a stock's price, the company is generating in profit. The earnings yield gives you a way to compare a company's profit generation with other investments. To get a stock's earnings yield, divide a stock's earnings per share over the past 12 months by its stock price. When a stock's earnings yield is well below the market or that of rivals, it might be a sign the stock is overvalued. I'll touch on this topic more in Chapter 10.

The earnings yield is especially valuable when trying to determine if the stock market is overvalued. You can get this by dividing the earnings generated by the S&P 500 over the previous 12 months by the value of the S&P 500. When the yield gets lower than what you can get by putting your money in safer securities, like government bonds, it's a warning you're not getting paid for the risk you're assuming.

Getting Familiar With the Price-To-Earnings Ratio

The granddaddy of all financial ratios must be the P-E. The P-E is an appealing ratio, because it's relatively easy to understand and can be used to compare the valuations of different companies with each other and to the market at large.

How to Calculate the P-E

When people refer to a stock's P-E, it's almost as if it's some sort of number that's etched in stone. Nothing could be further from the truth. A stock's P-E changes every day along with a stock's price. The formula is deceptively simple:

P–E = Stock price / earnings per share

The numerator, the stock price, everyone can pretty much agree on. That's set by the stock market and can be looked up. However, the denominator can be many different things and is subject to some interpretation. And that's why there can be several variants of the P-E including the:

- ✔ **Trailing P-E:** When you divide a stock's price by its net earnings per share over the past 12 months' earnings, or *trailing* earnings, you get the trailing P-E. This is considered one of the most conservative ways to measure P-E, since it's based on earnings that have actually been reported.

  Net earnings per share can be measured a few ways, as discussed in Chapter 5.

- ✔ **Current P-E:** When you divide a stock's price by what it's expected to earn in the current fiscal year, that's the *current P-E*. Typically, the forward P-E will be based on several quarters of earnings reported by the company, plus a few quarters of estimated earnings. This is a fairly common way to measure a stock's P-E.

- ✔ **Forward P-E:** When you divide a stock's price by what it's expected to earn in the next fiscal year, you're taking somewhat of a leap. Estimates can be pretty unreliable going out this far, meaning that investors should take the *forward P-E* with a handful of salt.

- ✔ **Operating P-E:** When you divide by a company's operating income, you are trying to get an idea of what investors are paying for the company's profit, excluding unusual and one-time charges. Current and forward P-E ratios are usually based on operating income, since these rely on estimates. There is usually no way to accurately forecast one-time charges.

- ✔ **As reported P-E:** When you divide by a company's net income, which includes all charges and one-time items. Reported P-E tends to be higher than operating P-Es during times of economic stress, since companies take many charges for restructuring.

If someone is trying to sell you on a stock by pointing to its "low P-E," be careful you know how it's being calculated. Future P-Es are infamously too low, making a stock look cheap, since the denominator may be based on an overly optimistic estimate.

What a P-E tells you about a stock

One of the beauties of the P-E ratio is its simplicity. With just one number, you can find out how much investors, on average, are willing to pay for a claim to $1 of a company's earnings.

The higher the P-E, the loftier the company's valuation is. When you see a P-E get high relative to peers in the same industry, you might begin to wonder if investors are overvaluing the stock. Similarly, if you see a stock's P-E fall below that of its peers, you might wonder if the company can make changes to its operations to win a higher multiple.

The long-term average P-E of stocks is about 15. If a stock rises above that, you need to be aware that you might be paying up for the stock. Be sure you're getting something for that extra price, such as growth. The PEG ratio, discussed below, explores how to adjust P-E to factor in a company's growth.

Putting the P-E into perspective

Now that you know how to measure a stock's P-E, the question is, what does it mean? The first thing you should do is compare a stock's P-E against the P-E of other companies in the same industry. You can calculate the P-Es of industries yourself, or if you want to save yourself trouble, use Web sites that do it for you. Reuters (www.reuters.com/finance/stocks) has a powerful ratio calculator. Enter the stock's symbol in the black, select the "Ratios" option and click the Go button. You'll get the stock's P-E based on trailing earnings, as well as the P-E for the industry and the S&P 500. This gives you something to compare the stock's P-E with, without having to do a single division problem.

Taking the P-E to the next level: The PEG

It's not uncommon for stocks with high P-Es to keep going higher. Many times, investors are willing to pay higher prices for companies that are growing more rapidly. Much of that has to do with the way the P-E is measured.

Imagine a company, which earned $1 a share, is trading for $20 a share. It has a P-E of 20, which might seem lofty if the rest of the stock market has a P-E of 15. But what if a year from now, the company's earnings rise by 30 percent? If the stock is still $20 a share, that means it would have a P-E of 15, which would be in line with the market. So in a way, the stock wasn't all that overvalued because it grows into its valuation.

The importance of a company's growth rate is one reason for the *PEG ratio*. The PEG compares a stock's P-E to its expected growth rate. You simply divide the stock's P-E by the expected growth rate. You can estimate a company's growth rate yourself by examining historical increases in revenue and earnings, as described in Chapter 5. Or you can read analysts' reports, which forecast growth, as explained in Chapter 14.

Investors generally consider a stock to be pricey if it has a PEG of 2 or more. Some investors also find a stock becomes attractive when its PEG falls below 1.

Sometimes, patience can be a virtue when using the PEG. During the severe market contraction of 2008, even some of the market's hottest stocks saw their PEG ratios plummet below 1. Internet darling Google surprised investors when its PEG fell below 1 in early 2009, as its stock price fell to $340, giving it a current P-E of 16. Meanwhile, the company's expected growth rate was 18.4%. Divide the P-E of 16 by the expected growth rate of 18.4, and you arrive at a PEG of 0.87. Investors who avoided the hoopla and watched the PEG got a much better valuation on the stock.

Evaluating the P-E of the entire market

One of the most valuable things about the P-E is that it is constantly evolving as stock prices move. Unlike other fundamental ratios, which are based on fundamental data from previous quarters, the P-E changes as stock prices move.

Table 8-3	P-E of the S&P 500
Year	*Trailing P-E*
2008	19.7
2007	22.2
2006	17.4
2005	17.9
2004	20.7
2000	26.4
1990	15.5
1980	9.2
1970	18.0
1960	17.8

Source: Standard & Poor's, based on reported earnings for past 12 months

The P-E of a stock can also be compared against the constantly changing P-E of the entire stock market. Knowing the P-E of the market is very valuable, because it lets you see how pricey, or cheap, a company's stock is compared with the market. You can get a general warning if the stock market might be overvalued and headed for a correction if investors are paying lofty amounts for earnings. Table 8-3 shows you how the P-E of the S&P 500 has changed over the years:

Chapter 9

Mining the Proxy Statement for Investment Clues

*W*hen you think of fundamental analysis, you're probably focused primarily on the number-crunching aspect of it. And there's no shortage of ratios and other quantitative measures to consider when evaluating an investment.

But fundamental analysis really is as much of an art than a science in many ways. Even when it comes to interpreting financial results and valuations, there's a great amount of judgment that goes into it. And judgment becomes even more important when considering the *proxy statement*.

The proxy statement, or *proxy*, is one of the more interesting financial documents. Interesting financial reports, now there's an oxymoron for you. But seriously, inside the proxy statement, companies lay out many of their deep, dark secrets that just don't fit into the neat rows and columns of the financial statements. Some of these details include executive pay, composition of the board of directors, and even how much the accounting firm is paid to watch over the financial statements.

Getting up to Speed with What the Proxy Statement Is

Every year, public companies hold giant shareholder meetings. Annual shareholder meetings give management the opportunity to lay out the company's *strategic plan* going forward.

The strategic plan is of upmost importance to shareholders because that will describe what kinds of products and services the company plans to push, and also how the company plans to finance the production and selling of those products and services. Certain matters are also brought to a vote during the shareholder meetings. I discuss the annual shareholder meeting, and ways to analyze them, in more detail in Chapter 13.

This section unearths the proxy statement, which is the document companies provide to shareholders before the shareholder meeting. The proxy is a key document that describes in detail the nitty gritty aspects of a company including its strategic plan and how it will achieve its financial goals.

Uncovering info in the proxy statement

The proxy statement is intended to brief investors on all the matters that are subject to a vote, in addition to other issues investors must be informed of. These documents are stuffed full of details that normally aren't discussed, including sensitive topics of how much executives are being paid. Fundamental analysts may be focused on the company's overall financial performance, but the proxy is worth paying attention to because it provides information about the:

- ✓ **Management's experience:** Fundamental analysts want to have a good handle on the people who are running the company. Detailed biographies of the management team are provided in the proxy.

- ✓ **Board of director composition:** If you invest in a company, the *board of directors* is your watchdog. This group is assigned the task of watching over the management team and making changes to the people or overall strategy when needed.

- ✓ **Compensation:** Want to know how much a CEO earns? It's not a secret; it's spelled out completely in the proxy.

- ✔ **Conflicts of interest:** A conflict of interest occurs when someone in the role of watching over the company may have a reason not to be very vigilant. Such potential conflicts must be broken out in the proxy.

- ✔ **Ownership details:** You can find out which officers or directors of the company are also big owners of the company's stock.

- ✔ **General thinking of other investors:** Shareholders may bring matters to a vote at the meeting. Sometimes these *shareholder proposals* get onto the proxy, allowing you to find out some of the concerns of other owners of the stock.

You may not think the information contained in the proxy is all that critical to fundamental analysis. After all, who cares what college a CEO went to, as long as the income statement shows robust profit and growth? And it's true that financial results are the crux of fundamental analysis. But getting a complete picture of a company's future requires you to take the time to understand the motives and oversight of the people running it.

Tyco's telling proxies

If there's a classic case of how the proxy statement may have been even more telling than the financial statements, it's Tyco International. The sprawling conglomerate dazzled investors through the early 2000s with stellar financial results for many years. Analysts and investors were certain the company's diverse mix of businesses, ranging from home security to electrical parts and industrial supplies was an unstoppable cash-flow machine. And had you just looked at the *income statement*, *balance sheet* and *statement of cash flows*, it would have been hard to find any fault with the company or its management.

But the proxy statements raised more than a few questions even before regulators called the company's management practices into question. For instance, in Tyco's proxy filed on January 28, 2002, the company disclosed it paid director Frank Walsh $10 million and gave another $10 million to one of his charitable foundations in connection to his help brokering one

of the company's acquisitions. The only problem was that Walsh was also a member of Tyco's board of directors, which is supposed to oversee the company's operations. Walsh later pled guilty to charges of trying to hide the fees he received.

Meanwhile, the proxy showed CEO Dennis Kozlowski continued to receive noticeable pay hikes in 2001, despite declines in Tyco's stock price. His pay jumped 36% to $5.7 million that year, not including 43% higher stock grants of $30.4 million and *stock options* valued at $76.4 million, according to a USA TODAY analysis of 2001 executive pay. And those were just a few of the alleged excesses at the company. Kozlowski and another top executive were accused in 2002 of looting the company of hundreds of millions of dollars and using the company as a "piggy bank." The stock cratered in 2002, and Kozlowski was convicted of fraud in 2005.

Getting your hands on the proxy

Before online access became so prevalent, you would normally need to contact a company to get a copy of its proxy. Even today, most companies will mail shareholders a paper copy of the proxy or send it to your brokerage firm, which would forward the proxy to you. But now, whether you own a stock or not, it's pretty simple to just download the proxy for free. The best way to obtain a proxy statement is by using the Securities and Exchange Commission's IDEA database. You can find step-by-step instructions on how to use the SEC's IDEA system in Chapter 4.

When using IDEA to access a company's proxy, just remember that the system lists the proxy statement under its technical name, the *definitive 14A*. When you're searching for a company's proxy statement, you'll want to scroll down for line item labeled "DEF 14A." That's the definitive proxy, and the document you will work with in this chapter.

Expanding Fundamental Analysis Beyond the Numbers

The income statement, balance sheet and statement of cash flows are highly formatted financial statements. You can quickly analyze them by applying scientific formulas and ratios, discussed in Chapter 8, to get insights and comparisons.

But the proxy statement is a little less rigorous. Certainly, rules and regulations stipulate what information must be included. But the information is more textual, in many cases, and less tabular. That means you need to have a general awareness of what to look for in order to know that it deserves your attention. You'll get that insight in this section of the book.

Appreciating corporate governance

If there's one overarching theme of what to look for in the proxy, it's corporate governance. Corporate governance is a catch-all term to describe the safeguards a company has in place to make sure that the management of the company is acting in the best interest for the shareholders. It's the way public companies deal with one of the greatest pitfalls of our financial system: the agency dilemma.

The basic idea of the agency dilemma is the fact that the people who own the company aren't the ones necessarily running it. When you buy 100 shares of a company, for instance, you're not given the right to tell the company what kinds of products it should sell. You're surrendering those key business decisions to the hired hands that run the business. And that includes the CEO and the rest of the management team, such as the chief financial officer and chief operating officer.

Not surprisingly, when there are hired hands running an enterprise on behalf of the owners, there's a potential for problems. And that's the case with companies, too. That's where corporate governance comes in. Companies are required to have a team of business experts, called a board of directors, that are supposed to watch over the management team. If the board feels management is making poor decisions with the company's resources, it's up to them to either reprimand or replace them.

The agency dilemma has become even more of an issue with the rise of massive mutual funds. Large money management firms, which own a vast majority of companies' stock, usually own a stock for less than a year, according to the Bogle Financial Markets Research Center. That's down from six years in the 1980s. What that means is that the big owners of stock are short-timers, and aren't all that vested in making sure the company is being properly watched over the long haul. Many of these large owners are in to make a quick profit, and don't have any reason to care whether the company is being run efficiently and for the long run. That's why it's up to you, the fundamental analyst, to realize when companies have poor corporate governance, and to steer clear when they do.

Getting to know the board

The board of directors is really your only advocate in the boardroom. Unless you own enough shares to get a direct hand on how a company is run, you're leaving it up to the board to make sure your money is properly handled. You, the shareholder, get to vote on the board members, and the company pays them sometimes large sums to conduct the job as watchdog.

So-called *activist shareholders*, like Carl Icahn, try to break through the agency dilemma by buying large blocks of shares and using the influence of a large position to force management teams to make changes.

Boards of directors also have a number of committees, which take on specialized oversight roles. These roles are of upmost importance to fundamental analysts because they get to the core of how professionals are chosen to run the company and how much they're paid. Those committees include the:

- **Audit committee:** If there's one board to pay most attention to, it's this one. The audit committee is responsible for directly connecting with the accounting firm that checks over the company's books and records. The members of the audit committee must be *independent*, meaning that they have no outside business dealings with the company.

- **Compensation committee:** The board members on this committee have the job of determining how much to pay the people running the company.

- **Nominating committee:** These board members evaluate candidates for key jobs at the company.

Paying attention to corporate governance can be a critical part of understanding what companies are worth investing in and which ones are best avoided. At 17 of the firms that suffered the biggest business problems and stock losses during the first part of the financial crisis in 2007 and 2008, most had poor corporate governance, according to research firm The Corporate Library. These firms had board members who received excessive compensation or who *over-boarded* by sitting on four or more corporate boards. Over-boarding is considered a corporate governance risk, since the directors are distracted and potentially unable to adequately watch over any one company. As a group, these 17 firms lost an average 80% of their stock value between mid-2007 and the end of 2008, twice the loss by the broader stock market.

Stepping Through the Proxy

When you invest in a company, you're entitled to vote on some of the company's corporate matters, most importantly, on the slate of people who sit on the board. Think of the proxy statement as your guide to all the matters that will come up for a vote at the company. Generally, most proxy statements will include several key elements, as described below.

One of the primary purposes of the proxy is to break out how much the executives are getting paid. This is such a critical part of your analysis, it will be explored in more detail in the next section of this chapter.

Bringing good governance to light

General Electric, in its 2008 proxy for its 2009 meeting, went to great lengths to assure investors that its board of directors were largely independent. At the time of the proxy, GE disclosed that 13 of its 16 directors were considered independent.

But the company took things a step further by detailing the tests it applied to the board members to determine whether or not they were independent. For instance, GE disclosed that a number of the board members were connected with companies that did business with GE. But the relationships were tested to ensure that none of the companies received more than 2% of their total revenue from GE.

GE, as required by regulations, further disclosed that none of the members of the audit committee received any sort of compensation from the company other than *director fees*. Director fees, or payments made to directors, will be explored in more detail later in this chapter.

Getting to know the board of directors

Typically, the first section of a proxy provides fairly complete biographies of the members of the board of directors. You'll usually see what kind of experience the members have, what kind of education they have, and what other corporate boards they sit on.

Pay close attention to how many corporate boards the directors sit on. As described above, if you notice several members of the board are sitting on three, four or more boards, you might wonder how much time they're able to dedicate to the company you've invested in.

Analyzing the independence of board members

Most companies will reserve a spot in the proxy, usually below the list of the directors, to outline steps that have been taken to make sure the board of directors are proper watchdogs. One of the most critical ways to do this is by ensuring that most of the board members are *independent*, or have no direct business relationship with the company.

Delving into the board's committees

The key aspect of this part of the proxy is to highlight which board members sit on which committees. You'll want to pay very close attention to who is sitting on the *audit committee*, since this is the group of people that's supposedly there to protect you from accounting fraud.

When looking over all the directors on the board, you want to pay particular attention to the members of the audit committee. Make sure they are financially literate. A look at their biographies will give you a decent idea if they're qualified for this extremely important job.

In addition to the competence of board members, you want to look for involvement and participation. In this section of the proxy, companies will often disclose how many times the members of the board met during the year. You want to see the board meeting at least four times a year, or once a quarter. In 2008, GE disclosed the board met 22 times.

You also want to make sure that the board members are actually showing up for the meetings. If you see multiple members missing 25% or more of the meetings, you might be concerned that they're not paying close enough attention to the matters at hand.

Finding potential conflicts between the board and the company

Most proxy statements will contain a section, often called *related-person transactions* or *related-party transactions*, which outlines any business relationships board members have with the company they're overseeing.

If you don't read anything else in a proxy, always check out the related-party transaction section. This is where a company must lay out any potentially sweet deals it has going with its officers and directors. Fundamental analysts who read this section of Enron's proxy statements got an early warning of some of the strange dealings between the company and its chief financial officer, Andrew Fastow. While many of the key details were left out, according to the Securities and Exchange Commission, there was enough of a vague description of the relationship between Fastow and the company to at least raise suspicions.

Understanding how the board is paid

The board of directors isn't overseeing the company you've invested in out of the kindness of its heart. The board members get paid, sometimes handsomely, for the service. Luckily, the payments received by directors are disclosed for all to see.

Pay for board members is a delicate balance. On one hand, you don't want to see board members receiving excessive compensation. If payment is over the top, the board members have an incentive to keep their mouths shut and not risk their gravy train by raising objections. However, qualified and savvy businesspeople aren't going to take the risk of sitting on a board for nothing. Sometimes you get what you pay for.

Just as you compare a company's net income and profit to its peers, you can do the same with board members' pay. For instance, the median board member at companies in the Standard & Poor's 500 in 2008 earned nearly $200,000, says The Corporate Library. That was an increase of roughly 12%. Keep your eyes open for sudden increases of pay to board members. A big spike in pay might indicate the company is trying to ensure a very amicable board of directors.

While it's helpful to compare how much directors get paid with the average of companies in the S&P 500, it's really best to compare against similar companies of comparable size. Sometimes disparities can be telling. For instance, the lead director at Freddie Mac, the lending entity that was essentially taken over by the government in 2008, was paid $100,000. That was well above the going rate of roughly $30,000 for directors at comparable companies, The Corporate Library says.

Sometimes board members are paid in cash. Sometimes they receive stock. Most of the time, though, they receive both cash and stock. And in some cases, companies may provide additional perks to board members. At GE in 2008, for instance, board members were permitted to receive GE appliances and other products, take part in programs to give gifts to charity, and enjoy events for the directors and their spouses.

While it might seem like a potential conflict of interest for the board members to take freebies from a company, just pay attention to the total amount of compensation. Be sure that the company clearly discloses all the benefits directors receive, including the perks, and make sure they're not excessive.

Auditing the auditor

While the board of directors is supposed to be your closest ally in the board-room, luckily, even the board has someone watching it: the auditor. The auditing firm has the job of checking over the books and records of a company to make sure it's representing everything accurately.

But it's kind of up to you, again, to make sure the auditor is on your side. One of the biggest inherent potential conflicts with an auditing firm is the fact it is paid by the company to provide the audited results. That's a conflict that you kind of have to live with, since that's how the system works.

If you see that the auditing firm is getting paid for all sorts of other services for the company besides conducting the audit, you should get concerned. You could imagine a situation where an auditing firm would get so reliant on these extra fees, it might not be as diligent as it should be. After all, Arthur Andersen had a very extensive relationship with Enron, which some say might have contributed to the auditor not raising flags at the company.

Luckily, the proxy makes digging up these kinds of details relatively easy. At the bottom of the proxy, the company must disclose all the fees it paid to its auditing firm. The fees are organized into:

- ✔ **Audit fees:** These are the direct costs the company pays to the audit firm for reviewing its books, including the 10-K.

- ✔ **Audit-related fees:** These are fees generally connected to the audit process, typically a review of the company's financial controls.

- ✔ **Tax fees:** Companies will often tap their auditing firm for tips on ways to manage their tax bills.

- ✔ **All other fees:** Here's the line item you want to pay close attention to. These "other" fees include consulting fees for information technology services and other advisory services that have nothing to do with the company's audit.

It's usually best when a company has a minimal amount, if not $0, in the line for all other fees paid to the auditing firm. You want to make sure the auditor is looking out for you, not itself and its partners' profits. In 2008, GE paid no fees outside of audit, audit-related and tax to its auditing firm, KPMG. GE also disclosed that the KPMG partners in charge of auditing it must be rotated at least every five years. That reduces the chances of the partners getting too cozy with GE management.

Finding out about the other investors in a stock

When you look to buy a house, you may pay close attention to who your neighbors are. It's helpful to find out what other people are investing in the same neighborhood and street. The same goes for stocks. The proxy will tell you which executives and directors are large investors in the firm. If you want to get a list of the biggest owners of a stock who aren't officers or directors, that information is available elsewhere as I'll describe in Chapter 14. Furthermore, you can get an idea of what's on the other investors' minds by reading the *shareholder proposals*. You'll find out how to check in on the other investors in the final section of this chapter.

How Much Are We Paying You? Understanding Executive Compensation

Some fundamental analysts might think examining executive compensation is a distraction. After all, the salaries of all a company's employees, including the CEO and management team, are subtracted from revenue to arrive at *net income*. Certainly, if a CEO's pay was completely outlandish, the profitability of the firm would fall and tip off fundamental analysts that way.

Even so, a key part of fundamental analysis is understanding the motives and ethics of the management team. After all, you're entrusting this team of men and women to take your money and invest it productively in ways to generate a return for you. If your money is being siphoned off for the big cheese to enrich himself, that's a problem for a fundamental analyst.

Studying executive compensation is a detailed science that could fill many books. And every year, major publications such as USA TODAY release comprehensive executive compensation reports that give you an idea of what's reasonable or excessive.

If you're interested in learning more about how much CEOs get paid and what is generally acceptable, check out USA TODAY's interactive graphic at www. usatoday.com/money/graphics/ceo-comp/flash.htm. To give you a general idea of how the other half lives, Table 9-1 shows the top-paid CEOs in 2007 and Table 9-2 shows the lowest-paid ones.

Table 9-1	Top-Paid CEOs in 2007			
Company	*Executive*	*Salary*	*Bonus*	*Total compensation*
Merrill Lynch	John Thain	$57,692	$15,000,000	$83,092,713
CBS	Leslie Moonves	$5,323,367	$18,500,000	$67,615,827
Freeport-McMoRan	Richard Adkerson	$2,083,333	$5,432,000	$65,193,723
Oracle	Lawrence Ellison	$1,000,000	$8,369,000	$61,180,524
XTO Energy	Bob Simpson	$1,312,508	$35,500,000	$56,614,936

Source: USA TODAY citing data from Salary.com

Table 9-2	Lowest-Paid CEOs in 2007			
Company	*Executive*	*Salary*	*Bonus*	*Total compensation*
Yahoo	Jerry Yang	$1	$0	$1
Apple	Steve Jobs	$1	$0	$1
Google	Eric Schmidt	$1	$1,898	$480,561
Duke Energy	James Rogers	$0	$0	$496,271
Symantec	John Thompson	$800,000	$350,000	$1,258,611

Source: USA TODAY citing data from Salary.com

Figuring out how much executives earn

If you've ever tried to find out how much a friend or coworker makes, you might get the answer, "It's none of your business." And that's probably the case. But guess what. Since you're technically paying the CEO's salary, as an investor, it is your business to know what he or she is paid.

CEOs don't typically just get a paycheck every couple of weeks. Generally, they receive a base salary plus a number of bonuses and other incentives that become valuable if they meet certain performance milestones. That's why most CEOs' pay is broken into these parts:

- ✓ **Salary:** This is the base pay received by the executive.

- ✓ **Bonus:** These discretionary payments are generally awarded at the end of the year for meeting certain performance targets.

- ✓ **Equity awards:** Top executives will often be given compensation that's tied to the company's stock price. These grants may become very valuable if the company's stock price rises in the future. Equity awards are generally stock options or *restricted stock*, which are both described in more detail below.

For instance, in 2008, GE CEO Jeffrey Immelt received a salary of $3.3 million and equity awards of $2.0 million for total compensation of $5.3 million. GE is one of the few companies to meticulously outline the goals the CEO needed to meet in order to earn bonuses and other incentive pay.

You can tell something about executives' motives by the way they handle their bonuses. Immelt, for instance, asked GE's board of directors not to pay him a bonus in 2008 due to the dramatic fall of the company's stock price. The board accepted the suggestion, even though GE meet the operational targets that were conditions for the bonus. The denial of the bonus cost Immelt millions, since his bonus was $5.8 million in 2007. Immelt also declined a $11.7 million long-term performance award.

On the other hand, former Merrill Lynch CEO Thain was subpoenaed to disclose details of more than $3.6 billion in bonuses that were handed to executives of that firm at the end of 2008. Those bonuses were paid just before the distressed investment bank was about to report a massive $27 billion loss for the year and was rescued by both taxpayers and Bank of America in a rushed merger. Interestingly, Thain was also the highest-paid CEO in 2007 according to Table 9-1 above.

Checking out the other perks executives receive

Oh, to live the life of a CEO. In addition to the pay, CEOs receive other noncash bonuses. The more forthcoming companies will break out all these perks, too. These perks generally include personal use of the corporate jet, leased cars, tax-preparation counseling, and discounts or free products from the company.

Going beyond the proxy to find executive perks

Just as you might negotiate for access to child-care or extra vacation time accepting a new job, the same goes for executives. Executives of large companies will very often seek non-monetary extras as part of their pay. These extras can range from a home-office setup to paid consulting gigs after retirement, paid insurance premiums or tickets to sporting events.

It's important for a fundamental analysts to pay attention to these perks, because they are a factor in determining an executive's total compensation.

When these extras are large enough the company should, in theory, disclose them in the proxy statement. But as you've probably noticed so far, companies go out of their way to keep details on executive pay as general as possible and not list or itemize specific perks. Most of these items are rolled up into a broad category in the proxy, usually called "other" or something vague. You can often find "other" pay listed in a table in the company's proxy. Some companies go a bit further and break out the value of certain expected perks executives receive such as use of aircraft, cars or financial or tax planning.

And that's why keen fundamental analysts interested in executive pay often find they must look beyond the proxy. Don't get me wrong, the proxy is extremely valuable and should be your starting point when researching executive pay. But remember companies will only go so far in listing details on perks executives are getting.

And that's why you need to know how to take your research one step further to get the full story on executive pay.

The first place to check after the proxy are court documents. Lurid details about executive pay are often fleshed out in divorce papers, legal skirmishes with business partners or in other legal battles.

One of the best examples of how you can get more details about all the benefits an executive is getting from the company occurred with GE and its former CEO Jack Welch. Court papers from Welch's 2002 divorce from his wife of 13 years revealed many never-before-seen details of perks Welch received from GE in retirement. Some of the perks included use of a multi-million dollar New York City apartment, a limo and security for his homes.

The case even got the attention of the Securities and Exchange Commission and has set a precedent for what needs to be disclosed regarding perks. The SEC in late 2004 settled charges against GE. The SEC alleged GE didn't adequately disclose the extent and details of perks given to Welch.

The SEC said GE's 1996 annual report didn't go far enough in describing the perks Welch would receive in retirement, instead, vaguely calling them "facilities and services." GE consented to the SEC's order. You can read more about this case here: http://www.sec.gov/news/press/2004-135.htm.

Where the real money comes from: Options and restricted stock

Just as restaurants make most of their money on the drinks, not the food, CEOs don't make most of their money from where you might think. Salaries for most executives, by and large, aren't where the vast majority of CEOs' compensation comes from. Instead, it's from stock options. Stock options are financial instruments that give their owners the right, but not the obligation, to buy a stock at a predetermined price.

Options are common tools to incentivize executives. For instance, a CEO might get an option to buy 100,000 shares of a stock for $30 a share when the company's stock price is $30. If the CEO is successful and the stock price rises to $50 a share, the CEO may exercise the option and buy 100,000 shares of stock worth $5 million, for $3 million. The difference, the $2 million, goes to the executive as compensation.

CEOs might also receive restricted stock. These shares are given to an executive, but cannot be sold unless certain criteria are met, typically after a period of time has lapsed. Restricted stock is designed to dangle a carrot in front of the CEO as an incentive to keep them at the company and working hard to increase the stock price and returns to shareholders.

Checking In on Your Fellow Shareholders

When you buy a stock, you don't get a directory of all the other investors in the company. You're free to attend a company's shareholders' meeting and do some glad-handing. But with that said, the proxy statement can be a useful tool in figuring out what executives are also big shareholders in the company.

Finding out who else owns the stock

Determining other investors who own a stock can be somewhat telling. For instance, if you are a *value investor*, looking to buy stocks at low *valuations*, you might take comfort in seeing whether any well-known mutual fund managers own a stock. You'll find out how to check in on these investors' moves in Chapter 17.

But some investors take comfort when the officers and directors own large positions in a stock, since they have some skin in the game and therefore stand to lose personally if the stock price falls.

The proxy is again your best friend in finding out whether the company's management is willing to eat its own cooking, so to speak. Most proxy statements contain a table, usually close to the bottom of the document, which spells out how many shares the officers and directors of the company own.

Some officers and directors feel so strongly a company's stock price is about to rise that they may buy the company's stock with their own money. These types of buys are viewed as bullish signals, because executives are reaching into their own pockets to buy shares, rather than receiving handouts as part of compensation packages.

These purchases are often disclosed and summarized in the proxy statement, described usually as *open market purchases*. GE's Immelt, for instance, bought 317,000 shares of the company in 2008, and at the end of the year owned 1.6 million shares, the proxy says. Additionally, Immelt has not sold any of the shares he received connected to stock options. You can learn more about the importance of watching what insiders do with their stock in Chapter 17.

What's on other investors' minds: Shareholder proposals

The proxy lists all the items of business that are up for a shareholder vote. The items may be presented by either the company or shareholders.

Generally, the issues presented by companies are pretty mundane. More often than not, they pertain to one of the following items:

- ✔ **Vote for board members up for re-election.** Shareholders may either vote for each nominated candidate or withhold their vote.

- ✔ **Approve the company's auditing firm.** Often, this is just an exercise of going through the motions, since companies tend to use the same accounting firm each year.

- ✔ **Authorize the issuance of shares connected with stock incentive plans.**

The most interesting proposals in the proxy are almost always the ones brought up by shareholders, called shareholder proposals. Some shareholders will go to the time and trouble to add items to the proxy for other shareholders to consider. While many of the items can be frivolous, many times they can signal to you, the fundamental analyst, concerns that other investors might have. These items might direct you to do further analysis on some portion of the financial statements.

Following the stock market crash in 2008, a number of shareholder proposals were directed at companies for issues ranging from excessive executive pay to concern about board with over-boarded directors. Many 2008 proxies raised the issue of *say on pay*, a proposal which would allow shareholders to directly approve the pay packages offered to executives. Shareholder resolutions also often target golden parachutes, or lucrative payouts to executives after they lose their job, including following a buyout by another firm. These proposals might be a gentle nudge for you to expand your fundamental analysis to check how reasonable the executives' pay is.

Don't discount and skip reading the shareholder proposals, especially the more outlandish-sounding ones. In the proxy, the company will generally urge shareholders to vote down such proposals and offer somewhat detailed insight on why the proposals are a bad idea. The defenses companies provide can offer useful insight for fundamental analysts. For instance, in GE's 2008 proxy, one investor called for the company to conduct a study on whether to cut itself up into four different businesses. The shareholder claimed the four separate companies housed inside GE would be worth 30% more than the combined GE. The company's defense outlined a number of divestitures the company made to streamline itself. And in the course of rejecting the idea, GE went into detail on how its business model, which tied together seemingly different businesses, continues to work.

Part III

Making Money from Fundamental Analysis

The 5th Wave   By Rich Tennant

"I've always used historical data analysis to rebalance my assets, but lately it's been pretty much hysterical data analysis that I've been working with."

In this part . . .

You probably wouldn't be taking the time to read about fundamental analysis unless you thought you could somehow benefit personally from it. And in this part, I show you how to apply the tools of fundamental analysis to how you manage your portfolio. You can use fundamental analysis for clues on when you might think about buying or selling an investment, for instance. I also show you how to do some of the more advanced types of fundamental analysis such as a discounted cash flow analysis and digging into the annual report of a company. You can also get clues on how to lean on the fundamental analysis done by professional analysts and also how to interpret pertinent comments made by a company's management team.

Chapter 10

Looking for Fundamental Reasons to Buy or Sell

· ·

In This Chapter

▶ Exploring fundamental indicators that give you some insights into an investment's attractiveness

▶ Understanding how to determine which companies have resources to endure tough times

▶ Uncovering warning signals of when might be a good time to consider selling

▶ Considering the importance of dividends and what they tell you about the value of a stock

· ·

Wouldn't it be nice if newspapers or financial Web sites put a big red dot next to the stocks that are going to fall in the next six months and a green dot next to the ones that are going to rise? Investing would be so simple.

Unfortunately, though, that's not the case. Deciding whether to buy or sell a stock is an excruciatingly difficult thing to do. There are dozens, if not more variables that go into this very important decision. You not only need to size up the health of the business and evaluate whether or not it has enough cash to survive, but also consider whether the stock price is attractive.

Fundamental analysis may not be a crystal ball. Cheap stocks can get cheaper and pricey stocks can soar. But fundamental analysis can at least give you some guidance on buying and selling. This section of the book explores some of the aspects of fundamental analysis that can help you intelligently approach investing with your eyes wide open. You'll discover how to apply many of the tools discussed in the early sections of the book to help you determine if you should be intrigued by investments, and when you should avoid them.

Looking For Buy Signals from the Fundamentals

When you go shopping for any big-ticket item, there's probably not one single factor that makes your decision. Before you buy a car, for instance, you don't just consider the color. You probably weigh all sorts of factors ranging from the reliability of the model to the quality of the interior and, perhaps most importantly, the price.

The same multistep approach applies when you're shopping for stocks. Very rarely is there a single factor that flashes a bright light to tell you that it's time to buy. As a fundamental analyst, you need to consider a variety of traits that, together, might give you an idea if it's worth taking a shot on a stock.

Fundamental analysts often concentrate on a few aspects of a stock, which might make it an attractive investment, including:

- ✔ **Staying power:** You want to make sure a company has the financial resources to endure a downturn and come out on the other side.

- ✔ **The trajectory of the fundamentals:** Since a stock price, over time, is connected to a company's revenue and earnings, fundamental analysts try to see improving trends in the company's revenue and profit. Trend spotting will be discussed at more length in Chapter 17.

- ✔ **Evidence of skilled management:** A management team with experience navigating through the ups and downs of a business may give the fundamental analyst more confidence in the company's future. Skilled managers can protect their company's business from competition with strong brands, service or quality.

- ✔ **Valuation:** Even if a company is performing poorly, the stock can still be a good investment if the bad news is already reflected in the price. Fundamental analysts spend a great deal of their time comparing a company's current stock price to its real value, based on what they think it's worth. You discovered how to use the P-E as a valuation tool in Chapter 8, and in this chapter you'll find out about the *earnings yield*. Fundamental analysts also look for good values using the *discounted cash-flow model*, explored in Chapter 11.

- ✔ **Dividend payments:** These seemingly small cash payments can quickly add up and become a significant consideration for a fundamental analyst. Fundamental analysts also use these dividends as a way to measure the attractiveness of some stocks, as will be discussed at the end of this chapter.

Now it's time for a disclaimer

Before you get too far into this chapter, it's a good time for a big fat disclaimer. Here goes. Fundamental analysis doesn't guarantee that you'll always make money on stocks by buying and selling at the exact right times. I know, that's not the kind of statement that's going to make this book a best-seller.

Just remember there's a paradox to using fundamental analysis as a tool to tell you when to buy or sell stocks, and you need to be mindful of it from the start. You're not the only one with instant access to a company's financial statements and performance. Scores of mutual fund companies, hedge funds, and other large investors get the same fundamental data you do and comb through them with armies of analysts and computers. If they see a stock that's undervalued, they may move quickly and push the stock price up. And when a stock moves up, other investors may pile on and push it higher.

All this means that many investors who try to buy and sell individual stocks at just the right times are often unsuccessful. And that's why it's often best for many investors to simply buy every stock on a stock market index, such as the Standard & Poor's 500, through an *index fund,* rather than try to time the market. Even the king of fundamental analysis, Warren Buffett, wrote in his 1996 letter to shareholders: "Most investors, both institutional and individual, will find that the best way to own common stocks is through an index fund that charges minimal fees."

Despite the warning above, fundamental analysis is still extremely valuable for many investors. There's no harm in understanding how investments you own are valued. And the market certainly has periods of indigestion. During asset bubbles, for instance, market prices can get pushed to extremes relative to their fundamentals. The 2000s have provided extraordinary examples of bubbles, including the dot-com bubble, tech-stock bubble and housing bubble. Fundamental analysis can be a tool of reason, helping you to at least recognize when investors appear to be paying more for an asset than they have historically or are betting on an overly optimistic future. Fundamental analysis is that one tool that may help save you from falling prey to a bubble, too.

Finding companies that have staying power

Let's face it. Capitalism isn't pretty. There are times of tremendous affluence when companies are reporting stellar profits. Fundamental analysis may help you find the companies that stand to steal away business from rivals during these boom times.

But, as a normal part of the ups and downs of business, or the *business cycle*, there will eventually be a downturn. And it's often during these tough times that companies demonstrate their lasting power. Since many investors give up on companies when they're down or out of favor, that can present tremendous opportunity to you as a fundamental analyst, too. If you take the time to find companies that are just down, and have the ability to recover, you can pick up good companies for low prices.

Typically, when you're looking for companies that have the resources to survive, you want to consider some key elements.

Liquidity: Cash is king

If you're trying to buy into a company on the cheap, you want to make sure it has the ability to weather the difficult times. And that calls for a close examination of *liquidity*, or ready access to cash. Make sure you pay close attention to a company's current ratio, as described in Chapter 6. This is a good approximation of whether a company will be able to raise enough cash to pay its bills due in a year.

There's a very important pecking order to investing you need to be very aware of. When you buy stock in a company that's on the decline, you're playing a bit of a game of chicken. In the case that the company *defaults*, or fails to pay its interest back to lenders, there's a chance that the company may be restructured or sold off. And if that happens, as a stock holder, you're the very last one in line at the asset buffet. Stock investors come behind everyone, including employees owed their salaries and bond holders, for any money that's left over. That's why when you invest in a company that is dangerously faltering, you must be absolutely sure that you've carefully measured whether or not it has enough liquidity to keep going.

Low debt loads and big piles of cash

When you're looking for cheap stocks of companies that may survive, be certain to consider the companies that have little to no debt. Companies that don't have an enormous amount of money to repay can tread water and get their operations in order before they have to worry about meeting onerous interest costs. Pay close attention to a company's *interest coverage ratio*, described in Chapter 8. The lower this ratio, the better the company will be able to handle a downturn. And make sure the total amount of debt a company owes is reasonable. Again, Chapter 8 will help you access this by considering the *debt-to-equity ratio*.

Don't think it's possible to run a company without borrowing? Believe it. Table 10-1 shows some of the largest U.S. companies in the S&P 500 that had no *long-term debt* at the end of 2008 and that also saw their shares outperform the market. Many of these companies were in relatively strong financial shape going into the brutal market correction of 2008 and 2009.

Table 10-1	Flush Companies With No Debt in 2008
Company	*Stock change in 2008*
Apollo Group	9.2%
CH Robinson	1.7%
QLogic	-5.4%
McAfee	-7.8%
Genzyme	-10.8%
S&P 500	-38.5%

Source: S&P's Capital IQ

Just because a company has no debt doesn't mean the stock will rise. That point is painfully clear in what you don't see in Table 10-1. There were plenty of companies with no debt that saw their shares fall. Apple and Google, for instance, had no debt at the end of 2008, but still saw their shares fall 57% and 56%, respectively. Again, I stress, there's no single indicator to tell you whether or not to buy a stock.

One trick that some fundamental analysts use to get a decent idea of the financial bedrock of a company is to compare its stock price to the amount of cash per share it has. Sometimes stocks get beaten up so badly, the company actually has more cash in the bank than its value in the stock market. This analysis is a good complement to studying a company's price-to-book ratio, which also considers how much debt a company has, as discussed in Chapter 8.

To compare a stock's price to its cash per share, follow these steps:

1. **Obtain a company's total cash and cash equivalents.** These data are available on a company's balance sheet. If you're not sure how to get this information, there are detailed instructions in Chapter 6.

2. **Divide the number from Step 1 by the number of shares outstanding.** You can get a company's number of shares outstanding from the balance sheet, too. The step gives you the company's *cash per share*.

3. **Divide the answer from Step 1 by the answer in Step 2.** If the answer is a negative number, that means the company has more in cash than its value in the stock market. Some consider this to be a potential sign the stock is undervalued.

When a stock price falls below a company's cash per share, don't assume it's a screaming buy. Sometimes a stock price gets beaten below cash levels due to excessive debt. In that case, the cash doesn't really belong to the company, but to the lenders. That's why the price-to-book ratio is so helpful, since it considers the role of debt. A stock with a low stock price to debt might also indicate investors have no confidence in the management team.

Stable cash flows

If a company is in a stable business where demand is relatively reliable, it may generate ample cash flow to undo many of the challenges it faces. You can discover how to measure a company's cash flow in Chapter 7. Unfortunately, many companies with stable cash flow feel inclined to boost their profitability by borrowing. Unfortunately, though, these piles of debt can haunt companies if business slows. Fundamental analysts may look for companies that have stability and the discipline to avoid excessive debt.

Case study of a survivor: Cisco

Sometimes it's helpful to consider history to see how fundamental analysis can help you identify attractive opportunities. Think back to 2002. A "Beautiful Mind" won the Best Picture in the Academy Awards. The soundtrack from "O Brother, Where Art Thou?" won a Grammy. But a less- pleasurable development was the brutal bear market in which technology stocks were suffering. The Nasdaq composite index, which is loaded with technology stocks, crashed 78% between March 10, 2000 and Oct. 9, 2002. Many investors gave up hope on technology stocks, figuring they were just overinflated fluff.

But fundamental analysts who took the time to find companies with staying power benefitted. One tech stock that fit the bill was Cisco Systems. Cisco was one of the darling stocks during the Internet bubble and suffered, too, as a result. As companies cut back on the amount of gear they bought, Cisco went from making a profit of $2.7 billion in fiscal 2000, ended in July, to losing $1.0 billion in fiscal 2001. And revenue dropped off 15% to $18.9 billion in fiscal 2002. The stock was punished brutally as investors questioned the industry's future.

Fundamental analysts, though, knew better. Thanks to cost-cutting, the company still reported a profit of $1.9 billion in fiscal 2002, during the industry's darkest days. In addition, Cisco had a pile of cash and no debt during the entire tech crisis in the early 2000s, meaning it had no interest expense to deal with. And Cisco's *cash flow from operations*, discussed in Chapter 7, actually increased during the tech crisis between fiscal 2000 and fiscal 2002.

Fundamental analysts who decided in 2002 that Cisco would be a survivor were richly rewarded. Investors who bought Cisco in late July 2002, after the end of the company's fiscal year, ended up seeing their investment rise in value by nearly 120% over the next five years, nearly twice the return of the S&P 500.

Looking for a company on the rise

If there's one thing many investors can agree on, it's that they want to see a company they're investing in is stable, if not growing. Companies with growing earnings and revenue can be attractive investments if the price isn't too high.

Fundamental analysis can be extremely helpful in pinpointing companies where the earnings and revenues are in an upswing. Some investors, called *momentum investors*, like to buy into companies when they're reporting faster and faster growth. These investors are betting they can grab on to a company with lots of good things going for it. But even *value investors*, who try to buy stocks on the cheap, are betting that a company will eventually start to do better, and the stock will catch up.

Finding companies that are growing rapidly is usually done using trend analysis, which is described in detail in Chapter 17.

Betting on the brains behind the operation

When you invest in a company, you're not just investing in its brands, products, and assets. You're having faith that the management team is properly equipped to best manage the company to deliver outstanding results.

Return on equity and *return on capital*, both discussed in Chapter 8, are the best and quickest ways to figure out how well a company is managed. But many fundamental analysts dig even deeper by dissecting *return on assets*. Return on assets, by itself, is a helpful thing for fundamental analysts to consider. It tells you how much profit the company is generating from the assets it has under its control. Return on assets helps you see how well a company is running itself without any financial distortion caused by the use of debt. If you compare a company's return on assets to that of its peers, using the same techniques applied to return on equity in Chapter 8, you get a good idea of how well the company is managing your money.

But dissecting return on assets into parts can reveal even more about a company's management. To show you want I mean, first consider the formula for return on assets:

Return on assets = Income / Assets

Income, in the numerator of the formula above, means different things to different fundamental analysts. Some use *net income*, since it's easily obtained from the income statement. Yet others use *earnings before interest and taxes*, or EBIT, instead of net income to measure return on assets. You can refresh your memory about the advantages and disadvantages of both net income and EBIT in Chapter 8.

You might try testing out return on assets on industrial company 3M, using the company's 2008 financials summarized in Table 10-2.

Plugging in the numbers in Table 10-2, you determine 3M's return on assets to be 13.8%:

Return on assets (0.138) = Income ($3,455) / assets ($25,121)

You can convert return on assets into a percentage by multiplying the answer above by 100 to get 13.8%.

Certainly, knowing 3M generated a 13.8% return on assets is helpful. That is a tremendous return, compared with the rest of the stock market and other industrial conglomerates. During the early 2000s, the average company in the S&P 500 generated a return on assets of 5.8%, and a 3% return was the norm for industrial companies as a group, Reuters says.

Table 10-2	3M's Vital Stats for 2008
Line item	*Amount in $ millions*
Revenue	$25,269
EBIT	$5,528
Tax-adjusted EBIT (assuming 37.5%)	$3,455
Total assets in 2008	$25,547
Total assets in 2007	$24,694
Average assets at end of 2008	$25,121

Source: S&P's Capital IQ

It's one thing to know 3M has a high return on assets. But fundamental analysis helps you figure out why. You can do this analysis by breaking return on assets into its pieces. Bear with me as I present to you yet another formula. It's return on assets broken into its component parts:

Return on assets = Profit margin × asset turnover

And let's cut that formula down even further to say:

(Income / assets) = (Income / revenue) × (Revenue/ assets)

Once your eyes stop glazing over, you'll recognize the power of this formula. What it's telling you is that a company's return on assets is a function of its *profit margin* and its *asset turnover*. A company's profit margin is how much it keeps in profit from every $1 in sales, discussed at length in Chapter 5. And the asset turnover is how much revenue a company earns from its assets.

Breaking down the return on assets clearly shows you the two levers a company can pull to boost its return on assets: profit margins and asset turnover.

When you plug the numbers from Table 10-2 into the formula, you can see that return on assets for 3M breaks into these pieces:

$$(\$3,455 / \$25,121) = (\$3,455 / \$25,269) \times (\$25,269 / \$25,121)$$

I could have spared you from these formulas. But just as doing your own personal taxes helps you understand how your actions affect your tax bill, breaking down return on assets lets you see how a company's management can boost returns to shareholders, which is of great importance in fundamental analysis. Just know that when looking for stocks to buy, find those that are:

- ✔ **Boosting their profit margins:** Profit margins, however you measure them, are a key component to a company's future.

- ✔ **Putting their assets to full use:** The more revenue a company can generate from its assets, the better the returns.

- ✔ **Doing everything simultaneously:** Even a small improvement in profit margins and a modest improvement in asset use can have an explosive effect on a company's returns.

Minding the earnings yield

There aren't many things in life that are as useful upside down as they are right-side up. Many a child has shed a tear over an upside down ice-cream cone.

But the *price-to-earnings* ratio, or *P-E*, is one of the few things that can be of value upside down. In Chapter 9, you found how the P-E is a key tool to understand a stock's valuation and whether it's an attractive investment. When you flip the P-E ratio over, and look at the *reciprocal*, you get what's called the *earnings yield*. While the P-E gets all the attention, the earnings yield can also be easier to understand. The earnings yield tells you how much in earnings a company is generating for you.

Let's keep things simple and use 3M's net income during 2008 and stock price at the end of 2008 for an example. 3M's stock ended the year at $57.54 a share, and the company reported *diluted earnings per share* of $4.89 a share. Dividing the price by the diluted earnings per share, you arrive at a P-E of 11.8 times. If you'd like to review how to calculate a P-E ratio, flip back to Chapter 8, where it's described in detail.

But now, try instead, dividing the diluted earnings per share by the price and multiplying by 100 to convert it into a fraction. Go ahead, it won't hurt. You find out that the company is generating earnings of 8.5% on every dollar invested in it.

The earnings yield is so useful because it puts the P-E into a form that is easily understood and compared with other investments. For instance, if you could get 8.5% in a savings account, then the 8.5% earnings yield from 3M wouldn't be all that attractive. You'll want to make sure the extra risk is worth it, for instance, if you're convinced the company's earnings will skyrocket.

Knowing When to Bail Out of a Stock

If you thought trying to pick the right time to buy a stock was hard, that's nothing compared to trying to sell at the right time. Inevitably, when you sell a stock it ends up taking off and doubling; at least it feels that way most of the time. At the same time, you may have been in a situation where you held onto a stock and it just kept falling.

Knowing when to sell is tremendously important when you buy and sell individual stocks. When you buy individual stocks, as opposed to buying broad index funds, you're taking on company-specific risk. Not only are you subject to the normal ups and downs of the market, but you're adding the risk that the individual company will make mistakes. For that reason, you need to be very disciplined about when you part ways with a stock. Some investors who apply *technical analysis* (discussed in Chapter 19), urge you to sell a stock once it falls 10% from your purchase price. This will prevent you from taking any large losses.

Breaking down some top reasons to say bye to a stock

There are many reasons why a fundamental analyst might decide to part with a stock. Some of the major ones include:

- **Decelerating earnings or revenue growth:** When you start noticing a company's growth is stalling out, that can be a warning sign of trouble. Flip ahead to Chapter 17 on ways to isolate trends at a company.

- **Deteriorating financial ratios:** When companies start taking a dramatically longer time to collect cash from customers or pay their bills, that can tip you off to trouble. See Chapter 8 for more details on this.

✔ **Poor corporate governance or questionable management:** If the motives of a company's executives get out of line from those of investors, that can be a problem. Chapter 9 will show you how to do this analysis.

✔ **Overvaluation:** Even good companies can get overvalued. As hard as it is sometimes, you might be best off selling a stock when the company seems like it can do no wrong and the stock price is soaring to unsustainable heights. There are many ways for a fundamental analyst to measure valuations. The earnings yield, discussed above, is one way; another is the dividend discount model, discussed below. But don't forget about the P-E and PEG, discussed in Chapter 8, and the *discounted cash flow analysis* covered in Chapter 11.

✔ **Rising risk of default:** If you have any questions at all whether a company can pay its debt, sell first and ask questions later. Perhaps the first way to sense this is by analyzing a company's interest coverage ratio, as described in Chapter 8. But you also want to scour the annual report for the words *going concern* from the auditors. If the auditors are worried, you should be petrified. I'll show you where to look for this in Chapter 12.

✔ **Chronically missing expectations:** Wall Street analysts routinely forecast how much they expect a company to earn in a given quarter or year. Companies that miss these expectations are sometimes giving you a heads up that either the stock is too high or the company is struggling. You can read more about this in Chapter 14.

✔ **Your appetite for risk has changed:** Perhaps you have recently changed jobs or think you'll need your money sooner than you'd thought. You might consider selling some of your smaller or more speculative stocks, since they tend to be riskier over time.

Why selling stocks everyone else wants can be profitable

There are many aspects of investing that just don't make any logical sense. One thing that often perplexes investors is the fact that sometimes the best time to sell a stock is when it seems everyone else wants to buy it.

A good company's stock may turn out to be a bad investment if you overpay for it.

There are a few telltale signs that show too many investors are piling into a stock, perhaps making it overvalued and a candidate to be sold, including:

- ✔ **Inflated price-to-book ratio:** The price-to-book ratio, described in Chapter 8, is your first tip-off when a stock is getting driven up too much. The ratio compares the stock price to the value of a company, according to the accountants. The most basic way to think of book value is the total of a company's assets minus its liabilities. When you see a stock's price-to-book pull ahead of its industry peers, you might consider selling.

- ✔ **Lofty price-to-earnings ratio:** Unfortunately, there's no concrete definition of when a P-E is too high. But one thing's for sure. When a company's P-E gets high relative to the other stocks in the industry, you ought to be concerned and consider selling. Also, if the stock market's P-E is 15 and your stock's P-E is above 100, you might consider selling a bit.

Data have proven how investors are often best served avoiding the stocks that other investors are clamoring to buy, and stick with the ones that are being largely ignored. Table 10-3, for instance, shows how *growth stocks*, those with the highest valuations, have performed worse than *value stocks* with low valuations and the market in general. It's another reminder that when others are talking (or bragging) about a stock at a cocktail party, you might consider selling.

Table 10-3	Betting On The Favorites May Cost You
Type of Stock	*Return between December 31, 1998 and December 31, 2008*
All stocks	–0.8%
Growth stocks	–4.0%
Value stocks	1.7

Source: Russell Investments, based on Russell 3000, Russell 3000 Growth, and Russell 3000 Value indexes

What Dividends Can Tell You about Buying or Selling a Stock

Companies can, and often do, put their best spin on their financial reports. As discussed in Chapters 5 through 7, there are things companies can do to put their results in the best possible light. But there's one thing companies just can't fake: dividends.

Dividends are typically cash payments companies make to their shareholders. These payments are tangible. You can actually spend them. Dividends are real money that gets deposited into your account. Companies that pay large dividends often get popular during financial scares, as investors take comfort in the fact they're getting real cash from the company.

These cash payments, while seemingly small, are very important to the overall profit you can expect to reap from an investment.

Don't confuse a company's dividend with the interest you might get from a bond or a certificate of deposit. Dividends are not for sure. Companies can, and often do, slash their dividends to conserve cash. General Electric in February 2009, for instance, stunned investors when it cut its quarterly dividend by 68% from 31 cents a share to 10 cents a share.

Calculating the dividend yield

When you hear that GE, for instance, pays a 10-cents-a-share dividend, it doesn't tell you much. Sure, that means that you might expect to earn 40 cents in dividends in the year, but that's about it.

That's why the *dividend yield* is such a key aspect of fundamental analysis. The dividend yield tells you how much cash you're getting in the form of dividends for every $1 you've entrusted to the company. If the stock price were to remain flat and do nothing, the dividend yield would be your investment return. The formula for dividend yield looks like this:

Dividend yield = Annual dividend / Share price

Fundamental analysts measure the annual dividend in several different ways. Some add the actual dividends paid over the past year, while others *annualize* the current quarterly dividend, or convert the quarterly dividend into an annual one by multiplying by 4. When a company has recently cut its dividend, it's best to use the annualized current dividend.

Using GE as an example:

Dividend yield = (Current quarterly dividend × 4) / Share price × 100

On Feb. 27, 2009, the day GE cut its dividend, the stock price was $8.51. That means the dividend yield was 4.7%, measured this way:

4.7 = (.10 × 4) / 8.51 × 100

At 4.7%, GE's dividend yield, even after the cut, was slightly higher than the S&P's dividend at the time.

Knowing if you're going to get the dividend

Investors who are investing in a company need to pay close attention to the timing of the dividends. Companies are meticulous about which shareholders receive the dividend, and there are several key dates to know about:

- **Ex-dividend date:** This is the date that you must already be a shareholder or buy the stock by in order to make sure you get the dividend.
- **Date of record:** This is the date that the company looks at its records to see who its shareholders are and determines who's getting the dough. If you bought or own the stock by the ex-dividend date, you'll be on the list on the date of record.
- **Payable date:** This is the date you actually get your dividend.

Making sure the company can afford the dividend

It might be tempting to look for stocks with the biggest dividend yields. Some investors get dollar signs in their eyes, thinking about dividends as their portfolio's version of money for nothing. There's just one problem, though. There's no law saying a company must continue paying the dividend. And if the dividend gets cut, you may be sorely disappointed.

There's no for-sure way to know whether a company will cut its dividend. However, there are some telltale signs. For instance, if you see a dividend yield creep dramatically above the average for the S&P 500, that can be a tip-off a cut could be on the way. GE's dividend yield before the February 2009 cut was 14.1%, definitely lofty when the average for the S&P 500 was 3.1% at the end of 2008, S&P says.

When you start seeing a company's dividend yield creep up well above the rest of the market, that's a signal to you that either the dividend yield is about to get cut or the company is in a deeply distressed situation. Keep in mind, though, dividend yields are best compared to like companies. Utilities and banks, for instance, have historically paid larger-than-average dividends and need to be compared to one another.

Fundamental analysts will often use some financial footwork, called a *dividend payout ratio*, to see how affordable a dividend is to the company paying it. The formula is:

Dividend payout ratio = Annual dividend / Diluted earnings per share * 100

To calculate GE's dividend payout ratio, for instance, divide its annual dividend of 0.40 (40 cents) by the $1.72 a share the company earned in 2008 and multiply by 100 to arrive at 23%. In other words, 23 cents of every $1 in earnings are paid out as dividends. A 23% dividend payout ratio is reasonable, but you don't want to see it creep much higher than that since most companies need to retain some cash to reinvest in themselves.

Investors need to be very suspicious when a dividend payout ratio gets to 50% or higher. A dividend payout ratio that high might mean the company will not be able to increase the dividend or might have to cut it.

Some real-estate companies, including those structured as real-estate investment trusts or REITs, are required to pay out 90% of their earnings as a dividend. REITs are a special case, and the dividend payout ratios do not apply.

Using dividends to put a price tag on a company

You can tell a great deal about a company by its *dividend policy*, or track record of either paying a dividend or not. When a company doesn't pay a dividend, for instance, it's telling shareholders it still has plenty of profitable ventures to plow its extra cash into.

But using fundamental analysis, you can get even more information from a company's dividend. Using a technique called the *constant dividend model*, you can get a rough idea of what a company's stock price should be based on the dividends the company pays. The formula looks like this:

Value of a stock = (Next year's dividend) / (Required return – dividend growth rate).

You'll need to make a number of assumptions to use the constant-dividend model. First you need to approximate what you think the company's dividend will be next year. Secondly, you need to estimate what return investors are demanding in exchange for providing their cash to the company. This is a complicated analysis I'll discuss in more detail in Chapter 11. Lastly, you must guess at what rate the company will increase its dividends in the future.

At this point, let's just assume GE plans to pay an annual dividend next year of 40 cents a share, investors will demand a return on their money of 11%, and dividends will grow by 8% a year. You can measure the value of the GE's stock this way:

Value of stock ($13.33) = 0.40 / (0.11 – 0.08)

If all your assumptions come true, GE's stock price on February 27 of $8.51 would appear to be undervalued.

If you haven't noticed, the assumptions you make can dramatically alter the results of the constant-dividend model. For instance, if you assume dividends will grow by 3% a year, instead of 8%, the value of the stock falls to $5, which would make the current price appear overvalued.

Also, the constant-dividend model only works on companies that pay a dividend. Many smaller or faster growing companies do not pay dividend. With those types of companies, you'll need to use the discounted cash-flow model, as explored in Chapter 11.

Dividends are not money in the bank

Many investors make the grave mistake of thinking dividends paid by companies will keep rolling in year after year. In fact, some investors ask me if it's safe to replace their savings accounts, which often pay low interest rates, for dividend-paying stocks.

There's certainly a case to be made for dividend paying stocks. Even if you're an *income investor*, or someone looking for regular cash payments from your investments to pay bills, dividend paying stocks can make sense. Not only do dividend paying stocks give you a shot at making extra money if the stock's price rises, very often, companies might increase their dividends over time. The chance at getting extra cash is a good thing as you try to preserve your nest egg from the ravages of time and inflation.

But I cannot stress enough that even dividends paid by massive companies or even seemingly stable businesses are not guaranteed. Dividends are not to be considered a replacement for interest you receive through savings vehicles such as certificates of deposits, money market funds or bonds.

If the financial crisis that began in 2007 taught investors anything, and it did teach several painful lessons, is was just how fleeting dividends could be. As the financial crisis worsened, company after company slashed or downright eliminated their dividend payments. Even companies that had been paying dividends for decades were forced to slice their dividends to preserve precious cash. For some companies, cutting the dividend was the first thing to do as financial pressures mounted.

The dividend cut-fest reached historic proportions in 2009 as companies, especially banks that usually pay fat dividends, cut deeply. In fact, dividend payments from stocks in the Standard & Poor's 500 fell by 32% in July 2009 from their level in 2008, says S&P. That brutal decline made July 2009 the worst July for dividend payments since 2002. And as of July 2009, S&P estimated investors would get $61.5 billion less in dividend payments than they did in 2008. Talk about a financial hit.

And that's why, if you're angling for dividends, you need to be very mindful of which companies are most likely to protect their dividend payments. Again, fundamental analysis can be your best friend when you're trying to predict which companies are likely to keep paying their dividends. If you flip ahead to Chapter 17 you'll learn about computer-screening tools, which will help you pinpoint companies that have been paying dividends for a long time and have the financial strength to keep it up.

But if building a computer screen to find solid dividend payers sounds like too much effort, don't worry. I have a very valuable shortcut that will handle much of the heavy lifting for you.

A great place to identify the predictable dividend payers is S&P's Dividend Aristocrats list. To make this prestigious list, a company must have boosted its dividends every year for at least 25 consecutive years and be a member of the S&P 500 index. The S&P 500 is a much-followed list of 500 of the largest U.S. companies. You can download an Excel spreadsheet containing all the stocks on the S&P Dividend Aristocrat list here: `http://www2.standard andpoors.com/portal/site/sp/en/ us/page.topic/indices_dai/2, 3,2,2,0,0,0,0,0,2,3,0,0,0,0,0. html`.

Yes, I know. I can already hear you poking a potential hole in this list. Yes, it's true that during the financial crisis even some companies that increased dividends for decades cut their dividends. To help protect you further, you might want to find companies that not only have a long track record of dividend increases, but also have solid earnings so they can afford the payments. S&P has a list for this, too, called the Dividend Starting Place list. To make this list, companies must increase their dividend payments for 10 or more years and earn at least twice what they pay in dividends.

That list is harder to find. But I can tell you that in mid-2009, the stocks that made the list and had the highest dividend yields appear in Table 10-4. Remember, though, these aren't necessarily stocks to buy. Be sure to do your own homework, applying all the lessons in this book before deciding to buy a stock or not.

Table 10-4	Big Time Yields	
Company	Ticker symbol	Dividend yield in mid-2009
Universal	UVV	4.8%
VF	VFC	3.7%
Abbott	ABT	3.5%
FPL Group	FPL	3.3%
Johnson & Johnson	JNJ	3.2%

Source: S&P

Chapter 11

Finding a Right Price for a Stock Using Discounted Cash Flow

. . . .

In This Chapter

▶ Delving into what a discounted cash-flow analysis is and what it can tell you about a stock price

▶ Finding out how to measure a company's expected future cash flow

▶ Digging into how to use the results of a discounted cash-flow analysis to size up a stock

▶ Comparing doing a discounted cash-flow analysis by hand with online tools that do it for you

. . . .

"*I*s this stock cheap?" Those might be the four most commonly uttered words by the typical investor. Perhaps you even picked up this book hoping to find out ways to answer that burning question.

Certainly, fundamental analysis can help a great deal when putting a price tag on a stock. By evaluating everything from a company's profitability and debt load to its cash flow, you can get a pretty good window into a company and help form an educated opinion on its future. Looking into a company's valuation using common ratios like the *price-to-earnings ratio*, can help you figure out how much investors are paying for a stock.

But while all these tricks of fundamental analysis can help you find stocks to buy or even sell, one of the favorite tools of all might be the *discounted cash flow analysis,* or *DCF*. The DCF analysis brings an almost scientific approach to putting a price tag on a company. If you can perform a DCF, you'll be miles ahead of investors who simply buy an individual company's stock and hope it goes up.

How to Stop Guessing How Much a Company Is Worth

If you've ever watched a group of kids playing, you'll quickly learn some slightly unpleasant traits of human nature. The room could be filled with thousands of toys of all kinds. But, almost inevitably, if one child picks up a toy to play with, it's not long before the others notice and decide they must have that same toy. A chorus of "mine" quickly breaks out.

That same playground mentality often reaches Wall Street too. There are thousands of stocks available. But, quite often, just a few hundred stocks will get all the attention while the rest will get ignored. It's not unheard of for just a handful of stocks, for whatever reason, to become must-own stocks or *story stocks*. These are shares of companies that seem to do everything right. Investors buy into the company's promises and push the stock price to lofty valuations, only for the company to disappoint and the stock to fall back to earth.

It's very difficult, if not virtually impossible, to know when a stock is over or undervalued until after the fact. Complicating things further, even if you're able to determine a stock is undervalued, other investors probably will too. And if they do, and buy the stock before you, they will push the price higher, and the stock will no longer be undervalued.

But don't let the fact that trying to find undervalued stocks is difficult discourage you completely. If you're going to try to outsmart other investors and traders, you'll need to know how to do a DCF analysis.

Before getting to that, though, it's helpful to first consider how the value of a stock can be measured. There are two main ways to look at what a stock is worth, including the:

- ✔ **Market value:** An investment's *market value* is what most investors primarily pay attention to. A stock's market value is the price investors have attached to a company. Market value is measured by multiplying a stock's price per share by its number of shares outstanding. You can review Chapter 3 to learn more about how market value is calculated. The constant tug of war between buyers and sellers pushes a stock up and down to settle at a price where the demand for the stock equals the supply of share.

When you sell a stock, remember there's another investor who has just bought it from you. That other investor thinks the stock you're dumping is selling for a good price. Does this other investor know something you don't? Before selling a stock, it's not a bad idea to remind yourself that someone else finds it attractive.

✔ **Intrinsic value:** A stock's *intrinsic value*, sometimes called its fundamental value, isn't based on what other investors think it's worth as is market value. Instead, a stock's intrinsic value is based on all the fundamental data you're been reading about so far in the book, namely *earnings, cash flow* and *dividends*. A stock's intrinsic value is based on how much money the company is expected to earn over its lifetime.

The difference between an investment's market value and intrinsic value is best understood with an example. Imagine an inventor is auctioning off a machine that spits out a gold bar worth $1,000 every year for 10 years. As you might imagine, some bidders might be so enamored with the machine they might offer hundreds of thousands of dollars for it. Perhaps the bidders think they can tinker with the machine to make it spit out two gold bars a year instead of one. But in its current form, the machine's intrinsic value is $10,000, not adjusting for inflation, since that's the value of its output of 10 gold bars worth $1,000 apiece.

How minding intrinsic value can help you

One of the best ways to be successful in an auction is knowing what price you're willing to pay before even entering a bid. If you ever find yourself in a heated bidding war over a Pez dispenser on eBay, for instance, you'd better know how much that dispenser is really worth by consulting a price guide. Not knowing the value of a collectible can be perilous if you wind up losing your head and overpaying for it.

The same caution applies to stocks. You might pick up a newspaper and keep reading about how great a company's goods or services are. You might chat with your barber or cousin about a promising company. All these things might tempt you to be that person bidding up a stock's price and overpaying. "Buying dollar bills for $1.10 is not good business," wrote Warren Buffett in his 1999 letter to shareholders.

Knowing a stock's intrinsic value, though, keeps you honest. If you know how to determine how much cash a company is expected to generate over its lifetime, you know roughly what its stock is worth and can bid only when it's priced right. Going back to the gold-bar machine example, you want to buy the machine when you can get it for less than $10,000.

Warren Buffett is famous for paying close attention to a stock's intrinsic value before buying it. He's constantly searching for stocks that, for whatever reason, are trading at or below their intrinsic values. By buying a stock well below its intrinsic value, he gets a bit of a *margin of safety*, or a bit of protection if the stock price were to fall further.

Getting up to speed for the discounted cash flow

Now that you know what intrinsic value is, the question is how do you measure it? There are several methods of calculating intrinsic value, but the DCF analysis is one of the top methods used by fundamental analysts.

In the next section, I'll show you how to do a discounted cash flow analysis. But first, it's important to understand some of the most basic parts of how it works, including:

A company's cash flow

Companies brag about their earnings, but it's cash flow that really matters. Unlike earnings, which are a measure of profits based on accounting rules, a company's cash flow is the amount of cold hard cash it generates. You can remind yourself of the importance of cash flow in fundamental analysis in Chapter 7.

But to save you from having to flip back in this book, just know that there are many ways to define a company's cash flow. Still, fundamental analysts often focus on what's called *free cash flow*. Generally speaking, a company's free cash flow is the amount of cash it throws off from its daily business, minus any cash it needs to spend on self-improvement, or *capital expenditures*.

All the information you need to calculate a company's free cash flow is available on the *statement of cash flows*. The formula for free cash flow looks like this:

Free cash flow = Cash from operations – capital expenditures

Being able to calculate a company's free cash flow is the first step in building a DCF analysis. The entire analysis is based on the company's free cash flow.

Understanding the time value of money

The term discounted cash flow analysis might sound strange. When you think of a discount, you probably think of that sweater that just went on sale at the mall. But in finance, *discount* means something different.

A discount in fundamental-analysis-speak is a way to describe the phenomenon that a dollar received in the future isn't worth as much as a dollar received today. If someone offered to give you $100, you wouldn't want to wait around 100 years for it. You'd want it now.

There are a number of reasons why a future dollar is worth less than a dollar now, including *inflation* and *risk*. Since prices generally rise every year, a dollar won't buy as much in the future as it would today, known as its *present value*.

Most years, inflation eats into the purchasing power of currency. In addition, there's a risk you won't actually get the dollar in the future. A dollar bill in your possession now is more valuable than the vague promise you'll get one in the future.

This matter of the present value of a dollar is critical to the DCF analysis. For instance, let's say you correctly forecasted how much cash a company will generate in its lifetime. Here's the problem: You don't actually get all that cash now. You need to wait many years to collect cash as it's generated by the company.

Unless you have a time machine and can collect the future dollars, you'll have to rely on some good old-fashioned fundamental analysis to tell you what those dollars in the future are worth today. Sounds pretty Twilight Zone, I know. But measuring the present value of a company's future cash flows is exactly what a DCF analysis does.

There are many ways to measure present value, but we'll start with the basic formula to show you how all this works. Trust me; it looks scarier than it is:

Present value = Future value / (1+interest rate) ^ time

The ^ is the way to designate an exponent. Must calculators have a key, y^x, which will allow you to take a number to a power.

It's easiest to get your head around this whole present-value concept with a simple example. Imagine you win $1 million in the lottery. Now, imagine the state makes you an offer. You can either get the whole $1 million in five years, or the state will pay you $950,000 right now. What's a better deal?

At first, you might feel like it's a no-brainer. Why accept just $950,000? You wouldn't even be able to call yourself a millionaire.

But guess what? Using the concept of present value, you quickly find out you're actually better off taking the $950,000 now. Let's say interest rates are 3% and expected to remain there for the next five years. Using the present-value formula, you calculate that $1 million received in five years is only worth $862,608 in present value. Here's what I mean:

Present value ($862,608) = $1,000,000 / (1 + 0.03) ^ 5

In the example above, the future value of the problem is $1 million. That's what you're receiving in the future.

I've only subjected you to the torture of the present-value formula to show you how it can be calculated by hand. Most fundamental analysts, though, aren't so masochistic and tend to use financial calculators or spreadsheets to calculate present value. It's a very good idea, if you plan on doing DCF analyses, to invest in either a financial calculator or a copy of Microsoft's Excel.

Using a financial calculator, such as Hewlett-Packard's HP 12c, the problem above is a snap. Simply enter 5, then press the n key for the number of years. Enter 3, then hit the i key, for the interest rate. Lastly, enter 1,000,000 and the FV key for future value. When you press the PV key, you'll get the answer instantly.

Microsoft's Excel spreadsheet software can also handle the problem pretty easily. You would just enter a function that looks like this:

=PV(interest rate, number of periods, number of interim payments, future value)

Or, in this example:

=PV(0.03,5,0,1000000)

Performing a Discounted Cash Flow Analysis

Now that you understand what a discounted cash flow analysis is and why it's critical to fundamental analysis, it's time to do one yourself. To perform a discounted cash flow analysis, you'll need a few pieces of information, including the company's:

- ✔ **Current free cash flow:** This is how much cash the company generated during the most recent year.

- ✔ **Number of shares outstanding:** This is the number of shares a company has put into shareholders' hands. A company's number of shares outstanding is available from the annual report.

- ✔ **Expected growth rate in the intermediate term:** You will need to estimate how rapidly a company's cash flow is likely to grow over the next five to 10 years. You can either estimate this yourself or get it from financial Web sites.

- ✔ **Expected perpetual growth rate:** Over time, most companies *mature* and start to grow at the pace of the economy. Over a company's very long term, this more moderate growth rate is assumed to continue into the future.

- ✔ **Discount rate:** This is how much return investors, in exchange for providing their cash to the company, expect to receive.

Financial analysts love the '80s

Ah. The 1980s. You might think of legwarmers and New Wave music when you think of the decade of Flashdance and Duran Duran. But for fundamental analysts, the decade wasn't all lost. In 1982, Hewlett-Packard introduced the HP 12C financial calculator, which revolutionized fundamental analysis. Even to this day, in the age of laptops, an HP 12C is almost required equipment for any self-respecting fundamental analyst. You've probably seen the calculators, which have a retro look to them, kind of resembling something used to launch the Apollo spacecraft. The 12C is hard to miss with its industrial style and gold metal band at the top. Lore has it that fundamental analysts snapped up the HP 12C, in part, because it's used horizontally, unlike most calculators that are used vertically, making it look like a miniature computer. HP still sells the calculator today, making it the company's longest-selling calculator. If you're curious, you can download and read the HP 12C's owner's manual, which is actually an excellent primer in business math. It's available for free at http://h10032.www1. hp.com/ctg/Manual/c00363319. pdf.

You're about to start one of the most math-intensive chapters in this entire book. Calculating a stock's intrinsic value using the DCF analysis requires several formulas and steps. Don't get frustrated if it seems confusing at first. Just reread the Chapter and practice, and soon, it'll make sense. It can also be helpful to build a spreadsheet, so you can see how all the calculations fit together. This chapter will calculate the intrinsic value of a well-known consumer products company, Procter & Gamble.

Starting out with free cash flow

Before you can measure all the cash a company is expected to generate in its lifetime, you need to know how much cash it generated in the just-completed period. This is the base of the DCF analysis.

Take P&G's 2008 results, for instance. During fiscal 2008 ended June 30, P&G generated cash from operations of $15.8 billion and spent $3.0 billion on capital expenditures. Subtract the $3 billion *cap ex* from the $15.8 billion in cash from operations and you determine the company had free cash flow of $12.8 billion in 2008.

Getting the company's shares outstanding

A company's number of shares outstanding tells you how many pieces a company's ownership is cut into. The number of shares outstanding is readily available in a company's annual report, or closely related 10-K, and the quarterly reports, or the related 10-Qs. At the end of fiscal 2008, P&G had 3.03 billion shares outstanding. You can review what data are in the 10-K and 10-Q in Chapter 4.

Estimating the company's intermediate-term growth

Up to this point, the data you need to do a discounted cash flow analysis are based in fact. A company's free cash flow last year, for instance, is in the financial statements in black and white. The number of shares outstanding is also a matter of fact.

But in this step, you'll need to start making some guesses. Clearly, there's no way to know for sure how rapidly a company's cash flow will grow in the next five years, much less 10. You'll need to estimate this future growth rate.

There are two main ways to estimate a company's future growth, including:

✔ **Historical trend analysis:** A company's historical growth rate is a good place to start when trying to see how fast it will grow in the future. If the company is in a pretty stable business, looking at its historical growth trends can be a good way to forecast the future. After all, consumers will generally buy P&G's toilet paper, detergent and soap in the bad times, and they probably won't stock up during the good times. Using a historical trend analysis, explored in more detail in Chapter 17, you can get an idea of how quickly a company's cash flow has grown over the years.

✔ **Listening to the analysts' forecasts:** The second method of estimating a growth rate is by considering what analysts say. Most stock analysts' reports will provide an expected long-term growth rate. Many financial Web sites also provide an average of the analysts' earnings growth forecasts, which can be a good proxy for guesses at the company's future cash flow growth. P&G was expected to grow by 10% a year over the next five years, according to MSN Money as of early 2009. I will use 10% for this example.

The difficulty in estimating expected future growth rates is a big reason why, as a fundamental analyst, you might stick with companies that sell products that have stable and steady growth. They are much easier to forecast growth for.

Going way out: Forecasting long-term growth

Companies are like rock stars. Even the great ones slow down over time. Even outstanding companies eventually succumb to the gravitational pull of capitalism when competitors crowd into their markets and drive down profits and eat into market share.

It's unrealistic to expect even a good company to keep growing at a double-digit pace forever. Generally, fundamental analysts assume a company's growth over its lifetime will moderate to the economy's growth. Over time, that super-long-term-growth rate is about 3%.

Measuring the discount rate

If you thought estimating a company's intermediate growth rate was tough, just wait until you try to estimate the *discount rate*, sometimes called a company's *cost of capital*. The discount rate is what you'll use to measure the present value of the company's future cash flows.

Measuring a company's discount rate can be an extremely complex calculation that could keep a supercomputer busy for a couple of days or weeks. I'm going to assume you don't really want to get into the gory details. If you do, "Valuation: Measuring and Managing the Value of Companies" (Wiley) will delight you and your pet supercomputer.

For our purposes, though, it's important to get in the ballpark for the discount rate calculation. There are two primary ways to do this, including:

Taking a cue from bond investors

One way to estimate the discount rate is by taking the *yield* being paid on some of the company's bonds that mature in five years or longer. The yield is the return investors would get if they bought the bond at the current price. The current yield on thousands of companies' bonds are available for free at brokerage firms' Web sites. Bond yields are also available on the free corporate bond tracking system, TRACE, which is operated by securities regulator FINRA at cxa.marketwatch.com/finra/BondCenter. Here's how to get a bond yield from TRACE in four easy steps:

1. **Enter the stock's ticker symbol in the "Symbol" blank, located under the light blue bar that says "Quick Bond Search."**

2. **Choose the Corporate option next to where it says "Bond Type:".**

3. **Select 5 to 10 years in the Maturity space.**

4. **Click the Search button.**

You'll see a list of the company's bonds and their yields, giving you an idea of what returns bond investors are demanding. In early 2009, the average on P&G bonds was about 4.5%.

Don't assume that a bond's yield is equal to the discount rate for a stock. After all, you're taking more risk buying a company's stock than a bond investor is taking, since you don't get a guaranteed return. As a result, you must add anywhere between one to three percentage points to arrive at a discount rate. In this example, you might assume the discount rate to be 7%. The riskier the company, the more you'll want to add to this yield.

Using the Capital Asset Pricing Model (CAPM)

So, are you sorry you started reading this chapter yet? Hang in there.

You might not like using a bond yield to approximate a discount rate. After all, bond buyers are taking much less risk, since they're guaranteed a return and get first dibs on the company's assets in case of trouble.

That's where the Capital Asset Pricing Model, or CAPM, comes in. This formula states a company's discount rate should be relative to the risk taken by investors and what return they could get for taking no risk. The formula looks like this:

> CAPM discount rate = risk free rate + (expected market return – risk free-rate) × stock's beta

That's a scary-looking formula. But it's not bad if you break it down into its parts:

✔ **Risk-free rate:** This is the return you'd get for taking very little risk with your money. Generally, this is the yield on U.S. securities maturing in 10 years. This yield is available on nearly any financial Web site. Yahoo Finance (finance.yahoo.com) lists it on the top left-hand side of the page next to the label, 10 Yr Bond (%). The yield was 2.819% in early 2009.

✔ **Expected market return:** This is the return investors generally expect from investing in stocks. Generally, investors use the stock market's long-term return of 10% as a reasonable long-term expectation.

If you don't like using the 10% long-term average, you can consider measuring the expected market return by adding the dividend yield to the earnings yield. If you'd like to find out how to measure dividend yield and earnings yield, that's covered in Chapter 8.

✔ **Stock's beta:** Some stocks are riskier than others. Beta is a statistical tool used to quantify how risky a stock is relative to the market. When a stock's beta is greater than 1, the stock is considered to be riskier, or more volatile, than the market. When a stock's beta is less than 1, it's thought to be less risky.

You can get stocks' betas from nearly all financial Web sites. For instance, using MSN Money, money.msn.com, enter the stock's symbol in the blank in the upper left-hand corner of the screen and click the Get Quote button. You'll see the stock's beta on the right-hand side of the screen. In early March, P&G had a beta, for instance, of 0.63.

Still with me? If so, it's just a matter of doing some plugging and chugging. The discount rate for P&G looks like:

$$0.0730 = 0.02819 + (0.1 - 0.02819) \times 0.63$$

If you multiply 0.073 by 100, you can convert it into a percentage: 7.3%.

When using the CAPM to calculate a discount rate, you must convert all the interest rates into decimals before inserting them into the formula. You can do this by dividing the interest rate by 100. For instance, 10% is 0.1, or 10 divided by 100.

Putting it all together

Now that you've gathered all the raw data, it's time to put them into a full-fledged DCM. The primary objective is to estimate a company's future cash flows and then figure out what those cash flows would be worth today. This section will show you do to do this.

Forecasting the cash flows for the first five years

You'll start by creating a table of what the company's cash flows will look like in the future. All you need is the company's free cash flow from the just-completed year and its expected growth rate.

Going back to the P&G example, start with the company's 2008 free cash flow of $12.8 billion. To estimate what the following year's free cash flow might be, multiply the previous year's figure by 10%, or simply by 1.1. So, to estimate 2009's free cash flow, multiply 2008's ($12.8 billion) by 1.1 to get $14.1 billion. And for year two, just repeat. Multiply the estimated 2009 free cash flow of 14.1 billion by 1.1 to arrive at an estimated 2010 free cash flow of $15.5 billion. Keep repeating this procedure for five years until you get something that looks like Table 11-1.

Table 11-1	Forecasting P&G's Future Cash Flows ($ billions)				
Year	1 (2009)	2 (2010)	3 (2010)	4 (2011)	5 (2012)
Expected free cash flow in future dollars	$14.1	$15.5	$17.0	$18.8	$20.7

Forecasting the cash flows for years five and beyond

You might be wondering how long you have to keep multiplying by 1.1. After all, P&G will likely be around a very long time. Luckily, though, yet another formula will bail us out and help us figure out how much the company is expected to earn in perpetuity, known as its *residual value*. The formula looks like this:

Residual Value = Cash flow in year 5 × (1 + long-term growth rate)/ (Discount rate – long-term growth rate)

For P&G, that's $495.8 billion, as calculated by just plugging the variables into the formula like this:

$$= 20.7 \times (1 + 0.03)/(0.073 - 0.03)$$

Discounting all the cash flows to current value

At this point, you've estimated how much cash the company is expected to generate in its lifetime. There's just one problem. Those cash flows will be received in the future. And as you discovered above, a cash flow received in the future is worth less than one received now.

To solve this mind-bending dilemma, you'll need to discount the future cash flows using the discount rate. That's right. That's a big reason why this whole tortured exercise is called a discounted cash flow analysis. All you need to do now is determine the present value of all the future cash flows you've estimated. Starting with the first cash flow, $14.1 billion, you would use this formula:

Present value = Future value / (1+interest rate) ^ time

By hand, you would calculate the answer, $13.1 billion, by inserting the numbers in the present value formula like this:

Present value = $14.1 / (1+0.073) ^ 1

Had enough of all these formulas and prefer to let your calculator do the work? Using an HP 12C calculator, you would follow these steps:

1. **Set the number of years.** Enter 1 and the n key.

2. **Set the discount rate.** Enter 7.3 and the i key.

3. **Enter the future cash flow.** Enter 14.1 and the FV key.

4. **Calculate the present value.** Press the PV key.

If Excel is more your speed, the following formula will do the trick for you:

=PV(0.073, 1, 0, 14.1)

Be sure to calculate the present value of all five of the years. And when you're done with that, don't forget to calculate the present value of the residual value. When you calculate the present value of the residual year, in this example, it's considered to be in year five.

You should get something that looks like what you see in Table 11-2:

Table 11-2   Present Values of Future Cash Flows ($ billions)

Year	1	2	3	4	5	Residual
Present value	$13.1	$13.5	$13.8	$14.2	$14.6	$348.6

Finally, you add up all the present values to arrive at an intrinsic value of $417.8 billion. This number can then be compared with the market value to see whether the stock is cheap or expensive based on intrinsic value.

Comparing intrinsic value to market value

Many investors like to think of stocks in terms of their per-share stock prices. And now that you have the stock's intrinsic value, you can finish the analysis by estimating what its intrinsic value, per share, is. To do this, simply divide the intrinsic value of $417.8 billion by the number of shares outstanding, which you figured at the beginning of this section to be 3.03 billion. The answer: P&G's intrinsic value is $138 a share. You then compare the stock's intrinsic value to the current stock price, using the rules in Table 11-3:

Table 11-3   Sizing Up Intrinsic Value

If a stock's intrinsic value is . . .	. . . the stock may be . . .
Greater than the current stock price	Undervalued
Less than the current stock price	Overvalued

At the time this chapter was written, amid the bear market of 2008 and 2009, P&G's stock price was $45.71. Using the discounted cash flow analysis, that would make the stock appear to be very undervalued.

Don't assume that just because a stock looks undervalued using the DCF analysis, you should run out and buy it. The DCF analysis is highly reliant on the multiple assumptions and estimates you've made, as I'll explain more at the end of the chapter. Fundamental analysts use the DCF analysis as one of many tools before deciding whether or not to buy a stock.

Making the Discounted Cash Flow Analysis Work for You

Perhaps your brain shut down as soon as you hit the first formula above. Certainly, the discounted cash flow analysis is one of the more math-intensive things you'll do with fundamental analysis.

Don't let the parade of formulas, though, discourage you from using the theory of the discounted cash flow analysis. Many people, fearing they're paying too much for a stock, love how the discounted cash flow model gives a framework to measure a reasonable value for a stock. But the math just scares them away.

And that's one reason I recommend beginners to use a variety of Web sites that will help them do the analysis for you.

If you'd like to practice doing another DCF analysis and read through another explanation, I've made one available here: http://www.usatoday.com/money/perfi/columnist/krantz/2005-06-29-cash-flow_x.htm.

Web sites to help you do a DCF without all the math

Given just how much calculation goes into the DCF analysis, it's not surprising you can just let a computer do all the work for you. A couple of sites worth checking out include:

- **Moneychimp's Cash Flow Calculator** (www.Moneychimp.com/articles/valuation) attempts to turn the DCF analysis into a matter of plugging in the data. The site asks for you to enter a company's earnings. However, the analysis works the same if you enter the company's free cash flow instead, if you'd prefer. After you fill in the blanks, click the Calculate button, and the site will calculate the intrinsic value.

- **Valuation Technologies' Discounted Cash Flow** (www.Valtechs.com/r2.shtml) takes more of a tutorial approach. There's quite of bit of text that coaches you on what to enter, and the site does the calculations for the DCF analysis.

- **KJE ComputerSolutions' Business Valuation tool** (www.dinkytown.net/java/BusinessValuation.html) is made with a fundamental analyst in mind. You can enter items from the statement of cash flow, and the site helps you process the data to arrive at the intrinsic value.

✔ **Damodaran Online's spreadsheet templates** (`Pages.stern.nyu.edu/~adamodar`). If you click on the Spreadsheets option on the left-hand side of the screen, you'll find a treasure trove of financial spreadsheets. There's a section on the site, called Focused Valuation Models, which offers a variety of pre-made valuation tools.

✔ **TransparentValue** (`www.transparentvalue.com`) takes a unique approach with the DCF model. Rather than analyzing a company's cash flow, and indicating what the stock price is worth, Transparent Value tells you how many products a company must sell to justify its current stock price. For instance, you can find out how many iPods Apple must sell to justify its valuation, based on the DCF model.

✔ **Newconstructs.com** (`www.newcontructs.com`) provides an extremely powerful DCF tool designed for professionals. The system automatically calculates companies' cash flow, so you don't even have to crack open a 10-K. While the system is designed for professionals, individual investors may buy reports the company generates using its methodology.

Knowing the limitations of the DCF analysis

Ever hear the expression, "Garbage in, garbage out?" That's really the best way to describe the DCF analysis. While the analysis gives the impression that you're measuring a stock's intrinsic value to the penny, it's highly based on the few assumptions you've made.

For instance, you can get just about any stock to look cheap if you jack up the discount rate. And while the discount rate seems like it's based in science, that, too, is subject to estimation.

Chapter 12

Using the Annual Report (10-K) to See What a Company Is Worth

In This Chapter

▶ Understanding what data fundamental analysts should be on the lookout for in the annual report

▶ Getting a game plan on how to logically read an annual report and find the things that matter

▶ Pinpointing seemingly minute details that have large meaning for fundamental analysis

▶ Tuning into valuable information auditing firms share about companies

Mail carriers around the country know exactly who the fundamental analysts in the neighborhood are. The tip-off? Every spring, hundreds of companies publish and mail out the *annual report to shareholders*, which are hefty documents full of just about everything fundamental analysts search for. The annual report to shareholders and the closely related official annual report called the *10-K*, for many fundamental analysts, are the single most important documents a company provides to investors all year. Think of these annual reports as the company's printed State of the Union Address, a source of information of where the business was and where it is headed. And just as the State of the Union Address is a chance for the president to stir up hopes for the nation, the annual report is a company's chance to do a bit of flag-waving for itself, too.

The annual report to shareholders and the 10-K annual report are so important that I'm dedicating an entire chapter to them. While the 10-K has been touched on in previous chapters in the book, this chapter will give you a road map on how to read these massive documents when they arrive.

I'll share with you techniques used by fundamental analysts to skip past the fluff in the 10-K and get to the meat. You'll also find out how to find the subtle, but important pieces of data buried in annual reports. After reading this chapter, I hope that you'll know exactly what to look for when delving into these sometimes intimidating documents.

Familiarizing Yourself with the Annual Report

Plunk. The annual report to shareholders for the company you own shares of has just arrived in your mailbox or in your e-mail. You'll probably notice scores of colorful photos and pictures of happy executives and employees at the front of the document. But if you flip through pages long enough, you're sure to hit the meat of the report, which is a pile of financials, legal disclaimers and seemingly endless footnotes. You might feel tempted to stuff the document back into the mailbox or delete the e-mail and pretend you never got it.

But while it would seem you need some sort of decoder ring to make any sense out of the annual report to shareholders and 10-K, after a little guidance you'll know exactly what to do. And if you're already experienced at reading annual reports, it's a good idea to know what kinds of things companies can easily bury in these documents and hope nobody notices.

First, a word on the difference between the annual report and the 10-K

The term annual report is somewhat of a misnomer. When investors mention the annual report, they are either confusing or grouping together two separate documents that have similar purposes. There's the annual report to shareholders, which is usually just called the annual report, and the annual report required by regulators, usually referred to by its legal name, the 10-K.

You may notice most fundamental analysts use the terms annual report and 10-K somewhat interchangeably. And that's usually okay, since both the annual report to shareholders and 10-K generally contain the same information; they just look different.

When the term annual report is mentioned in this chapter, you can assume I'm referring to the 10-K unless I state otherwise.

Introducing the 10-K

The 10-K is the annual statement companies are required to file with the Securities and Exchange Commission. These closely monitored documents are required as a result of a company being publicly traded, or having shares of stock trading on a major market *exchange*. Companies that have more than 500 shareholders may also need to file a 10-K.

The 10-K is a document giving investors and regulators an update on the company's financial standing each fiscal year. The 10-K isn't much to look at. The document is almost always printed entirely in black and white, and is very sparse when it comes to graphics and other pretty stuff. The 10-K is the document both regulators and *auditors* look over to make sure the company is *disclosing*, or informing, investors of all the *material*, or important, facts about its business.

Highlighting the annual report to shareholders

The document known as the annual report to shareholders is essentially the glam version of the 10-K. The annual report to shareholders is usually a slick, highly produced document companies mail out to investors every year to kind of show off a little bit. Many companies make an online version, which features fancy graphics and interactive pages. Generally, the printed version of the annual report to shareholders looks almost like a magazine, with the first few pages covered with photos of beaming employees and giddy customers all beside themselves with happiness about using the companies' products.

Some companies are trying to remove confusion between the annual report to shareholders and the 10-K. A growing number of companies are simply using the 10-K as their annual report to shareholders, a move that is also saving companies money. But companies, such as Coca-Cola, appear to be making the annual report to shareholders more of a high-level and highly readable summary for investors. Coke, for instance, calls its annual report to shareholders its *annual review.* In addition to pages of beautiful people in many countries drinking soda, Coke's annual review summarizes the financials in a bird's-eye view.

If you've ever read an annual report to shareholders, you'll notice there's kind of a Jekyll and Hyde thing going on. The first part of the annual report is colorful and fun. Keep reading, though, and the back half gets pretty serious and no-nonsense. In fact, the back portion of the annual report to shareholders is very often a carbon copy of the 10-K, but printed on nicer paper and in a more hip font. And in an increasingly common trend, many companies are simply putting a colorful promotional folder around the 10-K, called a *10-K wrapper*, to create a less expensive annual report.

Some fundamental analysts say the annual report to shareholders is a worthless marketing document. That's probably a bit of an overstatement, though. Certainly, the 10-K is where you want to spend most of your time as an analyst. But the marketing portion of the annual report may contain some useful background to help you understand a company. Just know that the annual report to shareholders is written to be flattering toward the company and its executives.

Getting your hands on the 10-K

Obtaining a copy of the 10-K annual report is surprisingly simple. The document is available in several formats, depending on what you're most comfortable with, including:

- ✔ **Downloading from the Securities and Exchange Commission:** The most direct way to get the 10-K is from the SEC's IDEA database. This is the official database of corporate filings required by the SEC. Downloading the annual report from IDEA assures you that you're looking at the same document as the regulators. You can get step-by-step directions on navigating IDEA in Chapter 4.

- ✔ **Downloading from the company:** Most companies will put an electronic version of their annual report to shareholders on their Web site. You can either view it online or download a PDF file. Many companies will also provide access to the 10-K.

- ✔ **Requesting a paper copy from the company:** If you're the kind of person who likes to take a pencil to paper, you can either call or e-mail most companies' investors relations departments and request a copy of the annual report to shareholder or 10-K, or both. Some brokerage firms will automatically send paper copies of these documents to shareholders.

Dissecting the main sections of the annual report

Most 10-Ks follow a pretty standard list of things to be covered. While 10-Ks are usually slightly different, and some may contain different items, usually you'll find most include the basic items listed below.

Business

Here, the company describes in excruciating detail exactly what it sells, where it sells, and how it makes money. Even if you think you know what a company does, taking a spin through the business section of the 10-K can be eye-opening. For instance, did you know that Coke sells Kildevaeld mineral water in Denmark? Now you do.

The business section also gives you, the fundamental analyst, a high-level view of the company's business model. Coke, for instance, primarily sells beverage concentrate to bottling companies. It's up to the bottling companies to deal with actually turning the concentrate into drinkable beverages, and get the bottles and cans to the stores.

Understanding the specifics of a company's business model is critical to fundamental analysis. For instance, since Coke doesn't actually bottle many of its beverages, a fundamental analyst might be careful before comparing the company with another beverage company that does its own bottling. The bottling businesses requires large investments in machines and trucks, which tend to be less profitable than selling concentrate. And speaking of competitors, in the 10-K's business section, companies will usually spell out all the companies they deem to be their rivals. This list of rivals is very helpful for fundamental analysts, since it's a list of *comparables*, or other companies to benchmark against each other.

Companies will also state, in the business section, who their key suppliers are. Fundamental analysts pay attention to suppliers, checking to make sure they're sound and able to keep providing materials the company needs. Also, sometimes it can be a better idea to invest in a company's suppliers than in the company itself. Since the suppliers aren't as well-known, they might have a lower valuation than the company itself.

Risk factors

Cigarettes contain health warnings as do roller coasters and even some food. The same goes for stocks. Companies must clearly spell out everything that possibly could go wrong. Many of the risks are *boilerplate*, meaning cut-and-pasted legalese, but sometimes the warnings can be useful in fundamental analysis.

Ignoring the risk factors in companies' 10-Ks can be a big mistake. The risk factors section in the 10-K filed by Lehman Bros. in January 2008 was stunningly clear. The first risk stated that Lehman stood to suffer if real-estate values were to continue to fall. Lehman also pointed out that being unable to borrow would "impair our liquidity." The risks were prescient as the housing market fell further and a *credit crunch* occurred, and Lehman was unable to borrow, causing it to collapse just a few months later in September.

Unresolved staff comments

If the SEC has a problem with any way the company handles its accounting, you'll see the details described here.

Make sure this part of the 10-K is blank. If the SEC disagrees with a company's books, you should probably find another stock to invest in.

Properties

Here you'll get a rundown of all the major property the company owns and where it's located. Coke, for instance, gives the square footage of its 35-acre office complex in Atlanta, as well as discussing facilities it leases in Georgia.

Legal proceedings

You can't go into business without getting sued, a fact that's painfully clear from this section of the 10-K. Here, you can see all the lawsuits that are pending against the company and the company's own estimate of the odds of winning or losing.

If you're interested in a company's environmental record, this is a great place to look. You can see whether or not a company has been sued for violating environmental rules.

Executive officers

Curious who's running the company? You'll get a rundown here, with bios of all the major executives of the company.

Market for registrant's common equity

Investors have gotten so used to getting stock information from financial Web sites, they often forget the company itself provides some basic, but sometimes useful stock price information. In this section of the 10-K, companies generally provide a chart showing how high and low their stock price got in each quarter of the year, and the value of dividends paid. The company also provides an estimate of how many investors own the stock.

Some companies even tell you how many shares of their own stock they issued, or bought back. Information on stock buybacks is extremely valuable, since you can find out whether a company is using its cash on the bet that its stock will rise. The importance of stock buybacks to fundamental analysis will be covered in more detail in Chapter 12.

Sometimes, investors need to find out a stock's price after it no longer trades. For instance, a stock you own may have been *acquired*, or bought, by a rival. After a company is bought, you can no longer look up its stock price on most investing Web sites because it no longer actively trades. The Market for Registrant's Common Equity section of the 10-K can help you get a ballpark estimate of a stock's value in the past.

Selected financial data

Here, you'll find a handy reference to the company's most important financial data over the past five years. There may also be some comparative data for the industry. This section of the 10-K is very important for trend analysis, which is covered in more detail in Chapter 17.

Management's discussion and analysis

Imagine the CEO of a company was put on the witness stand to discuss, with little embellishment, what the company does and what its future looks like. That's the tone of this critical section of the 10-K, often called the MD&A. The company spells out in very plain language what the current standing of the business is.

Pay careful attention to the wording used in the 10-K. When a business development is called "challenging" in the MD&A, that's a clue to fundamental analysts to dig deeper.

Quantitative and qualitative disclosures about market risk

There are many risks a company faces that go beyond the business risks listed above. Companies face the risks of rising and falling currencies, and commodity prices, for instance. Some companies sell a great deal of product in foreign countries. That means these companies may be exposed to the risk of falling overseas currencies, which could hurt the bottom line when the profits are brought back home and converted into dollars.

Financial statements and supplementary data

Here you'll find the real meat of the 10-K. The company presents all the required financial statements, including the income statement (Chapter 5), balance sheet (Chapter 6) and the statement of cash flows (Chapter 7). At the bottom of the financial statements, you'll find a further description of each of the line items in what are called the financial footnotes. Some companies may also disclose in these footnotes if they used a slightly unorthodox way of calculating any of the items on the financial statements.

Some of the most important portions of the 10-K are stuffed into the footnotes. These various odds and ends are vitally important to fundamental analysis. Here, the company will disclose all the financial information that is either too specific or unusual to fit neatly into the rows and columns of the financial statements. In either case, you'll want to pay very close attention to the footnotes, as I'll show you later in the chapter.

Changes in and disagreements with accountants

Just as getting into a tiff with your boss or teacher is generally not a great idea, the same goes when it comes to a company and its auditor. If a company and its accounting firm has a, shall I say, difference in opinion over the financials, you'll find it here. As a fundamental analyst, you want to see this part of the 10-K blank, and it usually is.

Controls and procedures

After the accounting debacles of Enron and Worldcom, regulators leaned on all companies to improve the quality of their financials. One of the key areas of new financial regulation had to do with a company's *financial controls* and procedures. It wasn't good enough for a company to have faith that its financial reports were accurate. But companies had to take the extra step to say whether someone could easily cook the books if they wanted to. Companies are required to have safeguards in place to stop fraud from even occurring.

What was that again? Restatements

One of the dirty little secrets of accounting is the fact that companies make mistakes in their financial statements. Mistakes are pretty common, actually. It's not unheard of for a company, many months or years after reporting revenue and earnings, to tell shareholders the numbers are wrong and need to be changed. When this happens, it's called a *restatement*. Restatements are one of fundamental analysts' worst enemies. When you analyze a company's fundamentals, you're forced to somewhat take the company's word on the truth of the financial statements. When financials are restated, that throws into question all the work you did analyzing the company. Just see how common restatements are by checking out how many companies issued restatements in the following years (source: AuditAnalytics.com):

- **2008:** 778
- **2007:** 1,111
- **2006:** 1,565
- **2005:** 1,403
- **2004:** 875

Corporate governance

This part of the annual report is really just a placeholder for things you can find the in the *proxy statement*. This section pretty much refers you to the proxy statement, covered in Chapter 9, which is where a company lays out how well the company's *board of directors* is watching over the company, and how well everyone's getting paid.

Exhibits and financial statement schedules

Anything that doesn't quite fit into any of the categories above is stuffed into this part of the 10-K. Interesting items to look for here include the juicy employment contracts given to top executives.

Executive sign-off

All the top executives sign off on the 10-K. And in a somewhat new development, in the wake of Enron, a rule called Sarbanes-Oxley requires the CEO and CFO to certify that the books and records are accurate, as far as they know.

Auditor opinion

The company's accounting firm is required to give the company the Good Housekeeping Seal of Approval, or not. The auditor's opinion of the company's books will be covered in more detail later in this chapter.

How to Tackle a Massive Annual Report

When slogging through a company's annual report, you might start thinking *War and Peace* wasn't so long after all. Not only are annual reports usually around 200 pages long, they're stuffed with technical language, tables, and detailed footnotes that will make you wish you were reading about the Bezukhovs and the Bolkonskys instead of revenue and earnings.

But as a fundamental analyst, reading the 10-K is one of those things you'll quickly master. Don't worry. You don't need to be an accountant to get what you need from the annual report. In this section, I'll step you through things you should be looking for in the annual report.

Starting from the bottom up: The footnotes

Reading an annual report is very different than reading a book. With a novel, you probably wouldn't read the back of the book first, in case you ruin the surprise ending. But fundamental analysts hate surprises. Perhaps that's why many start reading the annual report near the bottom with the footnotes.

By reading the footnotes before reading anything else, you can quickly find out about all the unusual items going on at the company. It's usually the unusual items that might have the most sway over your final opinion on a company's future or health.

Some fundamental analysts intentionally do not read any of the commentary from the management until they've reviewed the footnotes of the annual report. Management's discussion, in both the MD&A and in the preface of the annual report to shareholders, will be full of positive spin. You don't want your unbiased opinion toward the company to be tainted until you have a chance to figure out what questions you have.

When reading the footnotes, you'll want to pay special attention to areas described in the sections that follow.

Assets and liabilities that aren't on the balance sheet

One of the strangest things about accounting rules is companies are allowed, for various reasons, to keep certain *assets* or *liabilities* off the balance sheet. As you can imagine, this is a huge issue for fundamental analysts. The balance sheet is one of the key financial statements fundamental analysts use to assess a company's debt load and access to cash.

Sometimes, what isn't on the balance sheet is more important than what is on it. Consider American International Group, or AIG. This massive insurance company all but collapsed until the government plowed tens of billions of dollars into the company. How could an insurance company be brought to its knees?

The answer was contained in a footnote buried in the company's 2008 annual report: *credit default swaps*, or CDS. CDS are extremely complicated financial instruments that are essentially insurance policies to protect investors from bum investments. Just as an insurance policy protects a homeowner from a loss from fire, a CDS would protect an investor, say, if a borrower couldn't pay back a loan. AIG made quite a bit of money selling CDS contracts to other investors and collecting premiums from them. But fundamental analysts who paid close attention to the footnotes saw that AIG was exposed to huge liabilities that weren't on the balance sheet.

Fundamental analysts who paid attention to AIG's footnotes saved themselves a bundle. When the 10-K was filed on Feb. 28, 2008, AIG's stock price was still trading for more than $50 a share. By the end of 2008, once other investors understood the risks of the CDS contracts, the stock cratered to $1.57 a share.

Understanding pension liabilities

One of the biggest landmines faced by many companies is the huge pension benefits they owe to their retirees. During the 1950s, many companies attracted talented workers by promising to pay them big portions of their salaries well into their golden years. Those promises have come back to haunt many companies.

The size of the pension obligations are disclosed in companies' footnotes. Pension costs can take a big bite out of profit remaining for shareholders. When a company's pension is underfunded, for instance, it is required to divert some of its profit to fund its pension plan. Not only can big pension shortfalls eat into a company's profits, they can also cut into how much a company can afford to invest in new products, which may dent future growth.

It gets even trickier. Companies invest much of their pension funds. That means if the stock market takes a big nosedive, as it did in 2008, companies not only may see their business falter but also be forced to pony up money to put into the pension fund to cover the investment losses. For instance, in 2008, pension plans at the largest U.S. companies were nearly 18% short of the funding they need to cover future expenses, says S&P.

This shortfall of $459 billion is a direct hit on companies' profitability. During 2009, for instance, large U.S. companies may need to contribute an estimated $70 billion to the pension plans in 2009, up from just $10 billion in 2008, says consulting firm Mercer. Table 12-1 shows how companies' pension liabilities change over time. Notice how the shortfall in 2008 got so large, the pension deficit was larger than companies' total profit.

Table 12-1	The Rise and Fall of Companies' Pension Plans		
Year	Pension (shortfall) or surplus $ millions	Percentage (shortfall) or surplus	Net income of companies
2008	–$256,736	–17.9%	$222,007
2007	$63,380	4.4%	$587,232
2006	–$40,184	–2.7%	$708,486
2005	–$140,430	–9.6%	$599,571
2004	–$164,328	–11.5%	$545,143

Source: Standard & Poor's, based on S&P 500

Pension expenses can severely curtail companies' profitability. If companies do contribute $70 billion into pension plans in 2009, that would reduce the profitability of the largest U.S. companies by 8%, Mercer estimates.

Changes to accounting and inventory

Companies have a certain amount of leeway in deciding how to keep their books and records. That flexibility is part of the U.S. accounting system. But as a fundamental analyst, you want to keep a close eye on when companies make a change to their accounting rules. You should always ask yourself why a company might decide to change its accounting treatment. It's also a good idea to compare a company's accounting treatment with other companies in the same industry. Watch out when a company uses accounting methods that make its earnings look better.

Be extremely suspicious if you see that a company changes the way that it accounts for inventory. *First in, first out*, or *FIFO*, allows the company to consider the oldest goods in its warehouses to be the ones it sold first. In a period of rising prices, the oldest goods will have been the cheapest, so the company's cost of goods sold under FIFO will be lower, and profits higher.

Under *LIFO*, or *last in, first out*, companies consider that the newest inventory is sold. When prices are rising, LIFO tends to decrease profits. Be suspicious when a company voluntarily switches from LIFO to FIFO, since that's a quick and easy way to artificially boost the bottom line.

Debt repayment timeline

During the credit crunch of 2008, it became clear that some homebuyers and companies simply borrowed too much money.

A key part of fundamental analysis is understanding whether a company has borrowed too much. And an important part of assessing this is knowing when a company's debt *matures*, or is due. When a company's debt matures, suddenly it must either pay off the debt with cash, or *refinance*, by replacing the debt with a new loan at the higher current interest rates.

Chapter 6 shows you how to use the balance sheet to find out how much of a company's debt load is due in more than a year, or *long-term debt*. But the footnotes provide even more detail on when a company must repay its debts.

If you notice in the footnotes that a big chunk of a company's long-term debt is due in 13 months, and interest rates have risen, that's a tipoff that the company's profits going forward might be lower. If a company doesn't pay off the debt, it may have to replace the older debt with newer debt carrying higher interest rates.

Effects of tax rates

You might assume U.S. companies pay the standard 35% tax rate. But in reality, very few companies pay that much. Here, companies must state what their actual effective tax rate was and why it differed from the standard 35% tax rate. Typically, the effective tax rate might be decreased if a company does a large portion of its business in countries with lower tax rates.

It's critical when sizing up a company's earnings to compare the tax rate the company told investors it would use to the one it actually used to measure its profit. It's possible for companies to artificially boost their earnings by using a lower tax rate than investors are expecting. Fundamental analysts, too, should pay attention if the result a company's tax rate is lower is due to a temporary reason, such as a short-term tax incentive to open a plant in a certain country. If the tax rate rises in the future, the company's profitability might take a hit.

See what management has to say for itself

The MD&A is one of the most clearly written portions of the 10-K. It's where management spells out, in English, all the important factors facing the company and summarizes all the key elements investors should be aware of.

For beginning fundamental analysts, the MD&A is a good place to start reading the 10-K. Management will step through many of the portions of its business that are of most interest to fundamental analysts. A few of the things you should be looking for in the MD&A include the:

Forward-looking information

If there's one knock against financial statements, it's that they are historical documents. The income statement and balance sheet, for instance, tell you what the company did, not what it's going to do. And as an investor, you're more concerned about a company's future than its past. Stock prices tend to rise when a company does better in the future than people expect. Look for any indication from the company about how it expects to perform in the following year.

Don't expect to see the words, "This is what our business will do next year" in big, bold letters. Management signals this kind of thing more subtly.

An examination of the real risks

There's an entire discussion of the risks a company faces inside its MD&A. Many investors assume this is just a duplication of the dedicated risk section in the 10-K. But that's not always the case.

In the dedicated risks section, the company spells out every single possible thing it could imagine going wrong. Some might even say the CEO could get hit by lightning. (I'm kidding about that, but some companies go almost that far). Many of the risks are pretty generic and probably cut-and-pasted from other places.

But in the risks section of the MD&A, management highlights a few of the risks and provides more detail on why they're so scary. These risks, I've found, tend to be more of the high-level things that might keep a forward-thinking CEO up at night.

Don't get tripped up over whether you agree the risks highlighted in the MD&A are really the biggest concerns. What's important is that management thinks these risks are significant. Knowing what keeps the CEO up at night gives you a look into the decision-making of a company. For instance, the risks of obesity and changing tastes go a long way in explaining why Coke paid about $4.1 billion to buy rival Glaceau in 2007. The company was a leading competitor in less sugary drinks, such as Vitaminwater, perceived by some consumers to be healthier than soft drinks.

Comparing a company's promises with reality

One of the top secrets of many fundamental analysts is to always have last year's annual report handy when reading this year's. By comparing the two reports side-by-side, a fundamental analyst might pick up some interesting information about how well a company executes on its promises.

A Coke and a risk

While much of Coke's annual review focused on the exciting things going on with the company, Coke's 10-K highlights some of the real risks the company faces.

The dedicated risk section of Coke's 10-K provides a laundry list of concerns. But perhaps interesting for fundamental analysts is seeing which risks the company decides to focus on in the MD&A. The MD&A discussion pulls out four distinct risks that the company calls its "four key challenges." Those include obesity and inactive lifestyles, which the company in not so many words says could lead to closer scrutiny of where high-calorie sugary soft drinks may be served. Secondly, water quality and quantity. The company points out water is its primary raw material and expresses concern about its availability in the future. Next is evolving consumer preferences, something the company learned in the 2000s as many younger consumers started drinking new sodas instead of the traditional brands their parents consumed. Lastly, is increased competition.

Company executives love to make big claims about the future. Especially in the glossy annual report to shareholders, a company might say that it's investing big-time in its future. Fundamental analysts, though, have long memories and the ability to check the facts. When a company, for instance, claims in 2007 it's going to invest in its future, you can find out what really happened by reading the 2008 10-K. Simply look up the company's research & development spending and see how its compares with 2007 levels.

Johnson & Johnson is a good example. In the CEO letter at the front of its 2007 annual report to shareholders, the health care company stated "We continue to invest aggressively in research and development." But interestingly, in 2008, J&J actually reduced its research expense by 1.3% to $7.6 billion. Certainly, $7.6 billion is a huge amount of R&D spending. But the fact R&D spending fell reflects a slightly different reality than indicated in the letter to shareholders.

Being aware of legal skirmishes

Since companies seemingly get sued all the time, it's easy to get jaded about lawsuits. A vast majority of legal claims get dismissed with little cost to the company, other than the time of the legal staff.

However, if you're investing in a company involved in an industry that's especially vulnerable to legal action, you want to pay attention to this section. Altria, the parent company of cigarette maker Philip Morris, is named in so many lawsuits that it provides a table of the number of suits and what type they are. Altria also breaks down how many of the verdicts have been ruled in its favor.

If you're going to invest in a so-called *sin stock*, or a company that makes products deemed to have a potentially harmful effect on society, you'll want to understand the litigation risks it faces.

Paying close attention to amended 10-Ks

You might assume the 10-K is practically chisel onto stone and preserved for the ages. But many fundamental analysts are surprised to find out that companies periodically modify numbers that appear in the 10-K and other financial documents for that matter. This is very important for you to remember, since it's possible, that data on an old 10-K is outdated and has since been revised. You must monitor such changes since they can greatly affect your opinion on a company and its stock.

Revisions and restatements are more common than you might think, as you read above. And even large companies have been known to go back and change numbers in the 10-K either to fix errors or update numbers with more accurate data that became evident after the 10-K was filed.

General Electric, for instance, made a number of modifications to its past financials between 2005 and 2008. Much of the changes pertained to changes in the way the company accounted for complex financial instruments called swaps as well as sales from locomotives and aircraft engines.

When you see a company making changes to financial data that appeared in the 10-K, you need to pay close attention. As a fundamental analyst you want to be sure you understand why the changes were made, how significant the changes are and whether the modifications indicate any more serious issues at the company. Most importantly, you want to get an idea of whether or not the company may have padded financial results in order to make itself look good and keep its stock price moving higher.

Fundamental analysis who paid close attention to GE's restatements, for instance, were right on the money. In August 2009, the Securities and Exchange Commission charged GE of fraudulently misrepresenting its financial performance in 2002 and 2003 in order to make sure it topped the expectations of investors. GE paid a $50 million penalty to settle the charges without admitting or denying guilt.

Examining What the Auditor's Opinion Means For Investors

Investing takes a bit of faith. After all, you're not permitted to stroll into the headquarters of a company and look over its financial books and records, even if you've invested in the company. The role of oversight is left to the board of directors, as discussed in Chapter 9. But the other key watchdog for you, as an investor, is the auditor. This auditing firm's job is to look over the company's 10-K and ensure the books accurately represent the financial condition of a company.

While the auditing firm is your watchdog inside the company, keep in mind there is a potential for conflict, too. The auditing firms are paid by the companies, as discussed in Chapter 9, so there's a risk an auditing firm will not want to upset a big client. That's why if you see any red flag raised by an audit firm, that's a giant warning and should not be ignored.

Paying attention to tiffs between a company and its auditors

When a company and its auditors disagree in large degree, the squabble must be disclosed in the *Changes in and Disagreements with Accountants on Accounting and Financial Disclosure* section. Generally, you really don't like to see a company getting into a fight with its auditor. For an auditor to disagree to the point of putting the dirty laundry into a public filing, it must be a pretty big deal.

Keep a watchful eye if a company abruptly announces it's replacing its auditor. Some companies, which disagree with their auditor, go *auditor shopping* and try to find an accounting firm that's willing to sign off on the books. Replacing an auditor before the 10-K is put out helps a company get a clean *audit opinion*, as described below. Companies are required to file a Form *8-K* stating they've replaced the auditor and whether or not there was a disagreement at the time.

Understanding the importance of financial controls

Both the board of directors and the auditing firm are required to assess the company's financial controls. You may need to check two places in the 10-K to get the board's take on controls as well as the auditor's take. You will find the board's verdict on internal controls in the *Controls and Procedures* section of the 10-K. And many times, the auditing firm will attach a separate page called the *Report of Independent Registered Public Accounting Firm on Internal Control Over Financial Reporting.*

The 2007 10-K for computer maker Dell gave a lengthy discussion of the problems with financial controls at the company that year. The board of directors went a step further and described to investors changes that were made to accounting to prevent such problems in the future.

Reading the audit opinion

The Enron debacle put a new fear into the hearts of accountants everywhere. The alleged mistakes and omissions made by Arthur Andersen in the audits of those giant companies ultimately took the accounting firm down with it.

Ever since the fall of Arthur Andersen, auditing firms have been even more vigilant before signing off on a company's financial statements. And that sign-off, called the audit opinion and found in the *Report of Independent Registered Public Accounting Firm* section of the 10-K, is critical for fundamental analysis.

In this section, the auditing firm will say it gives its blessing to the books, usually using wording like "fairly represent the financial position" of the company. Don't just stop reading there, though. The auditing firm may point to some accounting changes made by the company it thinks investors should be aware of.

Always scan the audit opinion for the words *going concern*. Usually an accounting firm doesn't make a commentary on a company's prospects. The auditor is just in charge of making sure the books are accurate. So when an accounting firm has doubts a company may continue as a "going concern," that's a gigantic red flag to fundamental analysts that investing in this company is highly speculative.

Chapter 13

Analyzing a Company's Public Comments and Statements

*U*nless you belong to an exclusive country club, are in a Rolls Royce collectors' club, or jet out to Davos for the World Economic Forum every year, you probably aren't on a first-name basis with the CEOs of the companies you invest in. In fact, you might never have heard the CEOs' voices, even though you're entrusting them with your money.

With very few exceptions, most individual investors won't get a chance to sit down face-to-face with a company's CEO to discuss the future of the business. The relative unavailability of management to investors is one reason why a vast majority of fundamental analysis is based on closely examining a company's written financial reports and regulatory filings.

There are times, though, when members of a company's management team speak to investors. The most substantive meeting top-level executives have with investors is typically during analyst conference calls at the end of each quarter. These meetings, usually available to all investors on a limited basis, can contain critical pieces of information fundamental analysts need to be aware of. There's also the *shareholders' meeting*, an annual gathering of a company's executives and investors. These meetings are mostly marketing events, but can be worthwhile for fundamental analysts to monitor. Finally, companies may release important fundamental data while appearing in the media.

In this chapter, you'll find out how to extend your fundamental analysis beyond the financial statements to include monitoring conference calls, shareholders' meetings, and media appearances.

Using Analyst Conference Calls as a Source of Fundamental Information

Every quarter, investors eagerly anticipate when companies they're interested in will report their financial results. As soon as the results are available, fundamental analysts start poring through the quarterly *earnings press release*, as discussed in Chapter 4, to get an idea of how the company did during the most recent three months.

And while the earnings press release is pretty complete and usually provides the *income statement*, *balance sheet*, and sometimes the *statement of cash flows*, fundamental analysts still may have plenty of questions. Some analysts might wonder, for instance, why certain costs rose but can't find a reason for the increase in the earnings press release. Other fundamental analysts might notice a surprisingly large decline in cash.

That's where the analyst conference call comes in. Usually, shortly after the earnings press release is disseminated, the company sets up a telephone call for *Wall Street analysts*, who cover the stock, to call in and listen to a discussion about how the quarter went.

While most companies' analyst conference calls are designed for Wall Street analysts, that doesn't mean you should ignore them. I'll show you, later in this chapter, how you can listen into analyst conference calls and even access transcripts when they're over.

Understanding the purpose of analyst conference calls

Analyst conference calls aren't a chance for the CEO to trade recipes and golf stories with Wall Street analysts. While some of these calls sometimes seem oddly chummy, they are supposed to serve several primary purposes including:

✓ **Discuss and summarize the company's performance during the quarter.**
 Typically the CEO and *chief financial officer* will read key parts of the earnings press release and point out items of note.

✔ **Field questions from Wall Street analysts.** All the analysts who cover the company are usually permitted to ask questions about the quarter's results. Many of the analysts also try to extract more *forward-looking information* from the CEO, to get an idea of what the next quarter's results might look like.

Some companies are trying to give regular investors greater ability to ask questions during the analyst conference calls. Morningstar, a market research firm, for instance, allows any investor to e-mail questions to management. The questions are then collected and answered by the management team each month. It's a good idea to see if a company you're analyzing will allow you to pose questions.

✔ **Provide future guidance.** One of the most widely watched aspects of the analyst conference call is whether the company will indicate what it expects to happen in the immediate future. This tip-off to what the company thinks is likely for future financial results is called *guidance*.

The dimming guiding light of guidance

Some investors are initially surprised to hear some companies provide earnings guidance. It might seem somewhat strange to think CEOs would be willing to make promises to investors about the future, when the future is far from certain. And you might think that, if a CEO says the next quarter will be strong, that you can quickly make a profit by jumping into the stock.

But guidance isn't as mysterious as it might seem. For one thing, many companies have a pretty good idea of what their *book of business*, or expected deals with customers, will look like months in advance. And that's why when CEOs give guidance, they might not be taking as much of a leap as you'd think. Some CEOs, too, might give guidance they think will be easy to beat. That way, even if the quarter was just as expected, investors might view the financial results as better-than-expected and buy the stock.

Just because a company issues positive earnings guidance and says the future is bright doesn't mean investors have a license to cash in. Many times, by boosting investors' expectations, if the company either misses the guidance or sometimes doesn't top even the lofty expectations, the stock price can suffer.

Some companies, seeing the often perverse way some investors use earnings guidance, are not giving it out anymore. Companies including Berkshire Hathaway, Google, Coke, Citigroup and Ford have, at one point or another in recent years, stopped giving earnings guidance to investors.

If a company suddenly stops giving earnings guidance, there's reason to pay attention. Generally, investors assume companies stop giving earnings guidance when they foresee a rough future. And for that reason, typically, a company's stock price will suffer around the time it stops giving guidance, according to an academic research report called "Is Silence Golden? An Empirical Analysis of Firms that Stop Giving Quarterly Earnings Guidance." Also, when a company stops giving guidance, the growth forecasts from analysts for the company may be all over the map. You will want to keep in mind whether or not a company provides guidance when using analysts' forecasts for earnings, as described in Chapter 17. If you're interested, you can read more about earnings guidance here: http://papers.ssrn.com/sol3/papers.cfm?abstract_id=820644

Unique things to look for in analyst conference calls

During a conference call, you'll want to make sure the management team adequately steps through and describes the just-completed quarter's results. That's really the most basic reason for the call. But as a fundamental analyst, some of the others things you should watch for in the analyst conference call include the:

- ✔ **Tone of the executives:** Be on the lookout for CEOs and top management who act like it's their company instead of the investors'. One warning sign that a management team doesn't understand it's beholden to the public is if executives act agitated when answering questions from analysts or investors.

  The classic case study of what you don't want to hear happen in an analyst conference call occurred while Enron was discussing its quarterly results in April 2001. Prior to the discovery of the massive accounting scam, one analyst pressed executive Jeff Skilling for reasons why the company continued to provide scant financial details in the earnings press release. Skilling fired back angrily, directing profanity toward the analyst. That's not a good sign.

- ✔ **Lack of availability:** While nearly all companies conduct an analyst conference call, they are not required to do so by regulators. Regulators only require the timely filing of regulatory documents, including the financial statement. It's up to the company to decide whether or not to hold an analyst conference call.

  However, when a company doesn't provide a conference call with analysts, that lack of dialogue is somewhat problematic for the fundamental analyst. Some analysts also grouse when companies only provide highly scripted and pre-recorded conference calls.

  Wells Fargo, one of the largest U.S. banks, only provided a recorded statement and offered no opportunity for investors to ask questions when the company reported fourth-quarter 2008 results in January. Some found the lack of an opportunity for investors to ask questions amid the financial crisis to be problematic. That prompted some fundamental analysts, such as Gradient Analytics, to call attention to a "troubling lack of transparency." *Transparency* is an industry term to describe how forthcoming a company is with its financial information.

✓ **Completeness of answers:** If you start noticing the management team is constantly deflecting questions, refusing to answer queries or providing very canned answers, your fundamental analysis radar should start flashing. Company management should be forthcoming in providing information to shareholders.

How to access the analyst conference calls

Now that you've read about the analyst conference calls and discovered how they can tell you things you can't pick up from the financial statements, you might wonder how to get access to them.

Investors are increasingly demanding to be included in the analyst conference calls. And fairly recent regulations, especially Regulation FD, described in more detail below, prohibit companies from only sharing material information with Wall Street insiders and analysts.

Most companies make their analyst conference calls available to all shareholders in a variety of ways including:

✓ **Dial-in numbers:** Some companies provide a toll-free telephone number for anyone to use to listen in on the analyst conference call. Typically, though, unless you're an analyst, you are not able to ask questions. The phone numbers are available on the bottom of the earnings press release or on the company's Web site.

✓ **Web-streams of calls:** A growing number of companies allow investors to listen to conference calls using their computers. Typically, you'll find the links to the online audio broadcasts by visiting the investor relations section of companies' Web sites. Some companies, including General Electric, are also offering streaming video of the calls with investors. Can't listen to the call while it's going on? No problem. Some companies also let you download or stream previous analyst conference calls.

If you can't find a link to a company's conference call on its Web site, don't assume it's not available. Yahoo Finance provides many analyst conference calls, too. Log onto finance.yahoo.com, enter the company's ticker symbol into the blank in the upper left-hand corner and click the "Get Quotes" button. Next, click on the Company Events link on the left-hand side of the screen. And if you don't see an analyst conference call there, you can try BestCalls.com, a site dedicated to analyst conference calls.

> ✓ **Transcripts and FAQ:** Another popular way for companies to share their analyst conference calls with investors is by offering a typed transcript when they're over. These transcripts are typically posted on a company's Web site in the investors relations area shortly after the call is completed. Some companies, such as Morningstar, provide written answers to questions posed by all investors and analysts.

Companies will often conduct analyst conference calls before the stock market opens at 9:30 a.m. Eastern or after it closes at 4 p.m. Eastern. This is done intentionally to give companies a chance to fully explain their results before investors rush to conclusions and either buy or sell the stock.

Be highly skeptical when a company decides to release its earnings after the market closes on Friday. It's highly unusual do to this, since it leaves investors all weekend unable to buy or sell the stock during normal stock market hours. Generally, companies with very bad news try to slip it through late Friday and hope, I guess, that investors won't notice.

If you're not sure whether what's being discussed on the analyst conference call is good or bad, always check after-hours trading. Most financial Web sites will show you how the stock is behaving in special electronic trading that occurs the stock market exchanges close at 4 p.m. But don't think you need to start trading after hours yourself. Since the amount of stock being traded after hours is much lighter than during the regular hours, you might end up paying more for a stock you're buying or getting less for a stock you're selling than you would if you'd waited.

Getting In Tune with Fundamental Information from the Media

There's no question you get a bulk of your nutrients from your breakfast, lunch, and dinner. Those three core meals deliver most of what your body needs to get through the day. Even so, there's a chance that your diet might be lacking in some nutrient, which is why some people choose to supplement their meals with vitamins.

You can think of media reports as vitamins that some fundamental analysts take. Certainly, the regulatory filings and financial reports filed by companies provide most of the data a fundamental analyst need. But still, there might be some details that aren't fleshed out or are buried in the massive documents. That's how financial media can supplement and potentially enhance your knowledge about a company.

The fundamental investor's friend: Reg FD

For decades, analyst conference calls were almost completely closed off to individual investors. Wall Street analysts got top access to the executives of companies, and therefore had the best information. Analysts could often, for instance, get superior information about a company and its stock by being tipped off early on earnings guidance.

But in the 1990s, individual investors and fundamental analysts began to grouse about the one-sided nature of analyst conference calls. After all, if it was possible for individuals to execute trades electronically over the Internet, why were these important calls with management off-limits?

All that changed after the Securities and Exchange Commission passed Regulation Full Disclosure, more commonly called Reg FD, in 2000. This rule clearly stated if a company gives out *material*, or important information to analysts, it must be given to the public, too.

All of a sudden, those one-on-one calls between the CEO and his pet analyst at a Wall Street firm were essentially over. One important caveat, though, to remember is that company executives are still permitted to share nonpublic information with the media, since the press' mission is to distribute information widely to the public. And that's one reason why fundamental analysts should make it their business to monitor media reports, as described below, since there can be nuggets in the press you might not get elsewhere.

Bolstering your fundamental analysis with media reports

As you've probably noticed reading this book, there's not really one source of information that gives fundamental analysts everything they need to do their work. Getting a complete understanding of a company and its stock's valuation requires digging through many documents, looking for trends, discrepancies, and other anomalies. Media reports, available on financial Web sites, in newspapers, magazines and on TV and radio can help flesh out your fundamental analysis of a company. Some of the things media reports can assist you with include:

- **Breaking news:** Since financial wire services and newspapers are vigorously competing with each other, there are hordes of reporters covering companies and looking to get any bit of information first. Sometimes, these pieces of breaking news can have a significant impact on a company and its stock price.

- **Interpretation:** Since many reporters are either assigned to a specific company or trained to study financial statements, they may notice something about a company announcement that you missed. Many media outlets also have access to professional-level fundamental analysis tools, so they might be able to put numbers into context using data you might not have.

Media reports, too, might make it easier for you to quickly assess whether a company's quarter was considered to be better or worse then expected. Reporters who follow a company generally know ahead of time what analysts were forecasting for the company.

✔ **Deeper understanding of companies and the people who run them:** Some executives, hoping to get their messages out, might sit down with a reporter and more clearly spell out their companies' objectives or goals. Executive profiles might also give you more of an insight into the personalities of the people running the company you've invested in.

Some publications routinely provide profiles of company executives. It's important to recognize when these profiles are just CEO adulation, and when they're analysis.

✔ **Industry insight:** Just reading the financial statements doesn't really give you the buzz about a company or its products. Financial media, dedicated to specific industries, might give you a good early indication on how a company's new product, for instance, might be perceived. Some large companies, too, might have a Web site that's dedicated just to them. Reading these, and comments from other readers, might give you things to look for when analyzing a company.

Technology media can be especially helpful to fundamental analysts looking at tech companies. For instance, following the video-game industry's main conference in 2005, media were gushing over Nintendo's Wii game console. At the time, the concept of a game console operated with a motion-sensitive controller seemed odd. But the video-game press glowed over the device, and ultimately the console proved to be a big success and helped push Nintendo's profits higher.

What fundamental analysts look for in the media

Given the barrage of information available to fundamental analysts, it might be overwhelming to think that you need to read every financial Web site, newspaper and magazine in addition to studying a company's regulatory filings.

But savvy fundamental analysts know how to put the media to work for them. Rather than reading everything, much of which is duplicative, fundamental analysts use the media to zero in on developments such as:

✔ **New products:** One of the most difficult factors for fundamental analysts to deal with is a company's new products. With little financial track record to guide them, fundamental analysts may find it tough to figure out which new products are potential blockbusters and which ones are money-sucking duds. Media reports can help by offering comments from industry experts who can put the new products into perspective.

✔ **Bad news:** One thing that amazes me as a financial reporter is just how deft company executives are at spinning bad news. I've interviewed executives of companies at death's door, and the CEOs try to tell you how everything is fine. Good financial journalism, though, will help you look past the corporate spin and get a good grip on when a company's woes are alarming.

✔ **Availability (or over-availability):** Ever notice some companies' CEOs are constantly in the press while others' never are? As a fundamental analyst, it's important to monitor this kind of thing even through there's no way to qualify it. When you notice CEOs seem to be on TV a couple times a week, you really need to wonder why they feel so inclined to be constantly telling their story. But at the same time, you might wonder if an executive is being overly secretive, too.

When to be skeptical of executives' claims in the media

Just because an executive makes a claim in the media, don't assume it's true. Sometimes the media outlet, or reporter, isn't qualified or prepared to call out or correct an executive who makes a false or exaggerated statement.

This point was made clear when the CEO of Amplidyne, Devendar Bains, made a series of claims about the Internet company's products on financial TV in 1999. Bains said the company tested a new product to speed up Internet transmission over a 50-mile distance and the company was ready to sell it, a complaint from the SEC says. But the SEC alleges Amplidyne never field-tested the products and the company, in fact, didn't even have finished products ready to sell.

Fundamental analysts should be especially cautious of companies that seem to be in the business of issuing press releases. Some companies, especially those that trade on the largely unregulated Pink Sheets market, attempt to stoke interest in their stocks by constantly putting out promising-sounding press releases. If trading is light in the stock, meaning there aren't many buyers and sellers, a stock's price can be fairly easily manipulated by seemingly positive press releases.

If you're afraid of missing when a company or its executives appear in the media, you can set up electronic *alerts* so you will be e-mailed notifications. Go to news.live.com, for instance, and click on the "News alerts" link located to the right of the search blank. You can then enter the name of a company or executive you want to track, and you'll be e-mailed when any news breaks that mention those keywords. If you're interested in learning more on how to efficiently scan online news for information about a company, you can get some pointers in my book, "Investing Online for Dummies." How's that for a shameless plug?

Knowing When to Pay Attention at Shareholders' Meetings

If you're a U2 fan, you probably swear by the live show put on by the band's four members: Bono, The Edge, Larry Mullen Jr., and Adam Clayton. Or perhaps you've seen endless photos of Germany's Neuschwanstein Castle, but there's nothing quite like seeing the towering spires in person.

For some fundamental analysts, the annual shareholder meeting is the face-to-face chance to interact with a company's management team.

Getting tickets to a U2 concert may practically require you to hock your wife's wedding ring. Luckily, getting into an annual shareholders' meeting is much easier. As long as you own at least one share of a company's stock, you get a ticket to attend a company's annual shareholder meeting.

What to expect during a company's annual meeting

The annual shareholder meeting is kind of like a corporate version of show-and-tell. Nearly all these meetings are held in large conference halls or auditoriums, and not on the companies' premises. The companies often use these meetings as a chance to showcase all the products they offer. You can find out when and where a company's shareholder meeting is held usually in the proxy statement, which is discussed at length in Chapter 9.

While companies generally don't conduct their annual meetings at their headquarters, you might be a little concerned if a company seems to go out of its way to hold it somewhere it knows might be difficult to visit.

Annual shareholder meetings often follow a script like this:

> ✔ **Flashy introduction:** Many meetings kick off with a flashy slideshow or video presentation showcasing just how cool the company's products are. There's very little value to these shamelessly promotional presentations.

✔ **Presentations from company management:** The CEO and perhaps chief financial officer and chief operation officer might give a speech outlining their goals for the company in the year ahead.

There's rarely any new information released at the annual shareholder meetings. Anything of material interest has already been disclosed in the proxy statement or the 10-K, which is explored in Chapter 12.

✔ **Shareholder question-and-answer period:** Some companies allow shareholders to stand up and ask the management team questions. Other companies require questions to be submitted ahead of time and will only be posed to management if they are selected. In some cases, investors who have put proposals for a vote on the proxy are permitted to give a presentation of their views.

Putting the "Fun" in fundamental analysis

Typically lacking substantive information, the annual shareholders meetings are generally designed to make investors get a warm fuzzy feeling about being investors. Generally speaking, that's the kind of feeling you, as a fundamental analyst, don't want to have.

It's dangerous to get so attached to a stock that you lose your objectivity. Falling in love with a stock, as it's called, may cause you to stop asking the tough questions when owning a stock. Remember, stocks don't love you back.

A few companies are especially famous for their annual shareholder meetings. Shareholder meetings of Warren Buffett's Berkshire Hathaway are especially legendary. Scores of Berkshire investors descend on Omaha (the Qwest Center was the location of the 2009 meeting) to try to get close to the Oracle of Omaha.

The Berkshire Hathaway annual meeting is such a big deal it's almost like a weekend getaway. At the meeting in 2009, events included Warren's Western Cookout, dinner at a steakhouse, and tours of corporate planes sold by a Berkshire company called NetJets. There are also plenty of opportunities to buy and try products sold by Berkshire companies ranging from See's Candies to Borsheim's Fine Jewelry. Buffett usually refers to the event as the "Woodstock for Capitalists."

Don't feel like you need to attend an annual shareholders' meeting or you'll be out of the loop. You can vote on all the important items by mailing in your proxy statement form or by voting online. Also, most companies provide the presentations from the shareholders' meeting on their Web site after the event.

Chapter 14

Gleaning from the Fundamental Analysis Done by Others

In This Chapter

▶ Digging into analyst research reports for clues on whether a stock is attractive or not

▶ Finding out which other investors own a stock and guessing what they might see in it

▶ Using reports from credit-rating agencies to bolster your own fundamental analysis

▶ Discovering social networking and how to use knowledge of others to help you

*F*undamental analysts generally don't travel in packs or flocks. Fundamental analysts, almost by nature, approach investing as a solitary pursuit. Some fundamental analysts even fear getting the input of too many people, as biases might distract them from financial ratios and numbers and cause personal opinions to taint pure objectivity.

With that said, though, part of the job of fundamental analysts is to survey the financial landscape for any information that might affect the value of a company or change its future prospects. And that's where it can be worthwhile to look into the fundamental research done by others. Fundamental analysis from *Wall Street brokerage* firms and *credit-rating agencies* can provide details that you might have missed in your own work. Similarly it can be helpful to find out which other investors are buying a stock you're interested in and what they're saying about it.

Certainly, as a fundamental analyst, you shouldn't let the moves of others dictate what you do. But the findings of others can provide fresh information for you or act as a check against yourself to make sure you don't miss anything critical in your analysis.

Reading Analysts' Reports for Fundamental Analysis Clues

It might seem strange to suggest you take a look at research reports from others in a book about doing fundamental research on your own. After all, perhaps you're interested in learning how to analyze stocks because you've gotten bad investing advice from a broker or analyst in the past.

You're wise to be skeptical of research coming from anyone else, including Wall Street brokerage firms. Often times analysts get paid by companies, either directly or indirectly, to generate research to convince others to buy a stock. In 2003, for instance, the nation's biggest brokerage firms were ordered to pay $1.4 billion to settle charges that they misled investors with biased research.

With all that said, research from professional analysts can provide you with very helpful information to accompany your own fundamental analysis. You just need to know how to read analyst research reports and how to extract genuinely helpful information from them. And that's precisely what I'll show you how to do in this chapter.

Why reading analysts' reports can be worth your time

Sadly, most investors fixate on the wrong thing when reading analyst reports. Nearly all the time, investors will look at the top of an analyst report for the *stock rating* and see if the stock is deemed *buy, hold,* or *sell.* The simplicity of those ratings makes them irresistible, and investors may feel tempted to follow them. Unfortunately, many investors get themselves into trouble and risk losing a large sum of money when they blindly follow the ratings they read in analyst reports.

The stock ratings from analysts are infamously poor. During 2008, for instance, just 49% of the stocks with buy ratings from the top five analysts rose, according to analyst tracking service Investars.com. That means even if you buy a stock recommended by a top analyst, you still have a coin-flip chance of losing money.

Despite their problems, though, analyst research reports can contain some solid information. Some of the reasons why you might want to take a look at analyst reports include:

> ✔ **A way to double-check your own analysis:** Most of the analysts who write these reports are highly trained financial professionals who know how to do everything from discounted cash flow, or DCF, analysis (as covered in Chapter 11) to) to advanced valuation measurement. You

might want to compare the results of your DCF model with those created by professional analysts to see if they're in the same ballpark.

✔ **Industry insight:** Many times the analysts assigned to cover an industry either have studied that field for a long time or even worked at a company in the business. This in-depth industry experience can help you improve your analysis of an industry, as discussed in Chapter 16.

✔ **Dissenting point of view:** If you're convinced a stock is a screaming buy, it might make sense to seek out analyst reports that are less bullish on that stock. Perhaps the bearish analyst will point out things you didn't notice in your own analysis.

Analysts' reports are infamously overly bullish. For a variety of reasons, research reports from Wall Street brokerage firms tend to rarely slap a dreaded sell rating on a stock, as you can see in Table 14-1. The table, though, shows how analysts have been getting more skeptical in recent years. Even so, the fact so few companies get a sell rating underscores why you need to remember that when a Wall Street firm rates a stock a hold, that's actually a fairly negative recommendation you might consider to be a sell.

Table 14-1	Analysts Rarely Give Stocks a Sell Rating		
Year	*% of stocks rated buy*	*% of stocks rated hold*	*% of stocks rated sell*
2008	39%	47%	14%
2007	42%	47%	11%
2006	38%	49%	13%
2005	37%	50%	13%
2004	36%	49%	15%
2003	44%	42%	14%
2002	47%	41%	12%
2001	62%	35%	3%
2000	73%	25%	2%

Source: Investars.com, using data from the major brokerage firms

Understanding the types of firms that put out stock research

Not all analyst research reports are created equal. While the term analyst report is a catch-all used to describe nearly all investment research generated by professional analysts, there are many flavors of research to be aware of.

Giving analyst reports a bad rap

It's long been understood by those familiar with investing that the ratings given to stocks by Wall Street analysts are to be ignored at best due to the conflict mentioned above.

But the potential for significant conflicts of interest became very clear in the early 2000s, when 10 investment banks agreed to a sweeping $1.4 billion settlement with regulators for allegedly putting out misleading research reports to investors. Some individual analysts were also penalized. Henry Blodget, a former managing director at Merrill Lynch who made a name for himself publishing glowing reports on Internet companies, was barred from the industry and hit with a $4 million monetary punishment by the Securities and Exchange Commission in 2003. The SEC concluded that these firms and analysts routinely published reports that encouraged investors to buy stocks, giving them "buy" or "strong buy" recommendations, despite knowing the companies being recommended had fundamentals that were not sound. Investors who trusted the research and followed the recommendations, in many cases, lost large amounts of money. These charges are more reason why you want to know how to do your own fundamental research, rather than rely on the work of others.

The first way you should differentiate research in your mind is based on the source. Knowing where research is coming from, and how the person or firm generating the report gets paid, is vital to understanding what the potential biases and shortfalls in the research might be. Typically, research reports are put into one of two categories based on their source, including:

Broker research

Research generated by the analysts at large brokerage firms, such as Bank of America, Citigroup, Goldman Sachs, and UBS, is usually what investors think of first when its comes to analyst research. These large firms hire armies of analysts who have a *coverage universe*, or set group of stocks, to constantly monitor.

Never overlook the potential conflict of interest when it comes to broker research. Many of the same Wall Street firms that put out research on companies also have large *investment banking arms*. The investment banking portions of these Wall Street firms get lucrative fees performing services for companies, such as selling stock or bonds to investors. If a brokerage firm were to put out negative research on a company, it could risk upsetting management and jeopardize the future investment banking business.

Luckily, if you pay attention you can spot signs of potential conflict in broker research. At the bottom of broker research reports, you'll find a number of key disclosures. In one section, the brokerage firm must tell you whether or not the firm receives investment banking business from the company covered in the report. Analysts, too, must tell you if they personally own shares of the company's stock. And the company must disclose what percentage of all its ratings are buy, hold, or sell. Clearly, if a company only gives out buy ratings, you know to take a double dose of salt when reading that firm's reports.

Independent research

Wall Street firms aren't the only firms that provide research on stocks. Analysts not connected with a big Wall Street firm are typically grouped into the category called *independent research.*

By definition, independent research is considered to be analysis that comes from a firm that doesn't have an investment banking unit. As you read above, the co-existence of research and investment banking has been problematic at times in the past.

Independent research often comes from *boutique* research firms, which may be operated by one analyst or a team of analysts who may have specific experience, such as a particular industry or type of fundamental analysis. Other independent research comes from *quantitative research* firms, which create automated computer programs to study different stocks using a series of tests.

But not all independent research comes from small research firms. In fact, one of the largest providers of independent research is Standard & Poor's, an investment research company that provides data and information on stocks, bonds and other investments. S&P's research is considered to be independent because the company does not do investment banking.

But just because research comes from an independent research firm, don't assume it's better than the research from a brokerage firm. In fact, after the settlement with Wall Street firms, the quality of some brokerage firm's research improved markedly. Similarly, some of the research from independent firms has been way off the mark. You should judge whether or not to listen to analysts' research based on how good the research has been in the past, not by whether it is independent or not.

Keying into the main types of analyst research

Just as there are many types of books, there are many types of analyst research reports. As a fundamental analyst, there are two main types of reports you need to concern yourself primarily with, including:

- **Idea reports:** *Idea reports* are usually lengthy pieces of research an analyst publishes to lay out everything investors need to know about the company, industry and the stock. These reports are often released when an analyst *initiates* coverage of a stock, or begins to regularly follow a company. Some analysts often publish idea reports every year, where they take a comprehensive look at the just-completed year for the company and forecast what might happen next year. These idea reports are usually chock full of industry statistics, which might come in handy when you dig into how to do industry analysis in Chapter 16.

Idea reports can be excellent ways for fundamental analysts to get up to speed on a company or industry they hadn't been aware of before.

✔ **Maintenance reports:** If idea reports are long and comprehensive, *maintenance reports* are just the opposite. Analysts usually dash out quick maintenance reports following major events at a company, such as the release of earnings or the announcement of a significant new product.

Maintenance reports are kind of like an episode of a soap opera: Unless you've been following along (and reading earlier reports) you might not be able to follow what's going on in a just-released maintenance report. It can be a good idea to review an analyst's idea report on a company along with the maintenance report.

How to read between the lines of an analyst report

After you determine whether or not a research report is an idea or maintenance report, it's time to start reading more closely. Since I urged you to essentially ignore the stock rating on most research reports, you might be wondering what you're supposed to pay attention to instead in the report.

Some of the key pieces of data you should be on the lookout for in an analyst report include:

✔ **Savvy comparisons of a company to its peers:** Analysts most frequently will be assigned to cover an entire industry, including both the large stalwarts in the business and the small up-and-comers. Sometimes analysts are able to pinpoint a company's strengths and weaknesses that aren't readily apparent from studying the financial statements.

✔ **Deep analysis of demand for a company's products:** The better analysts perform what are called *channel checks*. In a channel check, an analyst will call up a company's customers and suppliers to see how well a particular product is flowing through the distribution channel. Analysts might find out, for instance, that retailers are slashing prices on a company's products just to clear them off the shelves. That's not a good sign. On the contrary, a supplier might say a company is ordering a great deal of raw materials, which could indicate the company is ramping up production.

✔ **Forecast for long-term growth:** One of the most difficult aspects of fundamental analysis is getting a realistic expectation for the future. I'll give you some pointers on how to estimate a company's expected growth rate for the next five years in Chapter 17. But it's not a bad idea to check analyst research reports to see what five-year growth forecasts they have.

✔ **Exploration of a stock's valuation:** Understanding how to measure whether a stock is cheap or expensive is one of the top things investors try to do. There are many ways to attempt measuring a stock's valuation, including looking at price-to-earnings ratios (Chapter 8) and performing the discounted cash flow analysis (Chapter 11). Both of these analyses, though, are subject to numerous assumptions and educated guesswork.

Sometimes it can be helpful for you, then, to examine the valuation assumptions and results determined by professional analysts. Even if the results don't agree with your findings, you can compare what they measured to what you measured, see why there's a difference and adjust your model if needed.

If you're looking for help with the discounted cash flow model, stock reports from Standard & Poor's can be useful. A vast majority of the stock reports from S&P, which can be obtained using the directions I'll give you below, provide the stock's *discount rate* and *terminal growth rate*. The discount rate is the rate of return investors demand in exchange for putting their money at risk by giving it to the company. And the terminal growth rate is how much the company's earnings and cash flow are expected to grow in the very long term. Both the discount rate and terminal growth rate can have a major effect on the results of the DCF analysis, and both are somewhat difficult to calculate yourself.

Analyst research reports can be very helpful when their insights help you tweak your own fundamental analysis for the better. But, there's an ugly underside to analyst reports, too, especially when the authors are cheerleading or touting a stock. It can be difficult, until it's too late, to know when an analyst report is being more promotional than insightful. A few things to watch out for, though, include reports that attempt to say recent bad news isn't that terrible, without justification. Also, be suspect of analyst reports that try to say a company is so well-managed or well-positioned that it's not subject to the ups and downs of the economy. As you'll discover in Chapter 15, all companies are subject to the typical ebb and tide of the broad economy.

Getting your hands on analyst reports

By now you're probably tired of reading about analyst reports and ready to get your hands on some. Accessing analyst reports is very easy, and may even be free depending on which brokerage firm you use. There are four primary ways to get analysts reports, including:

- ✔ **Your brokerage firm:** If you're a client of the big Wall Street firms, one of the perks you receive is access to the firm's analysts' reports. You might be able to access the reports yourself, or you may be able to ask your individual broker for a copy.

  What if you're with a low-cost online discount broker? You're still in luck. A vast majority of the online brokerage firms provide you with research from both the Wall Street firms and from independent research firms. Charles Schwab, for instance, provides access to S&P research reports, as well as access to its own quantitative research model called Schwab Equity Ratings.

- ✔ **Directly from research providers:** Most boutique research firms and even the larger independent research providers will sell their research to you. You can buy S&P's stock research reports, for about $35, from this Web site: www.sandp.ecnext.com/coms2/page_industry2.

- ✔ **Research resellers:** A number of companies have created Web sites that let you shop for and order a variety of analyst research reports. Both Reuters and Yahoo Finance, for instance, allow you to enter a stock's ticker symbol to see what analyst research is available and purchase it if you choose to. Reuters provides its analyst-report bazaar here, https://commerce.us.reuters.com/purchase/default.do, and Yahoo Finance offers reports for sale here: http://screen.yahoo.com/reports.html. Most reports cost between $10 and $100, but they can be free or cost more.

- ✔ **Analyst research summary Web sites.** Several Web sites let you look at the high-level summaries of analyst reports. Most of these sites give you the average recommendation of all the investors who follow a stock, which may be more valuable than just the opinion of one analyst. For instance, MSN Money, at http://moneycentral.msn.com/investor/invsub/analyst/recomnd.asp lets you look up the breakdown in stock ratings for individual stocks.

Interpreting Credit-Rating Agencies' Reports For Fundamental Analysis

Stock investors commonly forget the fact that they're not alone in bankrolling a company. Generally, companies obtain the cash they need to operate from both stock investors and bond investors. And while stock investors look at analyst research reports, bond investors pay even closer attention to credit-rating agencies' reports.

Credit-rating agencies, including Moody's, Standard & Poor's and Fitch Ratings, look at companies very differently than stock analysts do. The role of the credit-rating agencies is to access how capable companies are of repaying the money they've borrowed by selling bonds.

The role of reports issued by credit-rating agencies

If you've ever compared a credit-rating agency's report with a stock analyst report, even for the same company, you might be surprised at how different they are. Certainly, both the credit and stock reports will take a look at popular financial ratios, such as the debt-to-equity ratio and various interest coverage ratios, discussed in Chapter 8.

But while stock analyst research reports try to help investors make money, the credit-rating agencies reports are primarily concerned with helping investors just get their money back, with interest.

Bond investors are very different from stock investors. They are lending money to a company, and get no piece of the upside if the company does better than expected. Bond investors simply want to get their money back from the company that borrowed from them. And for that reason, credit analysts look at companies very differently than stock analysts do. For instance, credit analysts have very little interest in a company's stock valuation. Bond investors don't care if a stock is overvalued, as long as they get their money back.

But while the credit-rating companies are serving a different investor, the bond holders, fundamental analysts interested in a company's stock can benefit from the reports. Some of the aspects of credit-rating agencies' reports that might be especially valuable include:

- ✔ **The credit rating:** The credit-rating agencies assign various letter grades to companies. These letter grades attempt to give investors a quick way to determine how likely it is for a company to repay its debt, or, on the contrary, to *default* or miss an interest payment. Table 14-2 summarizes the credit ratings from both Moody's and S&P, and what they mean.

  Just as you should never take too much stock in a stock analysts' rating, you should also exercise discretion when looking at a company's credit rating. Since the credit-rating agencies are paid by the companies to provide their ratings, there's long been suspicion that credit ratings give companies a great deal of leeway. It's the analysis behind the rating, instead of just the rating itself, that has the most value for fundamental analysts.

- ✔ **Analysis of how much and how often the company is borrowing:** The credit-rating agencies take interest, and sometimes concern, when a company borrows more money by selling additional bonds. New bond issuances are monitored and explored in most credit-rating agencies' reports.

✔ **Risk assessment:** While companies themselves pinpoint the risks facing their businesses in their *annual reports*, as described in Chapter 12, it's often better to get this information from a credit-rating agency report. Bond investors are a pretty nervous bunch, since they're petrified of not getting their money back. As a result, credit-rating agencies spend a great deal of time investigating things that could go wrong at a company instead of what could go right.

Table 14-2	Alphabet Soup: What The Credit Ratings Mean	
Quality of debt	*Moody's*	*S&P*
Best	Aaa	AAA
High	Aa	AA
Upper-medium	A	A
Medium	Baa	BBB
Lower-medium	Ba	BB
Low	B	B
Poor	Caa	CCC
Highly speculative	Ca	CC
Extremely poor	C	C
In default	C	D

Source: www.credfinrisk.com/ratings.html

The death of the AAA-rated company

Just as consumers have largely gone on a credit-binge since the 1980s, so too have companies. The borrowing boom by companies is extremely evident in how the number of companies with the coveted AAA credit rating has continued to dwindle. General Electric, which had its AAA rating from Standard & Poor's since April 26, 1956, saw its credit rating get cut one notch to AA+ in March 2009. GE's downgrade was a stunner, since it had the AAA rating longer than any currently operating company.

After S&P took GE down a notch, only five U.S. non-financial firms were still rated AAA by S&P, including Automatic Data Processing, Microsoft, Pfizer, ExxonMobil and Johnson & Johnson. Table 14-3 shows how the number of AAA companies has been in free fall.

There are many hypotheses on why AAA-rated companies are vanishing. Perhaps one of the best explanations for a fundamental analyst is how companies have increasingly elected to borrow more, or *leverage* themselves up. By using more borrowed money, companies can increase how profitable they appear to investors who study *return on equity*. You can find out how a company can use debt to goose its profitability in Chapter 8.

Table 14-3	AAA-Rated Companies Increasingly Hard to Find
Year	Number of non-financial companies with AAA rating
1980	61
1990	37
2000	16
2005	6
2008	6

Source: Standard & Poor's

Getting your hands on the credit rating

If you thought getting stock analyst reports was convoluted, that was simple compared with getting a credit-rating agency's report. Generally speaking, you'll need to contact your broker directly to get a copy of the credit-rating report.

However, there are some online resources that will help you get what you need from the reports, including the:

- ✔ **Credit-rating agencies' sites:** Both Moody's site, www.moodys.com and S&P's site, www.standardandpoors.com will let you look up the rating on most stocks for free. You just need to register, which is free. If you need the full reports, you'll need to contact the agencies yourself.

  Both Moody's and S&P provide free access to some of their broader analysis on trends in the credit market. These reports can be helpful with fundamental analysis of stocks, too, since they pinpoint many of the concerns bond investors have with the economy in general.

- ✔ **Media reports:** Most major news outlets have real-time access to the credit-rating agencies' full reports and routinely issue stories on them. News outlets also have access to personnel at the rating agencies and can ask questions that go beyond what's contained in the reports. For instance, when GE's credit rating was cut by S&P, there were many media reports providing a summary of the key information in the report. If you want to review how to use news reports to bolster your fundamental analysis, flip back to Chapter 13.

Knowing when a company's credit rating is suspect

It's never a good idea to take any analyst's report on a company as fact. Analyst reports are based on a heavy dose of estimation. But when it comes to credit-rating agencies' reports, and credit ratings, there's a good way to know when bond investors themselves don't believe what they see.

Companies' debt, including their bonds, trade during the day just like stocks. Just as stock investors buy and sell shares all day, bond investors buy and sell companies' debt securities. The constant back-and-forth determines the price of bonds, just as trading determines a stock's price.

Savvy fundamental analysts know how to check the price of a company's debt and compare that to the prices of debt issued by other companies with similar credit ratings. If the prices on a company's bonds are dramatically lower than those on debt issued by companies with the same credit ratings, fundamental analysts know investors think the company's credit rating is too high.

If you're investing in a company's stock, why should you care if its debt rating is too high? If a credit-rating agency ultimately decides to lower the credit rating on a company, or *downgrade* it, that could potentially increase the company's borrowing costs in the future. And higher borrowing costs could increase a company's *interest expense* and decrease its net profit in the future. And net profit, as you discovered in Chapter 5, is critically important to fundamental analysts.

There are several ways to see how a company's bonds are trading to determine if investors think the credit rating might fall.

One method to see if bond investors trust the credit ratings is to look up bond prices using the Web site, called TRACE, operated by the securities regulator called Financial Industry Regulatory Authority, or FINRA. You can enter any company's name and see the prices on its bonds here: `http://cxa.mar-ketwatch.com/finra/BondCenter/Default.aspx`.

A much easier way, though, to find out whether investors trust a credit rating is by using Moody's own site. It's free; you'll just need to register. Below are step-by-step instructions on how to see if bond and stock investors agree or disagree with a credit rating:

1. **Log into moodys.com.**

   You will just need to enter your username and password.

2. **Search for the company's rating.**

   Change the "search by" pull-down option in the upper right-hand corner to "Ticker." Enter the company's ticker symbol and click the "go" option.

3. **Locate the company's name.**

   Look through the list of company names until you find the one you're interested in. If there's a gold-colored icon to the right of the company's name, continue to step 4. If not, the analysis is not available for this company.

4. **Hover your mouse arrow over the golden icon.**

   When you do this, a small box titled "Market Implied Ratings" will pop up.

5. **Interpret the results.**

   The first line, called Moody's Senior Unsecured or Equiv, will show you the official credit rating from Moody's. For GE, that rating in early 2009 was Aaa, as Moody's hadn't yet downgraded the company's debt as did S&P.

   Below the line with the official credit rating, you'll see a line called bond-implied. This line tells you what bond investors think GE's debt should be rated, based on the current price. That rating on GE was Baa in early March 2009. Next, check out the "Equity-Implied" line. This line tells you what stock investors think the company's credit rating should be, based on a methodology used by Moody's. In early 2009, GE's Equity-Implied rating was Ba.

   Doing this analysis tells you that neither bond investors nor stock investors thought GE deserved the Aaa rating Moody's was giving it in early March 2009. That's crucial information for a fundamental analyst. And it was telling. Weeks later, on March 23, Moody's cut its rating on GE's debt to Aa.

Finding Fundamental Data about Companies Using Social Investing

Up to this point in this chapter, you've learned how to pick up fundamental analysis from professionals. The analysts who write both stock research reports and the reports that go with credit ratings tend to do this type of thing full-time.

But there's growing interest in using the so-called *wisdom of crowds*, or the collective opinion of a large group of investors and analysts, to learn more about companies and investments. The idea is that one analyst may make an incorrect assumption or may be influenced by bias. If you pool together the opinions of hundreds of analysts, consumers, and others interested in a company, though, the hope is the collective wisdom will be valuable.

And that's where *social investing* comes in. Social investing is the financial version of social networking sites, like Facebook, Linked In, and Windows Live Spaces. Just as social networking allows you to meet new people and share photos and ideas, social investing is an Internet-based way to connect with other investors and share ideas, including fundamental analysis.

The origins of social investing

Social investing traces its roots to the late 1990s with the rather primitive and crude concept of *stock message boards*. These online sites allowed investors to anonymously share ideas and hunches about stocks. When stock message boards started, they were a unique opportunity for investors to congregate and share ideas.

However, the obvious problems with these stock message boards quickly turned them into the investing equivalent of locker room gossip. *Touts*, or investors who try to artificially promote a company, would talk up a company's future with the hope of dumping their holdings at a profit to naïve investors. Likewise, *shorts*, or investors betting a company's stock would fall, could easily spread false rumors about a company and try to drive the stock price down.

Stock message boards are filled with all the things you, as a fundamental analyst, are trying to avoid. Rather than analysis based on fact, data and analysts, the boards are stocked with amateurs just trying to spread false rumors and baseless allegations about stocks. Such rumor-mongering in stock message boards is especially problematic with stocks that don't trade on a major *stock market exchange*.

Social investing has since evolved quite a bit. Today, there are social networking sites, which I'll discuss in a bit, that let you see actual trades make by other investors. These sites allow you to find other investors that have similar investing strategies, such as fundamental analysis, and trade notes and ideas. There are other types of social networking sites that compile the investment ideas of many other investors into a single report, which I'll discuss in this section, too.

Why it might be worth paying attention to non-professionals

It might seem counterintuitive and even a little amateurish to pay any attention to what lay investors think about a stock. And that's mostly true. But, as a fundamental analyst, you want to make sure you have examined a company and stock from every direction. And if a non-professional can direct you to a gap in your fundamental analysis, you might be better off as a result.

Some of the areas where social investing may be worthwhile for a fundamental analyst include:

- ✔ **Local demand information:** Some social networking sites allow investors to share potentially valuable information, such as how crowded a restaurant chain's locations are in various cities or how busy a retailer's stores are. This type of information, if reliable, may serve the same purpose as an analyst's channel check.

- ✔ **Industry insight:** Sometimes, investors who participate in social investing sites may work at companies that buy gear from a company you're interested in. Their comments on the quality of a company's products or demand for the products can be useful.

- ✔ **Employee's dirty laundry:** Sometimes, employees will log into social investing sites and provide data that may be helpful in fundamental analysis. For instance, between 1997 and 2001, there were more than 100 posts on a stock message board about Enron, many that outlined potential problems at the firm, according to research from James Felton and Jongchai Kim in their article "Warnings from the Enron Message Board." Some were startlingly prescient, including one in April 2001 that said Enron "is nothing more than a house of cards." At the time of that post, most Wall Street analysts rated Enron a "buy" or "strong buy."

How to plug into social networking

Unlike financial statement analysis, getting started in social networking doesn't require any training. You just log into a Web site and get started. A few types of stock message boards and social networking sites to consider include:

- ✔ **Stock message boards:** The more popular stock message boards include those hosted by Yahoo Finance (`finance.yahoo.com`), Raging Bull (`ragingbull.quote.com`) and Silicon Investor (`siliconinvestor.com`). Again, these stock message boards are filled with misinformation, so it's caveat emptor.

- ✔ **Broker-operated sites:** Online discount brokerages TradeKing and Zecco.com are some of the leaders in allowing their members to share investing ideas with each other. What these sites offer, which make them more credible than stock message boards, is that you can see the actual holdings of the members. That way, if an investor is talking up a stock, you can see if the person owns or is buying the stock. You can also see how successful an investor that person is.

- ✔ **Compilation sites and dedicated social networking sites:** Some sites try to spare you from having to read through thousands of messages posted by various members of social networking sites. For instance, if you enter a stock symbol at USATODAY.com's Money section (money.usatoday.com), you'll find a summary of fundamental analysis performed by other visitors of the site.

Following the moves of big-time investors

If monitoring the fundamental analysis by amateur investors isn't all that appealing, you might still be curious what the Warren Buffetts of the world are doing.

Using financial documents, you can extend your fundamental analysis to find out what other famous investors are doing with their money. And yes, you can find out if a stock you're interested in is owned by famous investors including Warren Buffett or well-known portfolio managers of mutual funds that use fundamental analysis.

Finding out who a company's biggest investors are

Some companies list all the investors who have the biggest stakes in their companies in their *10-K*, or annual report filing that's required by regulators, as discussed in Chapter 12. Others may include the information in their proxy statement, discussed in Chapter 9. Both of those places are worth checking.

But if nothing turns up, it's time to find out about a regulatory filing called a *13F-HR*. Large institutional investors are required to file 13F-HR filings when they take significant stakes of publicly traded firms.

Following 13F-HR filings from your favorite investors can be a great way to find out what kinds of stocks they are buying. Many investors make a pastime out of following Buffett's investments, for instance, by watching the 13F-HR filings from his Berkshire Hathaway.

You can access 13F-HR filings, for free, from the SEC's IDEA database. You can find step-by-step directions on how to extract filings from IDEA in Chapter 4.

Following famous investors moves using Morningstar

Perhaps you're interested in finding out what some of your favorite mutual fund managers, who use fundamental analysis, own. Maybe you'd rather not deal with navigating the SEC's Web site to find out the moves of other fundamental analysts.

When a CEO can't resist social investing

Don't assume the only people hanging out in stock message boards are frustrated stock analysts and investors. Back in the late 1990s, John Mackey, the co-founder and CEO of natural food store Whole Foods Market, started to post in the Yahoo Finance message board dedicated to the company. But he didn't announce, "Hi everyone, I'm the CEO." Instead, Mackey responded to posts using the pseudonym rahodeb, or his wife's name, Deborah, spelled backwards. Mackey's comments ranged from responding to questions or critiques about the company to some critical comments about Wild Oats Market, a rival firm Whole Foods ended up buying.

After Mackey's posting were discovered, the matter was looked into by the Securities and Exchange Commission. No punishment was recommended. But, since that time, Mackey, like many CEOs, maintains a blog on the company's Web site to give his point of view on matters. Mackey's blog is available here: `www2.wholefoodsmarket.com/blogs/jmackey/`.

Investment research company Morningstar makes it very easy to look up who the biggest owners of a stock are, as well as the largest investments by big money managers.

To look up the largest owners of a stock, log onto Morningstar.com, enter the stock symbol of the company you're interested in and click the Go button. On the left-hand side of the screen, click the Insider Trading option. Finally, click on the Concentrated Fund Owners tab at the top of the list to get details on the biggest owners of a stock.

What if you want to find out what your favorite mutual fund manager owns? It's the same basic procedure. Just enter the name of the mutual fund or enter the fund's symbol at Morningstar.com and click the Go button. Next, click on the "Portfolio" option on the left-hand side of the screen. Lastly, click on the "Top 25 Holdings tab" at the top of the screen.

Monitoring the buying and selling of stock by a company's officers and directors can also be telling. You can read more about such legal *insider trading*, and how that can be incorporated into fundamental analysis, in Chapter 17.

Chapter 15

Performing "Top Down" Fundamental Analysis

*E*ven the best company or investment can be tripped up by a lousy economy. This truth was demonstrated in brutal fashion during the stock market decline that began in 2007, as prices of all sorts of stocks were punished, with little regard to what fundamental analysis would tell you.

The harsh reality that companies are subject to the vagaries of the broad economy is a major reason why you may consider expanding your fundamental analysis skills beyond looking just at the health and prospects of individual companies. Understanding the ups and downs of the economy, and the resulting *business cycle*, is what's known as top-down analysis. And top-down analysis is a critical adjunct to fundamental analysis, helping you make sure you're investing in the right companies for the right price at a good time.

This chapter will show how the health of the broad economy is a factor in the health of individual companies. You'll also discover how changes in the economy may cause you to tweak the way you apply fundamental analysis. I'll show you what some of the most important pieces of economic data are and even how some, called *leading indicators,* may help forecast the future.

Broadening Out Fundamental Analysis to Include Monitoring the Economy

There's no question that with fundamental analysis, the primary goal is often to deeply understand the inner workings of individual companies. Investors who practice fundamental analysis are attempting to find those companies that stand to benefit the most given the current economic environment.

It's critical to recognize that changes in the economy may have big effects on companies and dramatically alter your fundamental analysis. A large economic downturn, for instance, can cause a company's revenue and earnings to plummet, turning all your expectations for the company upside down.

How the economy has an overriding effect on a company

The recession that started in late 2007, as painful as it's been, has provided a startling reminder to fundamental analysts of just how captive a company's fundamentals are to the economy.

When the economy slows down, and consumers and companies cut how much stuff they buy, companies' financial statements take a direct hit. Less spending by consumers and businesses translates directly into less revenue and earnings for companies. And *revenue* and *earnings* are precisely the things that fundamental analysts spend their time looking at.

Sometimes, a drop in business activity can be swift and vicious, as was the case in 2007 and 2008. Table 15-1 shows how the earnings per share of some members of the Standard & Poor's 500 index fell by startling amounts in 2008 as the recession ravaged the economy and their businesses.

Table 15-1	Big Drops In Earnings Amid a Recession	
Company	**2007 Earnings Per Share**	**2008 Loss Per Share**
Symantec	$0.37	–$7.52
Tellabs	$0.15	–$2.33
American International Group	$2.39	–$37.8
AES	$1.82	–$0.14
Apartment Investment & Management	$2.98	–$0.28
Standard & Poor's	$82.54	$49.50

Sources: Standard & Poor's and S&P's Capital IQ, diluted earnings on calendar year

When the economy tripped up Buffett

It might be tempting to think your deft fundamental analysis skills are so bulletproof, you'll be able to find stocks that defy gravity and do well even when the economy is lousy. And it's true. There were a handful of stocks that rose even during 2008, when the S&P 500 index crashed 38.5%.

But before you think your fundamental analysis can lift you above the woes of the economy, consider that even Warren Buffett faced problems during 2008. Buffett's Berkshire Hathaway posted a 9.6% drop in its *book value*, the company's worst year in its history dating back to 1965. Book value is the difference between the value of the company's assets and liabilities, and the way Berkshire Hathaway investors tend to evaluate performance.

And investors in Berkshire Hathaway's stock weren't spared, either. The value of Berkshire Hathaway stock fell 31.8% during 2008, as the per-share price of Berkshire Hathaway's Class A stock dropped from $141,600 a share to $96,600. Ouch.

Buffett, in his 2008 letter to shareholders, clearly explains how troubles in the broad economy can translate into a slowdown for businesses, even those with outstanding fundamentals. "By the fourth quarter, the credit crisis, coupled with tumbling home and stock prices, had produced a paralyzing fear that engulfed the country. A free fall in business activity ensured, accelerating at a pace that I have never before witnessed." Well said.

Ways the economy can alter your fundamental analysis

Considering the economy's health in your fundamental analysis might seem like a pretty daunting task. After all, how can you consider something as grand as the U.S.' economic growth when you're poring over one company's financial statements?

Still, it's important to recognize that the economy can have big-time effects on business, especially in regard to a company's:

✔ **Ability to service its debt:** A company's level of debt might look very manageable during normal economic times. In fact, as pointed out in Chapter 8, companies carrying a bit of debt will generate higher returns for stock investors. But that debt can come back to haunt companies when the economy slows.

It might be easier to understand how a poor economy can turn debt into poison for a company by thinking about a plain old mortgage. Let's say a young couple making $50,000 a year takes on a $1,000-a-month mortgage payment. That's really not too ridiculous. But if one breadwinner in the family loses a job, and the couple's annual income falls to $25,000 a year, suddenly that mortgage payment is going to be a big nut to deal with every month. The same concept goes for a company. If the economy causes net income to fall, what had been a manageable level of debt might become pretty difficult to handle going forward.

Capacity to borrow: During the credit crunch, which intensified in 2008, many companies were no longer able to borrow at favorable *interest rates* or to borrow at all. That *unavailability of capital* caused many companies to have to *finance*, or pay for, their expenses and needed improvements out of their cash balances. What if they didn't have much cash? Welcome to bankruptcy court.

During severe economic contractions, the companies with access to large sums of cash are often able to make moves to improve their position when the economy ultimately heals. Some companies, for instance, may use their cash to buy weaker competitors, giving them greater market share when the economy improves.

✓ **Cost structure:** Some companies are able to adjust their costs and expenses rapidly during a downturn, unfortunately, usually by laying off workers. Yet other companies, which are *capital intensive* or reliant on large and expensive facilities, may have a more difficult time reducing their overhead costs. Closing a plant or facility may take longer than just giving a bunch of workers pink slips.

✓ **Reliance on a strong economy:** Some industries are more subject to the health of the economy. For instance, companies that make *durable consumer goods* such as homes, appliances and automobiles, usually see the largest drop-off in business as spending on such big-ticket items cools. Companies with profits that are closely tied to the economy are described as being *cyclical*. The concept of cyclicality in business will be discussed at more length in Chapter 16.

How interest rates can alter what companies are worth

The condition the economy is in can have profound effects on how much a company — or its stock — is worth. As shown above, companies' earnings and cash flow may be held hostage by the ups and downs of the economy. Valuations of companies are based in large part on how profitable a company is, as you found out in Chapter 5.

But there's another factor you need to be aware of when it comes to incorporating the economy's health into fundamental analysis: interest rates. Perhaps you've puzzled over why stocks often jump when the *Federal Reserve*, or the nation's central bank, reduces *short-term interest rates*. If the reduction in short-term interest rates, or the rates banks usually charge each other to borrow money overnight, prompts interest rates on longer-term loans to fall, that can affect how much companies are worth.

Most people assume lower interest rates are good for stocks because the companies can borrow money at a more affordable rate. And that is true. Lower interest rates may reduce a company's interest expense, and boost profit. Companies might also borrow more money to expand their operations or build new stores, which might increase future profits.

But fundamental analysis shows a more sophisticated reason why interest-rate changes affect the value of stocks. Remember that one way to measure the value of a stock is the *discounted cash flow model*, or DCM, which is covered in detail in Chapter 11.

If you recall, the value of a stock today, or its *present value*, is a function of its expected future cash flows in today's dollars. Go ahead. Read that sentence one more time; I won't mind. Believe it or not, it's easiest to explain why interest rates are critical in fundamental analysis using the formula you discovered in Chapter 11. It looks like this:

Present value = Future value / (1+interest rate) ^ time

If you haven't read Chapter 11 yet, some of the explanation of interest rates might seem pretty technical. If you read Chapter 11, that will help, I promise.

Imagine that you invest in a company you know will generate $10,000 in cash 20 years from now. And consider for a moment that interest rates on savings accounts are 5%. That means you might reasonably demand an 8% return in exchange for investing your hard-earned cash in the company. The present value of the company is $2,145 right now, using a formula that looks like this:

Present value ($2,145) = $10,000 / (1+0.08) ^ 20

Now imagine the economy starts to sputter, and the Federal Reserve cuts interest rates. The interest rate for money in a savings account falls to 1%. You might now demand a return of 4% on your money invested in the company. Just this one seemingly small change in interest rates makes the company worth $4,564, or more than double its value when interest rates were higher.

Be careful not to confuse the short-term interest rates set by the Federal Reserve with long-term interest rates set by investors and lenders. While short-term interest rates affect long-term interest rates, they don't always move in lockstep.

Analyzing the Key Measures of the Economy's Health

When it comes to analyzing a company, you can zero in pretty precisely. Companies' financial statements allow you to dig into a company's operations and get a good idea of what's going on.

But when it comes to the economy, where can you start? After all, when analyzing the economy, you're not just examining the performance of a single company, but scores of businesses, consumers, and many other variables.

And that's why you might think of the economy as a lab specimen. Doctors, trying to understand the creature, might put probes and sensors all over the specimen to try to get in tune with its vitals. Economists and investors, too, try to closely monitor the economy's health by tracking a variety of indicators that all reveal clues.

Being aware of the business cycle

Booms are inevitably followed by busts. After things get so bad, smart companies and entrepreneurs inevitably launch new ideas, and the economy gets going again before it overheats all over. This constant boom-to-bust is characteristic of the *capitalist* system, and is called the business cycle. It makes things interesting, don't you think?

Fundamental analysts generally break the business cycle down into five primary *phases*, including:

- ✔ **Expansion:** At this point, the economy is starting to pick up steam. Economic activity is heating up, perhaps following a recession, and sometimes powered by lower interest rates.

- ✔ **Peak:** The economy is running at full tilt. Hotels and airplanes are full. Companies are pumping out as much product as they can handle.

- ✔ **Contraction:** Uh oh. Business activity begins to slow from the unsustainable peak levels, due to some negative event. Companies begin slashing costs, often by laying off workers. In 2007, business activity began to slow down after lending to home buyers started to slow and home prices fell, making consumers feel poorer.

- ✔ **Trough:** When it seems like there's bad news about the economy and things are only getting worse, the economy may have hit rock bottom.

- ✔ **Recovery:** Eventually, demand hits bottom, and consumers and businesses start spending. Improved demand for products allows companies to hire back workers and increase production. And so the cycle starts all over again.

It's not a recession until NBER says so

How do you know if the economy is in a recession or worse? The old rule of thumb was if your neighbor was out of a job, the economy was in a *recession*, and if you were out of work, it was a *depression*. Fundamental analysts, though, need a better indication.

And that's where the National Bureau of Economic Research, or NBER, comes in. The NBER is a private and nonprofit organization, founded in 1920, that researches the health of the economy. One of the NBER's roles is to officially pronounce when a recession begins and ends. You can see when every U.S.

business expansion and contraction started here: http://wwwdev.nber.org/cycles/cyclesmain.html.

While the NBER is extremely helpful, it has its limits. One of the biggest criticisms is that the NBER doesn't officially pronounce the beginning of a recession until the economy has been contracting for some time. For instance, the NBER didn't determine that December 2007 was the peak in economic activity until November 2008. Gee, thanks guys. And that's why, as a fundamental analyst, you can't rely solely on the NBER to signal when tough times are coming.

Using government statistics to track the economy's movements

When it comes to economic statistics, sadly, there isn't a single number or even source that will give you everything you need to know. Until an economist starts Economic Indicators 'R Us, it's up to you, as a fundamental analyst, to know which economic data are important and where to get them. Below is a checklist of some of the important measures of economic activity, or *economic indicators*, you'll want to be aware of.

- ✔ **Gross domestic product, or GDP:** *GDP* is arguably the most popular measure of a country's economy. GDP measures how much action an economy has going on by tallying up the amount of consumption, investment, government spending and difference between exports and imports within a nation's borders. The GDP of the U.S. is available from the U.S. Department of Commerce Bureau of Economic Analysis at www.bea.gov.

- ✔ **Inflation:** Have your grandparents ever told you how they were able to buy a carton of milk for a penny? The reason that carton of milk now costs $1 or more is *inflation*, or rising prices. Inflation is critical to fundamental analysis since it is connected to interest rates. For instance, if inflation starts rising uncontrollably, the Federal Reserve may need to increase short-term interest rates to slow down demand, which could hurt the value of companies.

  Key measures of inflation include the *Consumer Price Index, Producer Price Index,* and *wages.* Those measures track how much prices of consumer goods, industrial goods, and employee wages are rising. *Deflation* occurs when prices fall. Each of these measures is available from the U.S. Department of Labor Bureau of Labor Statistics at stats.bls.gov.

✔ **Interest rates:** You'll want to keep at least one eye on *interest rates* at all times while performing your fundamental analysis. The Federal Reserve lets you see where short-term interest rates are, based on the *intended federal funds rate*, at www.federalreserve.gov/fomc/fundsrate.htm.

✔ **Regional economic activity:** Sometimes it can be useful to see which parts of the country are doing better — or worse — than others. That type of regional economic activity is provided by the Federal Reserve in its *Summary of Commentary on Current Economic Conditions*, commonly known as the *Beige Book*. You may access these reports here: www.federalreserve.gov/FOMC/BeigeBook/2009/.

Getting a Jump on the Future Using Leading Economic Indicators

While fundamental analysts may appreciate the value of economic indicators, there's a major problem. Nearly all economic indicators are *backward-looking*, meaning that they reflect what has happened, rather than what is likely to happen in the future. Successful fundamental analysis is all about accurately forecasting what might happen to a company's profits and revenue over the next years to decades. You'll want to pay close attention to leading economic indicators, or those that are more revealing about how the economy might look in the future.

Paying attention to the Conference Board Leading Economic Index

Trying to figure out what's wrong with the economy is kind of like determining why a baby is sick. You might know the baby isn't well, judging by a 103-degree fever, but it's not like you can ask what hurts and get a coherent answer.

Similarly, determining what ails the economy, or trickier yet, what might make it sick in the future, is equally problematic. The economy may show signs of illness, with weakness in many of the indicators discussed above, but it can be difficult to pinpoint the source of the issues.

Don't feel bad if you're not very good at predicting when the economy is falling apart or when it's improving. Even leading economists routinely make bad forecasts about the economy's direction.

The *Conference Board Leading Economic Index* attempts to give everyone a way to see what's hurting the economy and whether or not things are getting better or worse. The indicator gets a forward-looking read on the economy by examining the following 10 factors:

- **Real money supply:** The number of dollars in the economic system ready to be lent and spent. Money supply is kind of like the lubrication of the economy. Money supply serves the same role as motor oil in a car engine.

- **Interest-rate spread:** This measures how costly it is to borrow money. When consumers and businesses can borrow at an affordable rate, economic activity tends to pick up.

- **Consumer expectations:** When consumers are worried about their jobs and financial futures, they cut their spending. That slows down the economy.

- **Manufacturers' new orders for nondefense capital goods:** If companies are feeling better about the future, they may purchase new equipment and plan to expand.

- **Manufacturers' new orders for consumer goods and materials:** Companies ramping up production need to buy more ingredients to feed into their factories.

- **Average weekly initial claims for unemployment:** Companies slash jobs when they don't see economic activity getting better. Plus, more people out of work means fewer consumers to buy goods and services.

- **Building permits:** Companies must get permits to construct new properties, so a slowdown in permits indicates a less bullish view of the future.

- **Average weekly manufacturing hours:** Large manufacturers may ask workers to cut back their hours if they need to trim costs or have employees work overtime if they expect a boom in demand.

- **Stock prices:** Investors will generally start buying stocks if they expect the economy to recover within six months or so. Watching the stock market's moves is such a valuable, early predictor of economic cycles. I'll discuss it more fully below.

- **Index of supplier deliveries:** One of the first things companies do when they expect things to get better is place orders with their vendors.

The Conference Board makes its Leading Economic Index available for free, as a press release, here: http://www.conference-board.org/economics/bci.

Using the stock market as your economic early warning system

If you're looking for an early tip-off to when the economy is either headed for the toilet or about to improve, it's tough to beat the stock market. Since investors are always looking to the future, traditionally, the stock market will signal roughly three to six months ahead of time, in what direction the economy will head.

Again, the stock market demonstrated its predictive power in 2007. The Standard & Poor's 500 set its bull-market peak on October 2007, and started sliding dramatically from that point. Investors who noticed the stock market topped in October 2007 were tipped off that the economy was struggling more than a year before the NBER made the formal announcement.

If you're interested in finding out more about using the stock market indexes to help you see where the economy is headed, check out Chapter 19, where I go over the techniques used by technical analysts.

Part IV
Getting Advanced with Fundamental Analysis

The 5th Wave   By Rich Tennant

"Hello—forget the company's financials, look at the CEO's Facebook page under '25 Things the SEC Doesn't Know About Me.'"

In this part . . .

After you study more companies, you'll get more proficient and start looking for ways to take fundamental analysis to the next level. This part covers some of the more advanced aspects of fundamental analysis worth taking a look at once you're comfortable with the basics. I show you how important it is to understand a company's industry and how to spot trends developing in a company's business. Because often the way to be a good investor is by sidestepping financial land mines, I show you how to spot companies with danger signs that are worth noting.

Chapter 16

Digging into an Industry's Fundamentals

. . . .

In This Chapter

▶ Understanding how a company's value may be affected by the industry it's in

▶ Getting in sync with the unique characteristics of different industries

▶ Comparing one company's fundamentals with its industry's to gain better insight

▶ Realizing how important the concept of market share is in powering a company's profit

. . . .

*1*f you want to know what your kids are up to at school, just look at their friends and you'll get a pretty good idea. It's also common for employees at a company to adopt similar behavior, called corporate culture.

As strange as it might sound, you can learn quite a bit about companies, too, by examining what other companies they're lumped in with. Oftentimes, companies in the same line of work, or industry, have similar financial characteristics and idiosyncrasies. The industry a company is in can also contribute to its stock price performance.

Understanding what kind of company a company keeps is an important piece of the fundamental analysis puzzle. While you may understand an individual company by reviewing its financial statements, it's vital to understand the environment that company operates in and the industry dynamics at work.

You'll discover the ins and outs of *industry analysis* in this chapter. Not only will you see how a company's industry can influence its value, but you'll also see how a company's fortunes may rise and fall along with the *business cycle*. Another key aspect of industry analysis is determining how well a company is doing relative to its peers. And the crucial topic of *market share* is discussed, as it shows how smaller companies can benefit if they can successfully steal away business from their larger and more entrenched rivals.

Realizing How a Company's Industry Can Influence Its Value

The rise and fall of companies and industries follows a pretty standard script. Generally, things kick off when entrepreneurs get frustrated with the products that don't seem to fit some kind of need they might have. By tinkering on the kitchen table or in the garage, these entrepreneurs may create a prototype of a product and often literally sell them out of the back of their cars.

Before you know it, this little company grows and, for whatever reason, the product might get so popular it threatens the survival of the companies that sold the undesirable products in the first place. Entire industries are born, and sometimes destroyed, by this constant upheaval in our economic system.

You want to be aware when a company you're investing in might be threatened by a game-changing company or new technology. Almost overnight, all the revenue and earnings on the financial statements might not be meaningful if the *business model*, or way the company makes its money, is turned upside down.

The constant assault against established industries is part of our *capitalist* system. Remember air travel threatened railroads, personal computers threatened large mainframe systems used in business, and the Internet is an attack on traditional media. The battle for companies, and entire industries, to remain relevant in light of new ways of doing things is something you need to account for in your fundamental analysis.

The rise and fall of industries

One of the biggest threats to fundamental analysis is the constant danger someone will come along with a groundbreaking new business that threatens the old way of making money in the industry. One of the classic examples of this is what has happened in photography. Eastman Kodak became a blue chip company, thanks to its dominance of photography, which relied on costly chemical processing and film. Rivals that tried to take on Eastman Kodak had difficulty competing.

But in the early 1990s, Kodak saw its industry get turned virtually upside down. Suddenly,

giant consumer electronics firms elbowed their way into the photography business with digital technology. At first, the photo quality of digital cameras was very poor. But that quickly changed and by 2008, 65% of U.S. households had at least one digital camera. Chemical camera sales became just a sliver of the market. Suddenly Kodak faced dozens of new competitors, such as Sony and Casio, it had never faced before.

What's in an industry?

If you tell someone in Los Angeles you're in "the industry" they might assume you're in the movie business and try to get you to look at their script. In Detroit, people in the Motor City industry are involved in making cars.

But when it comes to fundamental analysis, the term industry has a pretty precise meaning. At its most basic level, a company's industry is the line of work it's in. But that's not a scientific enough definition for fundamental analysts; they're pretty precise folks, if you haven't noticed already.

Instead of just saying, for instance, Ford is in the auto industry, fundamental analysts break things down into more detail. Most fundamental analysts use a classification standard called the *Global Industry Classification Standard*, or *GICS*, to put companies into their places. GICS puts every industry into a *sector*, *industry group*, *industry* and *sub-industry*. GICS was co-created by Standard & Poor's and MSCI Barra, two companies that specialize in creating ways to classify companies.

If you've ever seen Russian nesting dolls, or matryoshka dolls, you already know exactly how GICS works. The sector is the largest classification, inside of which fit the industry group, industry and sub-industry. Just as you open the largest Russian nesting doll and find a smaller one and so forth, the same goes with GICS. Once you see what sector a company is in, you can then see which industry group, industry and sub-industry it's in. All these classifications fit neatly inside of each other.

Ford is a good example of how all this GICS stuff works. The company falls into the *Consumer Discretionary* sector, which contains all sorts of industry groups that make big-ticket items consumers buy, such as consumer durables. Digging further, you find Ford goes into the Automobiles & Components industry group, which contains the auto components and automaking industries. Next, Ford fits into the *Automobiles* industry, which includes two sub-industries: automobile manufacturers and motorcycle manufacturers. And Ford makes cars and trucks, so it goes into the Automobile Manufacturers sub-industry.

The GICS system is pretty comprehensive. Table 16-1 shows you how many sectors, industry groups, industries and sub-industries there are.

Table 16-1	Breaking Down The GICS
Classification type	*Number of types*
Sectors	10
Industry groups	24

(continued)

Table 16-1 *(continued)*

Classification type	Number of types
Industries	68
Sub-industries	154

Source: Standard & Poor's, `http://www2.standardandpoors.com/spf/pdf/index/SP_Global_Sector_Indices_Factsheet.pdf?vregion=us&vlang=en`

Just as scientists periodically change their classifications to make room for new developments regarding heavenly bodies, the same goes for industries. I'm still shocked scientists stripped away the planet title from Pluto in 2006. The GICS changes a little over time, too. Sometimes industries, for instance, are added, deleted or merged to reflect changes in the economy. Sometimes individual companies, too, are moved from different industries or sub-industries.

It's probably easiest to see how all these GICS sectors, industry groups, industries and sub-industries fit together by looking at a table. There are literally thousands of sub-industries, but Table 16-2 gives you a very small summary of what the basic structure of the GICS looks like.

Table 16-2 **A Small Piece of the GICS Puzzle**

Sector	Industry group	Industry	Sub-industry
Energy	Energy	Energy equipment and services	Oil and gas drilling
		Oil, gas, and consumable fuels	Integrated oil and gas
Materials	Materials	Chemicals	Commodity chemicals
		Containers and packaging	Metal and glass containers
Industrials	Capital goods	Aerospace and defense	Aerospace and defense
	Transportation	Road and rail	Railroads
Consumer discretionary	Automobiles and components	Automobiles	Automobile manufacturers
			Motorcycle manufacturers

Sector	Industry group	Industry	Sub-industry
Consumer staples	Food, beverage & tobacco	Beverages	Brewers
Health care	Health care equipment & services	Health care equipment & supplies	Health care equipment
	Pharmaceuticals, biotechnology & life sciences	Biotechnology	Biotechnology
Financials	Banks	Commercial banks	Diversified banks
	Insurance	Insurance	Insurance brokers
Information technology	Software & services	Software	Application software
Telecom-munication services	Telecommunication services	Diversified tele-communication services	Wireless tele-communication services
Utilities	Utilities	Electric utilities	Electric utilities

Source: Standard & Poor's, `http://www2.standardandpoors.com/portal/site/sp/en/ us/page.topic/indices_gics/2,3,1,7,0,0,0,0,0,0,0,0,0,0,0,0.html`

Following the ups and downs of industries

Just as the economy expands and contracts along with the business cycle as discussed in Chapter 15, industries also have their ups and downs. Some sectors, for instance, tend to see their business rise and fall along with the economy. These are called *cyclical* companies, and includes industries such as the automakers. Then there are sectors that tend to be *noncyclical*, meaning that their performance tend to not be all that connected to the economy's shape. The health care industry is a good example of a sector that's usually noncyclical.

Some fundamental analysts use industry analysis to clue into what point of the business cycle the economy is in. By paying attention to which industries (or sectors) are posting the best results, or the strongest stock prices, you can get a hint as to where the economy is head.

You can see how different sectors and stocks tend to outperform during the different parts of the business cycle in Table 16-3.

Table 16-3	Using Sectors to Monitor the Economy
During this point in the business cycle . . .	*. . . This Sector Starts to Outperform*
Early expansion	Consumer discretionary
Early peak	Materials
Late peak	Industrials
Late expansion	Energy
Early contraction	Health care
Early trough	Consumer staples
Late trough	Utilities and financials
Late contraction	Information technology

Source: Standard & Poor's

You can review the different phases of the business cycle in Chapter 15.

How to Track How Sectors Are Doing

If you want to find out how an individual company or its stock is doing, it's relatively simple. A company's financial statements, as described in Chapter 4, can be dug out pretty easily. And you can get stock quotes on just about any company from your brokerage firm or from financial Web sites.

But what if you want to know which sector is leading the economy or stock market? That's what I'll show you next.

Keeping tabs on a sectors' fundamentals

If you wanted to tally up how companies in a sector are doing, you could, in theory, do it by hand. You could get a list of all the companies in a sector and open each company's financial statements and add everything up. But, man, that would be a great deal of work you can avoid.

It's much easier to get fundamental data on sectors from companies that track these types of things very closely. S&P is one of the companies with massive databases dedicated to tracking all the earnings reported by companies and compiling them into a resource you, as a fundamental analyst, may use. All the earnings for the companies in all 10 sectors are compiled and provided to you here: http://www2.standardandpoors.com/portal/site/sp/en/us/page.topic/indices_500/2,3,2,2,0,0,0,0,0,0,6,0,0,0,0,0.html.

You'll be amazed at how quickly you can process the sector data from hundreds of companies using the S&P's data. For instance, you can not only see how quickly earnings in the 10 sectors rose or fell in the past couple of years, but you can also monitor how rapidly analysts expect the sectors' earnings to rise or fall in the future. S&P also provides data showing the average price-to-earnings ratio of companies in the sector. You can review how to interpret the P-E ratio in Chapter 8. Some of the sector data you can obtain from S&P looks like what you see in Table 16-4:

Table 16-4	Digging into The Sectors' Fundamentals	
S&P Sector	*Change in earnings (2008)*	*P-E for 2008*
Consumer discretionary	-60.3%	25.5
Consumer staples	10%	11.9
Energy	10%	6.4
Financials	N/A (sector posted large loss in 2008)	N/A (no earnings, no P-E)
Health care	5%	10.7
Industrials	-0.5%	6.8
Information technology	-7.2%	13.3
Materials	-49.3%	14.4
Telecommunications	-0.6%	11.4
Utilities	5%	9.5

Source: Standard & Poor's based on operating earnings, `http://www2.standardandpoors.com/portal/site/sp/en/us/page.topic/indices_500/2,3,2,2,0,0,0,0,0,0,0,6,0,0,0,0,0.html`

When evaluating the profit and growth of individual companies, as discussed in Chapter 5, it's a good idea to compare the results to that of the sector. This might help you identify companies that are pulling ahead of their peers.

Tracking the stock performances of sectors

Studying sectors' fundamentals, such as earnings growth, is just one part of industry analysis. To get a full picture of how the sectors are faring, it's important, too, to monitor their stock price changes.

The stock market can give you an early signal to where the economy is headed three to six months in the future, as shown in Chapter 15. You can apply the market's same early-warning signal to industry analysis. When you start to see stocks in a sector rising or falling, for instance, that tells you investors think the sector's fundamentals will follow.

If you really want to keep yourself busy an entire weekend, you could get price quotes for every stock in a sector. But why go to all that trouble if someone else makes it so easy? There are a few sources that provide helpful industry performance data, including:

- **Summary of how the sectors have done over time:** Standard & Poor's provides the performance of all 10 of its sector indexes on a daily, monthly, quarterly and year-to-date basis. You can download the data into a spreadsheet for further analysis. The data are available here: `http://www2.standardandpoors.com/portal/site/sp/en/us/page.topic/indices_500/2,3,2,2,0,0,0,0,0,0,0,0,0,0,0,0,0.html`.

- **Up-to-date daily industry information:** Yahoo Finance provides an industry analysis page that shows you which industries are doing the best or worst during a trading day. The data are available here: `http://biz.yahoo.com/ic/`

- **Graphical view of industry group data:** If you're looking for an easy way to see which industry groups are leading or lagging over time, USA TODAY provides a large informational graphic every Monday. The chart lets you quickly find which industry groups are charging forward or falling behind. An online version of the graphic is available at money.usatoday.com.

Using exchange-traded funds to monitor sectors and industries

Exchange-traded funds, or *ETFs*, are one of the more exciting things to happen to the investment business. Investors who want to invest in a basket of stocks, for instance, can buy just one ETF and spread their money over dozens, hundreds or even thousands of individual stocks.

But what do ETFs have to do with fundamental analysis? ETFs are excellent tools to get real-time information on industries and sectors. Since most ETFs track various stock *indexes*, or mathematical calculations that measure the value of a group of stocks, they can be tremendously useful when tracking industries, too.

The beauty of using ETFs as a way to see how a sector or industry is doing is that you can get real-time stock quotes on ETFs as you would with any stock. Just enter the ETF's stock symbol into a financial Web site to get a price. The prices of ETFs show you how sectors are doing. Many financial Web sites will also provide fundamental details about the ETF, giving you a deeper look at how things are going in the industry. Table 16-5 lists some ETFs that track all 10 sectors.

Table 16-5	ETFs That Let You Analyze the 10 Sectors
S&P Sector	*ETF symbol*
Consumer discretionary	XLY
Consumer staples	XLP
Energy	XLE
Financials	XLF
Health care	XLV
Industrials	XLI
Information technology	XLK
Materials	XLB
Telecommunications	TTH
Utilities	XLU

Source: State Street Global and Merrill Lynch

Adding Industry Analysis to Your Fundamental Approach

You may have hated it when teachers announced, on the first day of class, that they were planning to use the dreaded curve. The curve is pretty brutal, since getting a 90% on a test doesn't automatically mean you get an A. If half the class gets a 90% too, you could very well end up with a C.

The same curve-like mentality applies in industry analysis. Sometimes it's not good enough for a company to post strong revenue, earnings and cash flow. If the rest of the industry is doing just as well or better, even a seemingly outstanding performance by a company may not be impressive.

Companies cannot be analyzed in isolation, but rather, relative to their peers.

Sizing up a company's financials relative to its industry's

Whenever you look up a piece of financial data, the first thing that should pop into your head as a fundamental analyst is "what does this mean?"

Generally, no single piece of financial data is meaningful by itself. Financial ratios, covered in Chapter 8, are especially irrelevant by themselves. Traditionally, fundamental analysis requires you to either compare a company's financial data with its historical results or against other companies in the sector or industry.

Virtually any piece of financial data you can extract from the financial statements can be compared against other companies in an industry. You can also compare financial data to industry averages to give you a better idea of where a company stands in its respective field.

Comparing a stock's valuation, or measure of how pricey or cheap it is compared to its fundamentals, is one of the easiest things for investors to do. After you measure a stock's P-E, you can then compare the P-E against the valuation of the industry or the stock market to get an idea of how richly valued a stock is.

You can even evaluate statements made by a company's management using industry analysis. Here's an example. For many years, Dell Computer often talked about just how efficient its factories were. Industry analysis lets you see if the company's claims are true.

One way to verify a company's efficiency is by comparing its *inventory turnover in days*, or how rapidly a company clears out inventory from its warehouses, to the industry. A more efficient production system would have a rapid turnover, so the inventory turnover in days should be a small number. The formula is:

Inventory turnover in days = Average inventory / cost of goods sold * 365

Dell in 2008 churned through its inventory every 7.5 days. You know that because inventory turnover in days is:

7.5 = Average inventory ($1,024) / cost of goods sold ($50,144) * 365

How does Dell's inventory turnover in days compare with the industry? It's excellent. The computer hardware industry turns over its inventory every 34 days using 2008 data, according to Thomson Reuters. So it seems Michael Dell does know a thing about running a tight ship.

You don't have to calculate the financial ratios for all the companies in a sector to get a comparison basis. Thomson Reuters provides industry data for you at www.reuters.com/finance/stocks. All you need to do is enter the stock symbol of the company you're studying, select the Ratios button and click the Go! button.

One thing to keep in mind, though, is sometimes you need to convert industry ratios generated by systems like Thomson Reuters to match your calculation method. For instance, Thomson Reuters doesn't convert inventory turnover in days, as I did above. For the computer hardware industry, Thomson Reuters gives a turnover rate of 10.69 for the industry. To convert that into inventory turnover in days, just divide 360 by 10.69 to convert the industry number into days.

Find out who a company's competitors are

Sometimes you might find yourself getting interested in learning more about an industry or a sector. Perhaps you want to perform fundamental analysis on several companies that are competitors to one you're looking into.

There are several ways fundamental analysts can get a list of the other companies in an industry, including the:

- ✓ **The 10-K:** Most companies will provide a list of all the companies they deem to be their archrivals in their 10-K, or the annual report required by regulators. Flip back to Chapter 12 to refresh your memory on where this information is located in the rather lengthy financial document.

- ✓ **Web-based research tools:** Several leading financial Web sites will give you a list of all the companies that compete with each other in a given industry. Enter any stock symbol at Yahoo Finance, at finance.yahoo. com, and click the "Get Quotes" button. Next, click on the "Competitors" link on the left-hand side of the page and you'll find a list of the top rivals and some of their fundamental data.

Considering industry-specific data

Financial ratios are among the favorite tools used by fundamental analysts. You can quickly determine whether or not a company has borrowed too much, wastes too much money or isn't growing very fast by studying financial ratios. Most of the popular ratios that will work most of the time are discussed in Chapter 8.

But, when performing industry analysis, sometimes the off-the-shelf ratios aren't enough. Some industries might have unique characteristics, which requires additional analysis.

Companies in the financial sector are an excellent example of how industry analysis may need to be tweaked to handle different industries. Most of the traditional free cash flow measures and cash burn techniques, discussed in Chapter 7, just don't apply to financials. Banks and brokerages, often, have cash on deposit from their customers. That cash cannot be used to fund operations.

Due to the special way fundamental analysis must be applied to certain industries, analysts often adopt unique methods. Such *industry-specific financial measures* can help you better analyze some of the oddities of certain industries.

Again, the financials are a great example. Many financial analysts know to truly see how strong a bank is financially, they must examine both its *Tier 1* and *Tier 2* capital. Tier 1 is considered to be a much more reliable measure of financial staying power than Tier 2 capital. Banks must disclose how much Tier 1 and Tier 2 capital they have, but getting that information requires digging into the *footnotes* to the financial statements.

Fundamental analysts who specialized on financial companies also study industry-specific measures such as a bank's level of loans that are 90 days past due, loans that have been completely written off, and the level of reserves a bank has taken to cover loans if they go bad.

Some of the fundamental analysts who took the time to do industry-specific analysis saw that many of the banks were less solid than the traditional ratios implied.

Taking stock of raw material costs

Much of fundamental analysis dwells on the end result. You assess a company's bottom line and see how many *assets* and *liabilities* it ends up with after selling goods and services to customers.

But industry analysis encourages you to examine a company, almost the way the executives running the firm would. And that includes paying attention to how much a company must pay for its raw materials. As you know from analyzing income statements, the amount of money a company spends to buy raw materials used to make products is considered a direct cost, and is included in its *cost of goods sold*, or *COGS*. The more a company pays for raw materials, the higher its COGS, and the lower its profit.

Sometimes, increased demand for a commodity, such as energy or agricultural products, can drive the price of raw materials up. As a fundamental analyst, if you see the prices of raw ingredients rising, that might be a tip-off a company or industry that buys those ingredients might see its future profits fall.

Bloomberg keeps an up-to-date list of prices of many commodities companies use as raw materials. You can access this information, for free, here: `http://bloomberg.com/markets/commodities/cfutures.html`.

Remember, just because the prices of a commodity a company relies on is rising doesn't mean profits will take a hit immediately. Many companies use *hedging*, or complex financial instruments that let them lock in raw material prices for many months, or even years. You can find out if, or how, a company is hedging the risk of higher commodity prices in the 10-K.

It's mine! Paying attention to market share

One of the most dramatic ways of paying attention to what's going on in a company's industry is market share. Market share tells you how much of a certain line of business a company controls.

You can measure a company's share of either large industries or smaller sub-sets of the industry. For instance, if you're studying a software company, you might want to find out what the company's share of the overall software industry is. Or, you might drill down, and find out what percentage of the Web-browser software market a company has.

While market share may be measured on very precise markets, that level of industry analysis usually requires analysis that goes beyond what's available in the financial statements. Sometimes, you need to consult with specialized market research firms if you want to know what percentage of total sales of a product type a company has.

For instance, going back to the software example above, the leading makers of Web browsers, including Microsoft (Internet Explorer), Mozilla (Firefox), Google (Chrome) and Apple (Safari) may or may not disclose what they estimate their market share to be. There are firms that estimate market share for this type of software.

Still, using routine fundamental analysis, you can get a pretty good idea when other companies are eating each others' lunches, so to speak. You can use the financial statements to monitor changes in revenue, for instance, to see who is benefitting from the weakness of some of the players in the business.

Market share analysis demonstrates the counterintuitive fact that a company may be able to increase profit, even in a tough economic environment, if it's able to steal business from rivals.

Table 16-6 presents a simple demonstration on how you can see whether one company in an industry may be taking business away from other players. The table shows total revenue reported by three large computer makers, Hewlett-Packard, Dell and Apple.

Examining this chart shows you how Apple, which is a smaller PC maker than the other two, may have profited by cutting into the computer business. Apple's slice of the total revenue generated by the big three PC makers doubled between 2000 and 2008 to 15.3%. Meanwhile, Dell saw its total share of revenue fall a bit to 29%.

Using total revenue to measure a company's market share is kind of a blunt financial analysis instrument. Companies may generate revenue from many different businesses. The companies listed in Table 16-6, for instance, don't just make computers. HP has a large computer services business, and Apple sells music downloads. But the analysis can give you an idea of the shifts between the industry players and how this type of industry analysis is performed.

Table 16-6	Battle between Three Leading Computer Makers			
Company	*2008 revenue ($ millions)*	*% of total*	*2000 revenue ($ millions)*	*% of total*
Hewlett-Packard	$118.4	55.8%	$48.9	59.5%
Dell	$61.1	28.8%	$25.3	30.8%
Apple	$32.5	15.3%	$8.0	9.7%
Total	$212.0		$82.2	

Source: S&P's Capital IQ, based on each company's fiscal year

Chapter 17

Pinpointing Trends Using Fundamental Analysis

· ·

In This Chapter

▶ Understanding why financial trends are an important aspect of fundamental analysis

▶ Discovering several popular methods to pinpoint trends in a company's fundamentals

▶ Spotting trends in legal insider trading information and what they indicate

▶ Using computerized screens to help spot notable company and industry trends

· ·

*P*art of what you're trying to do, as a fundamental analyst, is to understand what a company's future might look like. You're not poring through all of a company's financial statements because you enjoy it. Well, maybe you do. But the end game of all the work you're putting into fundamental analysis is to try to get an understanding of how profitable companies might be next year or beyond. That information will, hopefully, help you determine whether an investment is worth buying.

Monitoring financial trends is an important aspect of trying to forecast a company's future. Studying how a company has done, while not necessarily an ironclad predictor of its future, can give you a decent idea of what to expect. At least it's a place to start.

This chapter will drill down even further into how you can analyze a company's historical fundamentals to get a decent expectation for the future. Specifically, you will examine how to build a long-term *index-number trend analysis* and a *moving average analysis*. You'll also discover whether insiders are signaling a trend by either buying or selling shares of their companies' stock. And lastly, you'll get an introduction into computerized *stock screening tools*, popular databases used by fundamental analysts to find investments that might have potential and be worth more study.

Understanding Why to Consider Trends

Historians like to say that while history may not repeat itself, it definitely rhymes. And that's the same idea when it comes to searching for trends, or patterns, in a company's fundamentals. Companies that experience high profitability and have *large barriers to entry* are often able to protect themselves against the ravages of competition and deliver solid results to investors over time. Fundamental analysts who track a company's long-term record, or trend, can then get a decent estimate of what the future might hold. *Trend analysis*, therefore, can be a key part of fundamental analysis.

Businesses that are very difficult, or very costly, to start up from scratch are said to have high barriers to entry. Barriers to entry might also be the regulatory hurdles that must be cleared before a new company can get into business. Another barrier might be the existence of a company in the field with a dominant brand name or technology. Companies that enjoy barriers to entry tend to have financials that are more stable and predictable, since competition is less of a threat.

When trends can be very telling about a company's future

Everyone has a bad day once in a while, if not a bad month or even year. The same goes for companies. It's not uncommon for a company to hit a rough patch, perhaps due to an unexpected economic slowdown. A company's net income or revenue or both might take a big hit in any given year.

But when is a bad year something to get worried about? Investors who don't perform trend analysis might make the common error of placing too much focus on the latest data from a company. If a company reports a bad quarter, for instance, some investors might rush to conclusions and assume it's game over for the company, and its profits are about to go into free fall.

Trend analysis can save you from myopic and short-term thinking. Sometimes it's best to consider an example. Rewind back to 2002. Just to refresh your memory, that year, technology companies were suffering a dramatic downturn in their business. Technology spending fell off a cliff in 2002 as companies cut back. Technology stocks started to crash in 2000 and continued falling for years as investors figured the industry's best days were over.

Oracle, a dominant maker of corporate software, wasn't spared by the tech downturn. After years of delivering strong profit growth, Oracle stunned investors on June 18, 2002 with uncharacteristically weak financial results for the fiscal year ending May 31, 2002. The company posted *operating income*, or income excluding one-time charges and taxes, of $3.6 billion. That was a decline of 5.5% from the $3.8 billion the company posted in fiscal 2001. Some investors, buying into the tech-is-dead argument, didn't like what they saw.

But fundamental analysts who took the time to examine Oracle's long-term trend were unfazed. If anything, 2002 results were the anomaly, a disruption in what had been many years of steady growth. By studying Oracle's previous five years of operating income, fundamental analysts saw the company had grown by an *compound annual growth rate*, or *CAGR*, of 30.6% between fiscal 1997 (ended May 31, 1997) and fiscal 2001 (ended May 31, 2001). Table 17-1 below shows how steady Oracle's operating income had been leading up to the 2002 slowdown.

Table 17-1	Oracle's Steady-As-She-Goes Results
Fiscal year	*Operating income ($ millions)*
1997	$1,299.8
1998	1,411.3
1999	1,872.9
2000	3,080
2001	3,777

Source: Standard & Poor's Capital IQ

Hopefully you're wondering how I just calculated the CAGR, because I'm about to show you. CAGR is calculated using the same *present value* formula you discovered in Chapter 11, just rearranged a bit. The formula looks like:

CAGR = (Last amount / starting amount) $^{(1\,/\,\text{number of years})}$

Yikes. I know what you're thinking: That's one ugly-looking formula. You're right: it's not going to win any beauty contests. But using the Oracle data as an example, it won't be so bad. All you need to know is the:

- ✔ **Last amount:** This is the financial result for the latest year that you're studying. For Oracle, this is operating income for fiscal 2001, or $3,777.

- ✔ **Starting amount:** Here is the starting financial amount. For Oracle, this is operating income for fiscal 1997, or $1,299.8.

- ✔ **Number of years:** The sum of the years you're calculating the average return. This is a little tricky. While we're analyzing five years of Oracle's financial history, there are really only four full years of growth: from 1997 to 1998, from 1998 to 1999, from 1999 to 2000 and from 2000 to 2001.

The resulting formula looks like this:

$$CAGR = (3777 / 1299.8)^{(1/4)} - 1$$

After you run these numbers, you should come up with 0.306. To convert that into a percentage, 30.6%, simply multiply by 100.

The ^ symbol tells you to take the number in the previous set of parentheses to a power. Most calculators will help you do this using a key, usually labeled y^x.

If you and math just don't get along, this might be another reason why you might want to invest in a financial calculator such as Hewlett-Packard's HP 12C. The calculator can crunch these present-value problems down with just a few keystrokes.

Attempting to forecast the future using trends

Trying to forecast what a company might earn in the future is extremely difficult. Many Wall Street analysts get paid big bucks to attempt to forecast future revenue and profit.

Historical trend analysis can be a helpful way to approach this extremely difficult task of forecasting. Sticking with the Oracle example, you can see how trend forecasting could be used to get a decent idea of how things would turn out after the 2002 tech decline.

It turns out fiscal 2002's disappointing results were followed by another difficult year. Operating income fell another 3.7% in fiscal 2003, pretty much cementing the doubters' beliefs that even the biggest technology companies had finally hit a wall, and the growth was gone.

Trend analysis, though, would help you know that growth wasn't gone. It was just moderating a bit. Imagine that in 2002, when things looked bleak, you decided Oracle's days of increasing operating income by 30% might have ended. But what about half that? Wouldn't 15% growth be doable?

While 15% growth isn't 30%, that's still outstanding growth for a company of Oracle's size. A forecast of 15% growth, at a time when tech companies were struggling in 2002, would have seemed outlandish. But in reality, you would have been very close to what actually happened. Oracle's actual compound average annual growth rate between fiscal 2003 and fiscal 2008 was 18.4%, as shown in Table 17-2.

Table 17-2	Oracle's Growth Wasn't Dead After All
Fiscal year	*Operating income ($ millions)*
2003	$3,440
2004	$3,918
2005	$4,377
2006	$4,958
2007	$6,133
2008	$8,009

Source: S&P's Capital IQ

Paying close attention to Oracle's financial trends could have been very profitable for you. Had you invested in Oracle's stock on June 18, 2002, right after it announced the lower earnings, and held through the end of its fiscal 2008 (ended May 30, 2008), you would have gained more than 150%. The market during that same time period gained just 40%.

When forecasting a company's future profit, it's often best to use operating income, as I did in the Oracle example above. Operating income strips out one-time charges and gains, which are impossible to forecast, aren't repeated and can muddy up a historical analysis.

Attempting to forecast the future using index-number analysis

Following the tremendous downturn in business when many companies suffered in 2008, fundamental analysts began wondering about the value of forecasting based on trend analysis. After all, how can you trust a historical analysis when one bad year can come along and knock the whole model to smithereens?

One way to make sure your fundamental analysis has a long-term time horizon is by using index-number analysis. Despite the fancy name, index-trend analysis is just a way to see how a company's financial results are changing over time. This analysis includes recent drastic ups or downs, but also lets you see the broader, long-term trend. You found out how to apply index-number analysis to the *balance sheet* in Chapter 6.

Index-number analysis, though, can also be applied to the income statement to help forecast a company's growth rate into the future. The analysis attempts to help you put short-term declines in business into perspective.

To perform an index-number analysis, you just need to choose a year to act as a starting point, or *base year*. You then divide each year's results by the base year and multiply by 100 to get the index number for the year.

For instance, imagine using Oracle's fiscal 2000 operating income, $3,080, as the base year. To calculate the index number for fiscal 2001, simply divide that year's operating income of $3,777 by the base year of $3,080, multiply by 100, and you get 122.6. Table 17-3 shows you how the index analysis puts Oracle's downturn in fiscal 2002 and 2003 into perspective. Despite the downturn, the Oracle's operating income kept chugging along.

Table 17-3	Oracle's Index Numbers Tell the Full Story
Fiscal year	*Operating income index-number analysis using fiscal 2000 as the base year*
2000	100
2001	122.6
2002	115.9
2003	111.7
2004	127.2
2005	142.1
2006	161.0
2007	199.1
2008	260.0

Applying moving averages to fundamental analysis

Another technique used in long-term forecasts in fundamental analysis is the *moving average*. With this analysis, investors attempt to smooth out unusual bumps in a company's results. A moving average serves the same role as your seatbelt when your airplane hits turbulence.

Moving averages may be applied to annual results or to quarterly results, based on how volatile the company's profits are.

To conduct a moving-average analysis, you first must choose how many years you want to incorporate. A common time period would be three years. You add up the company's results over three-year chunks and then divide by the number of years, or 3. Table 17-4 shows you what a three-year moving-average analysis on Oracle's operating income would look like.

Table 17-4	Getting a Move On with Oracle
Fiscal year ended	_Three-year operating-income moving average at the end of . . . (in $ millions)_
2004	$3,643
2005	$3,912
2006	$4,418
2007	$5,156
2008	$6,367

Using this analysis, you can see that the company's compound average annual growth rate based on five moving-average periods is 15%. That might be a reasonable basis with which to make a forward-looking growth forecast.

A word about restated results and trends

Whenever you perform long-term trend analysis, as you've been practicing in this chapter, it's imperative to pull all the data from a company's most current annual or quarterly report. And that's due to a dirty little secret known as _restatements_.

From time to time, companies may come out and say, oops, remember when we said we made X in 2007? Scratch that. We actually made Y. If the restatement, or change in past financial results, is large enough, or _material_, the company may issue a formal statement. But other times, if they're small changes, a company may simply alter the numbers in the latest financial statements.

Restatements are another reason why the annual report required by the regulators, or 10-K, is one of your best friends in fundamental analysis. The portion of the 10-K called _Selected Financial Data_ is a very useful source of the freshest data, including any restatements. Most companies provide the most up-to-date numbers for key elements of the income statement, including revenue, operating income, net income and balance-sheet items going back at least five years.

Finding Trends in Insider Trading Information

In what's one of the harsh realities of fundamental analysis, no matter how carefully you examine a company's financial statements, you'll probably never know more than the CEO does. After all, the CEO is in constant contact with the company's customers, suppliers and employees, and has access to financial data you'll never see.

And that's why you'll want to know how to watch trends in what top executives are doing when it comes to their company's stock. Officers and directors of a company are permitted to buy and sell their stock, called *legal insider trading*, as long as they follow specific disclosure rules. Looking for trends in the transactions of executives, though, can sometimes tip you off to issues.

Legal insider trading is very different from *illegal insider trading*. When a company's officers or directors use knowledge of material, nonpublic information, or important financial data that have not been shared with everyone, they run the risk of committing illegal insider trading. Many executives try to avoid the appearance of illegal insider trading by instructing their brokers to sell the company stock they own at a prescheduled time each year.

When a CEO is bullish, should you be, too?

Ever go to a restaurant and notice the workers are eating the restaurant's food, too, on their lunch break? There's something kind of comforting about seeing the people in charge of a company using its products.

Fundamental analysts carry that same idea when looking at companies. It's often considered to be a positive sign when a company's top management, including the CEO, is buying shares of the company. If nothing else, it's comforting to at least know that the CEO stands to lose money, too, if things don't work out.

Even CEOs aren't perfect. Sometimes CEOs' own optimism can lead to not-so-great investments in their company's stock. In 1998, then-dominant PC seller CompUSA began reporting softening earnings, and the stock price was skidding. But James Halpin, an experienced retailer and CEO of CompUSA at the time, couldn't have been more bullish about the company. He spent $3 million of his own money buying 200,000 shares of the company's stock. "I didn't wake up one morning and say, 'Gee, I have this $3 million … what am I going to do with it?' " Halpin told *Investor's Business Daily* in 1998. "People (insiders) sell stock for a lot of reasons. But they buy for only one."

Turns out, though, the company's future wasn't all that bright. The company replaced Halpin just a few years later, says Hoovers.com. Eventually the company wound up selling most of its stores and was ultimately sold.

Paying attention to when a company buys its own stock

Some investors think the ultimate bullish signal is when companies announce they're buying back their own stock. What could be more bullish than a company investing in itself, right? From time to time, when a company feels especially flush with cash and deems its stock price to be too low, it might plan to buy outstanding shares.

Turns out, though, companies have had pretty lousy timing when it comes to buying their own shares. Companies spent a record $158 billion buying back their stock in the second quarter of 2007, only to pay peak prices ahead of the market's gigantic swoon. As companies were paying up for their stock, the Standard & Poor's 500 hit its bull-market peak on Oct. 9, 2007 and proceeded to fall into one of the worst bear markets since the Great Depression. So much for good timing. Table 17-5 shows you how much companies have spent buying back their stock in recent years.

2007 wasn't the first time companies had lousy timing buying their own stock. Stock buybacks surged in the first quarter of 2000 ended in March, just when the market was peaking and about to collapse.

Table 17-5	Tracking the Rise and Fall of Stock Buybacks
Year	*Buybacks ($ billions)*
2008	$339.7
2007	$589.1
2006	$431.8
2005	$349.2
2004	$197.5
2003	$131.1
2002	$127.3
2001	$132.2
2000	$150.6

Source: Standard & Poor's, based on the S&P 500

There are additional risks to stock buybacks other than bad timing. When companies use cash to buy their own stock back, that is cash that wasn't used to invest in future products or even to reduce the company's debt load.

Watching when the insiders are selling

When insiders sell stock, it almost instantly gets everyone's attention. Investors might fear the executives know something they don't when there's a great deal of selling going on.

Don't assume just because the management team is selling shares that you should dump your holdings, too. CEOs may sell their stock for lots of reasons, such as paying for junior's college or a new car or home renovation. But when you see a flurry of selling at a company, or an industry, it pays to be extra skeptical.

Many investors were shocked and surprised by the dramatic meltdown of the real-estate business and of homebuilders' stocks starting in 2005. Everyone, that is, expect the top executives at major homebuilding companies. Many of these executives, as a group, sold 4.8 million shares in July 2005, says Thomson Reuters. That was the largest level of selling in the industry since Thomson started keeping records in 1990. The timing couldn't have been better, since the homebuilders' stocks hit their peaks on July 20, 2005.

How to track insider selling

Now that you've seen how watching what the insiders are doing can be somewhat telling, you probably can't wait to get started. Here's the problem. You probably can't call or e-mail the CEOs of companies you're investing in and ask them if they're buying or selling.

Fundamental analysis, again, is your way to get the full story. There are two main ways to track the insider buying and selling at companies, including from:

✓ **Companies' regulatory filings:** Given how sensitive the topic of insider selling is, you can imagine how regulated it is. There is a whole array of filings executives must provide to the Securities and Exchange Commission when buying or selling company stock.

The most common form containing insider-selling activity is *Form 4*. When an executive buys or sells stock, that activity must be reported on Form 4 within two business days. Form 4 documents are available in the SEC's IDEA database. Flip back to Chapter 4 if you want to refresh your memory on how to get regulatory filings from IDEA.

✔ **Financial Web sites:** Several financial Web sites spare you the trouble of having to dig up Form 4 filings yourself and compile all insiders' buying and selling in one place.

The Nasdaq's Web site provides comprehensive insider-trading data. At Nasdaq.com, enter the stock's symbol and click the Info Quotes button. Next, click the Holdings/Insider option located toward the middle of the page. You'll get a summary of how much insider buying and selling is going on. You can also drill down and get the names of the executives doing the buying and selling.

Designing Screens to Pinpoint Companies

With thousands of stocks and companies to choose from, it can be intimidating for a fundamental analyst to choose which stocks to start studying. After all, it could take hours to completely analyze just one company and stock. It's not humanly possible to analyze every company available.

Fundamental analysts often use stock screening tools to help them scan through thousands of companies' financial statements, literally, with the push of a few buttons. These screening tools scan through massive databases of fundamental data on stocks to select those that meet characteristics you're looking for.

Stock screening tools help fundamental analysts find stocks much like online dating services help singles find potential mates. With online dating services, you can enter what particular eye color or hobbies you want your mate to have. The system then pulls up a list of people with those traits. Stock screening tools aren't nearly as romantic, unless you think calculators are cute. But they're just as useful. If you're in search of stocks with returns on equity greater than the industry average, for instance, the stock screening tool will show you with stocks fit the bill.

Examples of what screening can tell you

Screening is fundamental analysts' way of narrowing down the search for companies that have all the traits they are looking for. By carefully instructing the screening tool to filter out the universe of all stocks for only those with certain characteristics, fundamental analysts can get a shorter list of strong candidates that deserve closer attention.

Typically, stock screens fall into one of several categories, including those that look for:

- ✔ **Cheap stocks:** By searching for stocks with low valuations relative to their industry, such as price-to-earnings ratios or price-to-book ratios, investors can pinpoint potential bargains.

- ✔ **Fast-growing companies:** Investors who like to find companies that seem to have momentum on their side often seek out those with strong earnings or revenue growth.

- ✔ **Efficient companies:** Pinpointing companies with strong *efficiency ratios*, such as *accounts receivable turnover*, are often the ones handling their resources effectively. Chapter 8 discusses efficiency ratios and other ratios you may decide to include in a screen.

- ✔ **Well-managed companies:** Ratios like return on equity and *return on assets*, especially compared against peers, can give fundamental analysts an idea of which companies have an able set of hands behind the wheel.

- ✔ **Financial strength:** Companies with excellent balance sheets, filled with cash and light on debt, may be well-positioned to endure an economic downturn.

You may build screens that find companies that score well in all the areas listed above. Some professional fundamental analysts screen for companies based on dozens of criteria.

Step-by-step instructions on building a sample screen

Now you're ready to stop reading about screens and start building them. I'll give you an example of a basic screen in this section: A list of the largest companies, based on *market value*, in the S&P 500 that have return on equity that's greater than the average in their industries.

I'll be using MSN Money's Deluxe Screening tool for this example, but this is not the only stock screening tool that is available to you. Several Web sites offer screening tools; some are free and others require a subscription. You can read more about what stock screening tools are available in *Investing Online For Dummies*.

Building this sample screen requires taking these steps:

1. **Log into the screening system.** You can try MSN Money at money.msn. com. Scroll down and click on the "Stock Screener" option on the left-hand side of the page.

2. **Make sure you're running the Deluxe Screener.** If you haven't used the MSN Money stock screener before, you will be prompted to install the MSN Investment Toolbox. It's a small program that won't hurt your computer.

3. **Set your first criteria.** Here you tell the screener to only find the companies with the largest *market capitalizations*. You can review what market capitalization is in Chapter 3.

   In the first row of the screen, you can instruct the screener to filter its results for companies with market values of $3 billion or more. Click in the first block under where it says Field Name, choose Company Basics, and then choose Market Capitalization.

   Next, change the Operator to >=, which means greater than or equal to. Finally, change the Value block to read 3,000,000,000, which is $3 billion.

4. **Set the second criteria.** Here you want to limit your list to companies with better-than-average return on equity. Change the next blank, Field Name block, to Investment Return and then Return on equity. Set the operator to >=, for greater than or equal to. Lastly, click on the Value column and choose Investment Return, and then Industry Average Return on Equity.

5. **Set the third criteria.** To limit your search to companies in the S&P 500, go to the third row and change the Field Name column to Company Basics and S&P Index Membership. Next, change the Operator column to =. Lastly, change the Value column to S&P 500.

6. **Run the screen.** To see the results of your screen, just click the Run Search button. The results should look something like what you see in Table 17-6, but with updated numbers.

Table 17-6   Tracking the Rise and Fall of Stock Buybacks

Company name	Market Capitalization ($ billions)	Return on equity	Industry return on equity
Exxon Mobil	$341.8	38.5	23.5
Wal-Mart	$197.9	20.4	19.2
Microsoft	$150.8	50.0	34.3
Johnson & Johnson	$140.2	30.2	24.5
Chevron	$133.5	29.2	23.5

Source: MSN Money

Chapter 18

Avoiding Investment Blow-Ups with Fundamental Analysis

*I*n many sports, not messing up can be the best way to win. In tennis, for instance, mistakes you make yourself are called unforced errors. Too many unforced errors usually give your opponents an easy victory, even if they're not all that good.

Reducing the number of errors you make is also important in investing. As you'll discover in this chapter, making too many unforced errors in picking the wrong investments can sink your returns. Fundamental analysis, while not perfect, can be a vital tool in allowing you to avoid at least some colossal disasters.

Making big mistakes in investing can dig you into a hole that's extremely difficult, if not impossible, to climb out of in a timely fashion. If fundamental analysis prevents you from making just one blunder, it's well worth your time.

Part of the process of avoiding mistakes is steering clear of companies whose fundamentals just aren't right for some reason. Sometimes you might not know for sure that a company is about to implode. But fundamental analysis can give you the tools that may signal to you, at least, that something about the company's financial reporting doesn't smell right or displays some common red flags. By sticking with companies that have high *quality of earnings*, or reported results that accurately reflect the businesses' health, you can go a long way in avoiding the many landmines that are so easy to step on.

Uncovering the Dangers of Not Using Fundamental Analysis

It might seem like a cheap marketing gimmick in a book about fundamental analysis to claim that not using fundamental analysis might be dangerous. Maybe the word dangerous is a bit strong. After all, you probably won't die if you don't read a company's income statement or balance sheet before investing in it.

But, if you're assuming the risk of picking and investing in individual companies, not having a knowledge of fundamental analysis can expose your portfolio to some trouble. Buying individual stocks because you believe the company's prospects are strong may prompt you to pay sky-high valuations for untested companies with shaky fundamentals. And that's a recipe for poor returns, as you will see by reading this chapter.

Why investing in individual companies is risky business

By investing in individual companies, you're exposing yourself to *specific risk*, or unique business challenges faced by companies. Specific risk is very different than *systematic risk*, or risk faced by all stocks.

For instance, if there's a credit crisis, as there was in 2008, that's a systematic risk that will (and did) hurt just about every stock. However, if you own a company that makes widgets, and it's found that those widgets cause cancer, that's a specific risk to that one company.

By using fundamental analysis to choose individual companies to invest in, depending on what else is in your portfolio, you may be exposed to specific risk. In other words, if a company you're invested in makes a misstep, you will suffer a loss other investors won't. Table 18-1 shows you how investment *risk*, measured by a statistical measure called standard deviation, is much higher when investing in individual stocks rather than a broad *index* such as the Standard & Poor's 500.

 By investing in a broad mutual fund or exchange-traded fund, which owns hundreds of different companies, you can reduce or *diversify* away your exposure to specific risk. If fundamental analysis seems like too much trouble, you're probably best off investing in a diversified mutual fund with low expenses. Most investors get the best results investing in diversified *index funds*, or funds that own all the stocks in popular stock market indexes.

Table 18-1	Individual Stocks Are Riskier by Nature	
Stock	*Average Annual Return*	*Annualized risk (standard deviation)*
Disney	10.4%	25.8
Hewlett-Packard	12.1%	36.3
Pfizer	15.0%	24.4
AT&T	11.5%	24.2
S&P 500	11.6%	13.5

Source: Index Funds Advisors (www.ifa.com)

Standard deviation is a statistical method used to measure how risky a stock is by measuring how much it tends to rise and fall. The higher the standard deviation, the riskier the stock is. You want to make sure you're getting the highest amount of return for the amount of risk you're taking.

Ignore the fundamentals at your own risk

It's easy to get enamored with a stock. You might buy a pair of shoes, like them, and decide to invest in the company that makes them. Some fundamental investors believe it's a good idea to invest in companies that make things they like or understand, for that reason. And there's no question that having an in-depth understanding of an industry, as discussed in Chapter 16, can be a vital part of fundamental analysis.

Just because you invest in a company that makes products you understand or even use, doesn't mean you will make money. One of the great examples of the danger of buying what you know is Crocs, a maker of plastic clog shoes. During 2006 and 2007, these shoes, typically used by gardeners to keep their feet relatively clean, caught on with fashionistas. You'd see Hollywood celebrities and their kids wearing Crocs around, and soon they became popular, especially with little kids.

Investors, betting Crocs might be the next Nike, snapped up shares of the company when they were first offered to the public in an *initial public offering* in 2006. Shares closed on their first day of trading in February 2006 for about $14. And for a while, the investment looked like a real winner, and investors chased the stock all the way up to nearly $75 a share by October 2007.

But investors who ignored the fundamental signs showing Crocs' earnings growth wasn't going to last suffered greatly. The stock began to falter in late 2007 and crashed to less than $1 a share in March 2009. The company's auditing firm,

Deloitte & Touche, warned in March 2009 it had "substantial doubt" about the company's ability to stay in business. The importance of auditor warnings is covered in Chapter 12.

Curious what the fundamental warning signs of Crocs were? I'll consider Crocs, and ten other real-life examples in Chapter 20, where I discuss how fundamental analysis could have helped you avoid big blow-ups.

Why digging out of a hole is so difficult

One of the top reasons why you want to use fundamental analysis is that investment mistakes are incredibly difficult to recover from. Many times when companies start to stumble, they have a tough time regaining control. When you invest in an individual stock, you're betting that the company's *corporate governance*, covered in Chapter 9, will be strong enough to kick out the failing management team before things get out of hand. But you also need to have faith the board of directors will bring in a qualified replacement to fix the company.

And that's just the business risk of making an investment mistake. Don't forget the mathematical cruelty when it comes to digging out of an investment hole. Table 18-2 shows just how hard it is to make up for drastic losses.

Table 18-2	Digging Out of a Hole Is Hard to Do
If your loss on a stock is . . .	*. . . to break even you need a return of . . .*
10%	11.1%
20%	25%
30%	43%
50%	100%
90%	900%

Since large losses can be difficult, if not impossible, to recover from, some fundamental analysts borrow techniques from technical analysis and cut their losses. Technical analysis, covered in more detail in Chapter 19, often calls for investors to sell a stock if it falls 10% or more from their purchase price to avoid devastating losses.

The dangers of initial public offerings

If there's a time when investors often turn off their reasoning and fundamental analysis skills, it's with IPOs. With an IPO, a company that had been private offers its shares to the public for the first time. There's often a great deal of hoopla and excitement when a company's shares are in the public's grasp.

Some investors love to buy IPOs, practically sight unseen. And it's not because there's a lack of information on IPO. Companies going public for the first time must provide everyone interested in investing with a regulatory filing called the *prospectus*. A prospectus is a gigantic file of regulatory disclosures that are kind of like the 10-K, 10-Q and proxy statement all rolled into one. Prospectuses contain all the financial statements you could ever want.

But often, new companies coming public have such a positive story, investors can't seem to help themselves. Here's a startling fact: A huge number of companies aren't even profitable when they're launching their IPOs. In 2008, for instance, 43% of all companies launching an IPO lost money, says Jay Ritter, professor of finance at the University of Florida. And get this: Back in 2000, 80% of the companies that sold stock to the public weren't profitable. Investors, though, ignored the fundamentals and bought these IPOs anyway.

As you're probably guessing already, investors who buy IPOs with no understanding of the fundamentals are usually sorely disappointed. Investors who bought IPOs between 1980 and 2005, and held the stocks for three years, wound up lagging the rest of the stock market by 20.3%, Ritter says.

Some IPO wipeouts are especially stunning. One that comes to mind is Blackstone Group, a private-equity firm that sold shares to the public for the first time in June 2007. Private-equity firms were the hot thing on Wall Street in the mid-2000s, as they bought companies with borrowed money and sold them for a profit. Since private-equity firms had a cachet to them, many common investors couldn't wait to get a piece of Blackstone's stock. Blackstone closed its first day at $35.06. But, again, investors doomed themselves by paying top dollar for a risky business. The credit crunch hit, and Blackstone shares sank to $6.53 at the end of 2008 for a crushing 81% loss for investors.

Avoiding bubbles and manias

From time to time, stock investors lose sight of the fundamentals. Bubbles, or periods of time when prices of investments get disconnected from their fundamental value, are a reality in a market economy. When the public is allowed to set the prices on assets in a free-for-all auction, it's inevitable that sometimes prices in the short term are pushed to levels that are difficult to justify with reason.

When you start hearing other people who don't know how to study a company's earnings and revenue telling you what stocks to buy, the market may very well be in a bubble. Caveat emptor.

Sometimes the entire stock market enters a bubble. Sometimes a particular part of the stock market gets bubbly. And sometimes, just a few stocks or types of stocks see their prices shoot up to the stratosphere. Having the self-control to avoid these investments with inflated prices is extremely difficult, since everyone around you who is buying them keeps making money. But fundamental analysis can provide a few things to watch out for as a warning prices might be getting ahead of themselves.

Price-to-earnings ratios getting inflated

When investors start to lose their discipline and begin chasing stocks, you might start to notice P-E ratios are getting inflated. The long-term average for P-Es is generally 15, so when you notice a company's P-E get dramatically higher than that you'll want to take notice. You'll want to analyze a stock's valuation, including its P-E and PEG ratios, to get an understanding of how rich the price is.

If you're interested in trying to figure out when an individual stock's P-E is starting to get lofty, one approach is suggested by BetterInvesting, a large group for investment clubs. BetterInvesting provides electronic software and forms that help you measure how lofty a stock's P-E is relative to earnings forecasts and its historical P-E. A stock is considered to be a "buy" when its P-E falls into the lower one-third of its historical range. Stocks are considered a "sell" when the P-E lands in the upper one-third of the historical range. The methodology gives you a way to evaluate P-Es using a company's historical valuation.

Dividend yields sagging

A stock's *dividend yield*, or annual dividend divided by the stock's price, can give you a heads-up on a stock that may be part of a bubble. When a stock's dividend yield drops well below the average in its industry, or what's paid by other companies, you might start to wonder whether investors are paying up too much for promises. Similarly, you might be suspicious if one company is the only one in an industry not to pay a dividend.

The more investors pay up for a stock, the more the dividend yield drops, making the dividend yield a decent indicator to pay attention to. You can look up dividend yields paid by other companies to see what the norm is.

Dividend yields often get very low when investors get too bubbly about the prospects of the stock market, as they did in both 2007 and 2000, as shown in Table 18-3. Don't assume, though, when a stock's dividend yield gets unusually high that it's a screaming buy. When a stock's dividend yield gets very high, that may be a signal the company is about to cut the dividend or run into some serious financial difficulties.

Table 18-3	When Dividend Yields Sag, Watch Out
Year	*S&P 500 dividend yield*
2008	3.1%
2007	1.9%
2000	1.2%
1990	3.7%
1980	4.5%

Source: Standard & Poor's

Price-to-book ratios skyrocketing

If you ask an investor and an accountant how much a company is worth, they'd approach the question very differently. The accountant might start counting up all the *assets,* or things the company owns, and subtract all its *liabilities*, or things it owes. By subtracting the liabilities from the assets, the accountant would come up with the *book value* of the company. That, the accountant would attest, is the company's value.

Investors, though, approach the valuation question very differently than accountants. Investors might try to figure out how much someone else would be willing to pay for the company. The price at which a company would sell, the investor might say, is how much the company is worth.

 What happens when the accountants and investors disagree? You'll see it in the *price-to-book ratio,* which is covered in more detail in Chapter 8. If investors and accountants agree on the value of a firm, the stock's price-to-book ratio will be 1. If investors think the company is worth more than what the accountants are saying, the price-to-book will be greater than 1. And if investors think the value of the company is less than what the accountants claim, the price-to-book ratio will be less than 1.

When you see a company's price-to-book soar, sometimes it can be a tip-off its stock is in a mini-bubble. Google, for instance, was a stock that could do no wrong in 2006 and 2007. Investors drove the company's price-to-book ratio to about 10, as shown in Table 18-4, in 2007. Investors, though, found out the hard way that buying pricey stocks can be dangerous.

Table 18-4	Google's Price-to-Book Told the Story	
Year	*Price-to-book (based on year-end book values)*	*Stock price*
2008	3.5	$307.65
2007	10.3	$691.48
2006	9.7	$460.48
2005	13.7	$414.9
2004	19.7	$192.79

Source: Standard & Poor's Capital IQ

Here's one of the biggest problems with using fundamental analysis to avoid big stock declines: timing. Stocks' valuations can remain inflated for some time and correct with little warning. Consider Google. In 2004, the Internet search company's price-to-book ratio was nearly 20, but the stock still proceeded to nearly quadruple over the next three years. This is another reason why no single fundamental indictor can be completely relied on. And it's another reason why for many investors, stymied by the timing needed to pick stocks, might be best off simply buying and holding a diversified basket of many stocks.

Profitability becomes meaningless

When you start noticing companies that lose money hand-over-fist posting huge stock-price gains, it's time to be on bubble watch. A company's fundamental value is based on its earnings and cash flow, as you discovered in Chapter 11. Using that logic, if a company doesn't have any earnings, it doesn't have any fundamental value. Unless by performing industry and trend analysis, you can be confident the company can generate profits, you should steer clear.

We'll likely find out in a few years or so whether or not Buffett was right and Treasuries were actually in a bubble. But the lesson still applies: Bubbles can inflate in any corner of the financial markets, not just the places where the fast-money crowd hangs out.

Finding and Avoiding Financial Red Flags

It's a sad reality that despite all the protections provided to investors, buying stock is still largely a buyer-beware endeavor. That's especially the case when buying a large stake in a single individual company. If the company's management makes a mistake, whether honestly or dishonestly, shareholders may end up paying the price.

I cannot stress this enough. When you buy common stock in a company, you're last in line for any assets that might be left over if the company is sold off. Employees and bondholders are paid first, often leaving the stock investors in the failed company with nothing.

Bubbles can come from unlikely places

There's certainly a "type" of stock that ends up being caught in a bubble. Most of the time, bubble stocks come from an industry that seems boundless with possibilities that captures the imagination of the uninformed public. The Internet stock bubble of the late 1990s was the classic example of the type of stock with the potential to become a bubble. Investors had endless optimism for what the Internet, and companies taking advantage of it, could accomplish. There's no question the Internet itself proved to be a giant innovation and has completely changed global business. But most of the Internet companies investors bet on either suffered massive stock crashes or vanished completely.

Some investors, though, incorrectly figure they can avoid bubbles if they just steer clear of the overhyped stocks that are on the front pages of the newspapers or the favorite playthings of day traders. But that's simply not the case. It's not the type of investment itself that determines whether it's in a dangerous bubble. Any stock, bond, collectible or commodity can find itself in a bubble. It's the valuation, or price you're paying, that determines whether or not you're one of the investors helping to inflate an investment bubble.

One of the best examples of an unlikely bubble occurred in 2008. Investors got so worried about the health of the banking system during the financial crisis they piled into debt sold by the U.S. government, called Treasuries. To show you just now strange this situation was, Treasuries are just about the least exciting investment you can buy. It's odd to even have the words Treasuries and bubble in the same sentence. Treasuries usually pay relatively low rates of interest and watching their prices change is akin to getting front row seats for a turtle race. The lure of Treasuries is that they're backed by the U.S. government, and therefore, are considered a super-safe place to stash money.

But you have to remember the level of panic in 2008. Investors were practically stuffing cash under their mattresses, Treasuries became all the rage since they were seen as the last safe place to put money. Investors bought Treasuries with such ferocity they arguably pushed their prices to bubble-like levels. At one point in 2008, the prices on Treasuries were at such nosebleed levels investors were getting negative returns. In other words, investors were willing to buy Treasuries and lend the government $1, just so they could be sure they'd get 99 cents back in a few years.

The bubble prices of Treasuries even caught the attention of famous investor Warren Buffett. In his 2008 letter to Berkshire Hathaway shareholders, he wrote: "When the financial history of this decade is written, it will surely speak of the Internet bubble of the late 1990s and the housing bubble of the early 2000s. But the U.S. Treasury bond bubble of late 2008 may be regarded as almost equally extraordinary."

A real-life pattern for suit-worthy shenanigans

All sorts of shenanigans, both those that are pushing the limits and those that are outright fraudulent, often leave investors feeling cheated and caught off guard. Many investors, feeling there's no other recourse, may band together to sue a company or its management team in a *securities class-action lawsuit.* Table 18-5 shows how the number of federal securities class-action suits tends to spike amid a bear market for stocks, such as in 2001 and 2008.

Table 18-5	Shareholder Ire Follows the Stock Market
Year	*Number of Securities Fraud Class-Action Lawsuits*
2008	227
2007	176
2006	119
2005	182
2004	238
2003	227
2002	266
2001	498

Source: Stanford Securities Class Action Clearinghouse

The rationale behind shenanigans

The temptation to cook the books, or make financial statements look better than reality, is very big. Management teams running companies have a tremendous amount at stake when it comes to the financial results. One disappointing quarter could erode investors' confidence in the company's plan and knock the stock price down. And since executives and members of the board of directors often own big chunks of company stock, they don't want to see the value of their holdings fall. A vast majority of executives' pay is often tied to their company's stock price. If the stock falls, they just took a massive pay cut.

Flexibility in the accounting system may give executives the leeway they need to legally add a penny or two a share to earnings, helping them to make sure they meet Wall Street's ever-increasing demands. Some executives figure just a few pennies here or there won't hurt anyone.

Financial smoke-and-mirrors used by management teams can be very difficult for investors to detect, unless they get tipped off and know exactly what to look for in the financial statements. And the ability for management to *manage earnings*, or tweak financial statements to make them look more positive, is a huge issue fundamental analysts must contend with.

Red flags that signal shenanigans

In Part II, you'll find all sorts of troubling things that might show up in the individual financial statements. In this section of the book, though, I spotlight a few of the more common warning signs you need to be particularly vigilant to watch for.

Some of the red flags discussed below aren't illegal. But they all can cause financial results to be manipulated to the point that your fundamental analysis might be compromised.

Swelling accounts receivable

If you start seeing the *accounts receivable* item on the balance sheet skyrocket to the point where it's outpacing revenue growth, that can be a bad thing. The accounts receivable line item grows when a company sells product to a customer, and accepts an IOU in exchange. If you see accounts receivable growth outpacing revenue growth, you might wonder if the company is pushing product onto customers to boost revenue. The way a company decides when to book revenue, called *revenue recognition*, may have a profound influence on its results.

For instance, Internet software company PurchasePro in late 2000 reported a $13.2 million quarterly jump in accounts receivable to $23.4 million. That should have caught fundamental analysts' attention, since the company's revenue was just $17.3 million for the period. The company a year later restated results, and the Securities and Exchange Commission ultimately accused company executives of committing fraud.

Overvalued intangible assets

When you think of a company's assets and read about them in Chapter 6, actual property the company owns that can be touched or seen probably comes to mind. But those types of assets, called *tangible assets*, are only one part of what a company owns. Companies also have what are called *intangible assets*, or items believed to have value that cannot be seen or touched. When intangible asset values are inflated, fundamental analysts might believe a company to be worth more than it is in reality.

Many fundamental analysts completely disregard intangible assets when measuring the book value of a company. Since many of these assets probably couldn't be sold if the company were to be liquidated, it's often safe to leave them out of your analysis.

Massive big-bath and "one-time" charges

One commonly used trick by companies is the so-called *big-bath restatement*. When a company is about to report a poor quarter, it makes it really bad. A company's management writes down the value of assets or pays some expenses ahead of time, which makes the current results look really bad. But by getting all this bad news out, the company sets itself up for the illusion of a better future. Best of all, some investors automatically look past one-time charges, assuming they're just unusual events. But the fact is, these restatements can have a profound effect on inflating a company's future profits.

Be especially skeptical of companies, sometimes called *chronic restaters*, which seem to be regularly declaring big one-time charges. One-time charges are supposed to be just that. If you see them occurring frequently, you should wonder why.

Low "Quality" earnings

Accounting rules are supposed to make a company's financial statements more reflective of reality. For instance, companies are expected to book revenue when a sale is made, not necessarily when cash is received on the sale. Booking revenue this way ensures that the revenue is matched up with the costs incurred to generate that revenue.

But this accounting technique, while of merit, can open the doors to manipulation. Companies can push the limits of accounting by padding the financial statements with revenue and earnings that have no connection whatsoever to cash actually received or spent. Companies that do this are considered to have earnings of low quality. The *statement of cash flows* is a fundamental analyst's best weapon in finding and steering clear of companies with low-quality earnings. I give you complete instructions on how to perform this quality of earnings detection analysis in Chapter 7.

Increasing borrowing, or leverage

If the bear market and credit crunch that began in 2007 taught investors anything, it's the danger of borrowing too much. The same lesson was learned by investors. Some companies, including Bear Stearns and Lehman Bros., had so much exposure to debt, or *leverage*, they were unable to hold themselves together when business turned south.

And while entirely legal, debt can also distort some of the popular measures fundamental analysts consider when evaluating companies' profitability. *Return on equity*, a commonly used financial ratio used to measure the effectiveness of a management team, is especially vulnerable to distortion from the use of debt. You can read about return on equity, and how it's skewed by debt, in Chapter 8.

General Electric is an example of how some investors may not have fully understood how debt can have a big-time influence on fundamental analysis. GE's return on equity in March 2009, based on its financial returns from the previous 12 months, was a respectable 16.3, says Thomson Reuters. That was right in line with the industry's average of 17.8.

But if you look at the company's *return on assets*, a financial ratio which strips away the effect of leverage, you get a different picture. GE's return on assets during the same time period was 2.3, well below the industry's average return on assets of 5.2. GE's use of debt caused return on equity to be relatively high, even though its return on assets was relatively low at the same time.

Again, nothing is illegal about borrowing, and I'm not suggesting at all that it is. Debt can be a critical portion of a company's total *capital structure*, since it tends to be cheaper to borrow than to issue stock. But it's a crime for a fundamental analyst not to pay attention to the effect of a company's debt.

Chapter 19

Marrying Fundamental Analysis with Technical Analysis

In This Chapter

▶ Realizing the differences between fundamental and technical analysis

▶ Getting familiar with the primary tools used by technical analysts

▶ Understanding what to look for in stock price charts and how they can aid fundamental analysis

▶ Using the options market to see the true demand for stocks

*B*uying the right stock at the wrong time is often worse than buying the wrong stock to begin with. Many beginning investors get frustrated after studying a stock's financial statements, the analysts' and media reports, and valuation information, only to end up losing money anyway.

And that's the big drawback of fundamental analysis. Just because a stock might appear to be cheap doesn't mean it will rally anytime soon. And just because a company's historical fundamentals look strong doesn't mean its business can't deteriorate and put the company in jeopardy. On the flip side, sometimes companies that look like real dogs can turn things around and surprise investors on the upside. Don't forget, too, that no matter how good you might be performing fundamental analysis, your assumptions might be off, leading to poor investment decisions.

These complications of fundamental analysis are big reasons why some investors consider adding a dose of technical analysis to their technique. *Technical analysis*, the study of patterns in stock prices, is used by investors who think they can use the opinions of other investors to see something in a stock's future.

Marrying technical analysis with fundamental analysis, in some ways, is like trying to mix oil and water. They're very different approaches. But even fundamental analysts may improve their understanding of the way a stock behaves by taking a closer look at its *technicals*, or indicators technical analysts pay attention to.

Understanding Technical Analysis

If you've ever seen an investors' desk that's covered with all sorts of charts with squiggly lines or computer screens displaying graphs, you may have found a technical analyst.

Technical analysts are often called *chartists* because they spend their time poring over *stock price charts*. These charts show where a stock price has been over time and how many investors have bought or sold the stock. Technical analysts believe historical patterns in a stock price's movement can give solid clues about where the stock might be headed in the future.

It's important to remember many academics take strong exception to technical analysis. Studies have shown a stock price's movement in the short term is tied to news events, which are random. Stock price charts, academics say, tell you nothing other than what a price was in the past. Longer-term stock prices respond to a company's earnings and cash flow, which are not predicted by anything on a stock price chart, many academics insist.

Sometimes it does seem technical analysts get a bit carried away with the art of their craft. Some technical analysts read stock price charts almost like a clairvoyant studies the lines on a client's palm. With that said, technical analysis is often mentioned by investors, so it's worth knowing a bit about. More importantly for fundamental analysts, though, is that some of the methods used by technical analysts may be useful for investors who are focused on revenue and earnings.

Reading the stock price charts

The primary tool used by technical analysts is the stock price chart. These charts, available on just about any financial Web site, usually plot a stock's closing price every day. Charts usually come in several forms, including the:

- ✔ **Line:** Most of the stock price charts you see are usually line charts. Line charts, as their name implies, are simply a connect-the-dots line linking the closing prices of a stock each trading day.

- ✔ **High-Low-Close:** Line charts are simple, but they do obscure some of the relevant data from trading. If you look at a line chart, there's no way to know how high or low stock prices got each day. The High-Low-Close chart, shown in Figure 19-1, attempts to solve this shortcoming of line charts. On each trading day, there's a vertical bar, with the top portion representing a stock's high price and the bottom, the low. Then there's a line through the middle of the bar showing the price at which the stock closed.

✔ **Candlestick:** Candlestick charts pack even more information than line or high-low-close charts. Candlestick charts not only show you a stock's high, low and close, but also its open price. A stock's open price is the very first price in a trading day that buyers and sellers agreed upon. The indicator on a candlestick chart looks like a rectangle with a vertical line protruding from the top, to mark the stock's high, and from the bottom, to mark the low. You can take a look at a sample in Figure 19-2.

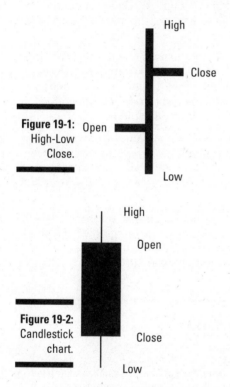

Figure 19-1: High-Low Close.

Figure 19-2: Candlestick chart.

What technical analysts are looking for in the charts

If you've ever heard a technical analyst speak, it might seem like a bit of voodoo. Usually, technical analysts have a pen or marker in hand, start scribbling all over a price chart and talk about all sorts of patterns that they see. If you've ever been to a star-gazing presentation at an observatory, you probably get an idea of what it's like hearing a technical analyst describe a stock chart. Technical analysts try to connect dots on charts to find patterns they say can be revealing about a stock's future. Technical analysts are looking for several things in the charts, including:

- **Price patterns:** If there's one thing that technical analysts fixate on, it's the shape of the charts. Technical analysts think investors, being human, follow predictable cycles of fear and greed. These emotions cause stock prices to follow predictable scripts, or patterns, that may indicate where the stock is headed.

- **What other people see:** Even if you do all the fundamental research possible, you can still be dead wrong. Technical analysts attempt to look at a stock chart to either confirm or deny their belief about a stock's future. If a stock is in free fall, technical analysts would assume other investors know something they don't and would avoid it.

- **Support and resistance levels:** Through the constant tug-of-war between buyers and sellers, a stock attempts to settle at a price investors agree upon. Sometimes a stock will have difficulty breaking beyond a high point, or *resistance level*, and will routinely bounce off a low point, called a *support level*.

- **Momentum:** Technical investors often try to capitalize on the tendency of some stocks to gain steam either going up or heading down. If a stock starts to rally, technical investors take notice and assume those in the know expect the company to report something positive.

A technical analysts' dictionary

If you ever find yourself speaking with a technical analyst, I'll warn you, you might need to bring a decoder ring. Technical analysts use all sorts of sometimes funny sounding words and terms to describe certain patterns that might appear on a stock-price chart. These terms are extremely useful for technical analysts because they can, very quickly, describe the ups and downs of a stock in a way that others can instantly picture and know what they're talking about.

These terms remind me a bit of the names of constellations in the heavens. If someone points at the Big Dipper in the sky, you know to look for a certain pattern of seven stars that looks like a soup ladle. Similarly, when a technical analyst says a stock pattern is showing a *head and shoulders* pattern, you know to look for a stock that has risen and fallen three times in a way that appears like a person's shoulder, head and other shoulder.

Just as there are countless names for constellations, there's practically an endless supply of terms to describe patterns in stock prices. Besides head and shoulders, there's the *cup and handle*, *neckline* and *throwback*, just to name a few. All these terms mean very specific things to the technical analyst. If you're interested in finding out more about these patterns, and what they mean, you might check out Technical Analysis for Dummies (Wiley).

How technical analysis differs from fundamental analysis

Technical analysts and fundamental analysts are diametrically opposed to one other. Get enough fundamental and technical analysts together in one room, and a fight is sure to break out. Technical analysts believe all information about a stock that's worth knowing is reflected in its stock price. Taking the time to study a company's fundamentals is a waste of time, a pure technical analyst would argue, because everyone else has access to the same information and has either bought or sold the stock already.

Fundamental analysts, on the other hand, claim technical analysts fall victim to groupthink and fixate over changes in stock prices that tell investors nothing about the future. What's more, fundamental analysts claim stock prices can get *overvalued* when investors become too optimistic about a stock and push its price above or below the company's *intrinsic value*. You can learn how to calculate a stock's intrinsic value in Chapter 11.

Blending Fundamental and Technical Analysis

While fundamental and technical analysis couldn't be more philosophically opposed to each other, there are ways to marry the two approaches together. In fact, the shortcomings of both fundamental and technical analysis, in some ways, balance each other out.

A few ways to potentially boost your fundamental analysis success using techniques from technical analysis include:

- ✓ **Cutting your losses:** One of the fatal flaws of many pure fundamental analysts is stubbornness. Fundamental analysts urge investors to do their homework, buy a stock and hold on for dear life no matter what happens. But during the ugly bear market that kicked off in 2007, many fundamental analysts learned the hard way that stocks can go to zero, or at least get very close.

  One thing technical analysts are often very good at is cutting their losses. When technical analysts buy a stock, they often have a stock price in mind that they'll sell at if things go south. Knowing how to cut your losses short can be vital when investing in individual companies' stocks, which is a risky endeavor. Some technical analysts suggest investors sell a stock if it falls 10% or more from their purchase price.

- ✔ **Improving your timing:** Some fundamental analysts like to buy stocks and just hang on. But sometimes stubbornness can be expensive. For instance, you might be sitting on a stock that's not moving, while the rest of the stock market charges ahead. Technical analysis attempts to help you avoid sitting still when there's money to be made in other stocks.

- ✔ **Helping you to spot manias:** Because technical analysis is so focused on what other investors are doing and what they're paying for a stock, it can help alert a fundamental analyst to manias and bubbles. Knowing when other investors are getting overly enthusiastic about a stock can be a good clue to explain why a valuation might be getting overly lofty.

Using stock prices as your early-warning system

Even a lifelong fundamental analyst, who looks at technical analysis as glorified palm reading, may still benefit from the art of reading charts. When forecasting how a company's revenue or earnings might look like a year from now, fundamental analysts need to take educated guesses at what shape the economy or the company's industry will be in.

Watching stock prices can be useful in helping a fundamental analyst form an opinion about the future. Since stock prices tend to foreshadow economic reality three, six or nine months in advance, paying attention to stock price movements may tell fundamental analysts something about what the economy might look like.

Monitoring industry *sectors*, as described in Chapter 16, may be especially helpful. If you start noticing shares of companies that make durable goods, or high-ticket items like houses and cars, falling, that may very well be a tip-off that investors expect the economy to slow. That's useful information you might consider when forecasting a company's future earnings growth.

Looking up historical prices

Even if the technical analysis tools discussed in this chapter seem a little too, well, out there for you, you can still benefit from charts and historical stock price data. Oftentimes, you might find yourself wanting to know what a stock price was in the past. Perhaps you want to look up your *cost basis* in a stock, or how much you paid for it when you originally bought it. You'll need to know your stock basis to measure your capital gain or loss for tax purposes.

You may also want to know what a stock price was, say, a year ago so you can measure how well or poorly a stock has done.

When you want to look up a historical stock price, it's time to break out the stock price chart. Most online Web sites let you plot stock prices going back in history so you can see what a stock price was in the past. All the major financial Web sites let you pull up historical stock charts.

Since so many investors ask me for tips on looking up historical stock prices, I'll step you through one way to accomplish this task. If you're looking to get a stock's price in the past, here's how you'd do it using the Money section of USATODAY.com:

1. **Log onto the Money section of USATODAY.com.**

   Enter money.usatoday.com into your Web browser.

2. **Enter the stock's ticker symbol.**

   Scroll down a bit until you see an area to enter the stock symbol on the left-hand side of the page. Click the Go button.

3. **Launch the historical stock quotes engine.**

   Click on the "Historical quotes" option on the green navigation bar.

4. **Choose the date you're interested in.**

   Enter the date into the blank and click the Get Quote button. The system will tell you the stock's high, low and closing price on that day.

The Primary Tools Used by Technical Analysts

Just as fundamental analysts pore over financial ratios and statements, technical analysts have indicators they examine as well. Many of the indicators technical analysts focus on are tied directly to a company's stock price or trading history. You might review some of the items that technical analysts pay attention to and determine how to best implement them in your fundamental strategies.

Getting into the groove with moving averages

One of the first things most technical analysts plot on a stock chart is the *moving average*. The moving average tells you what a stock's average price has been over a set period of time. Moving averages can be calculated for any period of time, but technical analysts usually use the following time periods:

✔ **10-day moving average.** The stock's average price over the past two weeks.

✔ **50-day moving average.** The stock's average price over the past quarter.

✔ **200-day moving average.** The stock's average price over the past year.

Technical analysts compare a stock's current price to its moving average. If the stock price is greater than the moving average, that's considered to be a bullish signal for the market. If the current stock price is less than the moving average, that's a bearish signal.

If you're going to choose a moving average to pay attention to, you should go with the 200-day. Technicians get very cautious when a stock price falls below the 200-day moving average, and may wait on the sidelines before buying back in until the stock rises above the 200-day moving average. When a stock falls below the 200-day moving average, that means that every investor who bought the stock within the past year, on average, is losing money. If the stock creeps upward, many of these disappointed investors are eager to dump the stock, making it difficult for the stock to rise.

Keeping an eye on trading volume

Technical analysts are very interested in a stock's price and the trend of the price. But most technical analysts also pay close attention, too, to how much *trading volume* is occurring. Trading volume measures how much investors are buying or selling a stock. If buyers and sellers are furiously trading shares back and forth, then trading volume is considered to be high, or *active*.

When trading volume is active, technical analysts figure they can trust the price movement to a greater degree. For instance, imagine a stock that soars to break into new high ground, but on low trading volume. A technical analyst would be skeptical of the move higher, since a relatively small group of investors powered it. Similarly, if trading volume is heavy, that tells the technical analyst there's a great deal of volume, or *conviction*, behind the trade.

Table 19-1 summarizes the way a fundamental analyst might couple reading volume with price movements.

Table 19-1	Putting Volume and Price Together	
If a stock . . .	*. . . and trading volume is . . .*	*Technical analysts are . . .*
Rises	Higher	Bullish
Rises	Lower	Cautiously bullish
Falls	Higher	Bearish
Falls	Lower	Cautiously bearish

Your next question, though, might be how you can determine whether trading volume is higher or lower. The major stock market exchanges, including the Nasdaq and New York Stock Exchange, provide trading volume for the day and the *average daily volume* to most of the financial Web sites. Technical analysts compare a stock's trading volume for the day with its average daily volume to determine whether buying and selling is active or not.

Using MSN Money's site, you can obtain a stock's daily and average daily volume following these steps:

1. **Log into MSN Money at money.msn.com.**

2. **Enter the stock's symbol in the blank and click the Get Quote button.**

3. **Read and interpret the volume.**

   You'll find the stock's volume, as well as its average daily volume over the past 13 weeks, listed on the page. When the day's volume is considerably higher than average, then you can use that insight to analyze the significance of the stock price's move.

The ABC's of Beta

Beta, or the *beta coefficient,* is one of those rare market indicators that both fundamental and technical analysts can agree has value. Beta is a statistical measure of how volatile a stock is relative to the stock market at large. You might recall, from Chapter 11, how beta is used in the *capital asset pricing* model used to build a *discounted cash flow model.*

While beta is based on a somewhat complex statistical technique, as an investor, most of what you need is pretty simple. If an individual stock has a beta of 1, that means it is equally volatile as the general stock market. If beta is less than 1, then the stock tends to swing up and down less than the market. And if a stock's beta is greater than 1, it is less volatile than the market.

A technical analyst might look at beta to provide clues on how wild to expect a stock's ups and downs to be. Beta is available from nearly all financial Web sites.

The long and short of short interest

It might seem strange, but there may be other investors who are hoping, and betting, that a stock you own will go down. These investors, called *short sellers*, use a series of maneuvers to position themselves to profit if a stock falls.

Investors short a stock by first borrowing shares from another investor who owns them. The short seller, then, turns around and sells the shares immediately, pockets the proceeds and waits. The short seller then must buy the shares, hopefully at a lower price, and return them to the investor they borrowed from. If the stock falls, the investor makes money by buying the shares back at a lower cost than they sold them for.

You might never decide to bet against a stock yourself. But it may be useful for a fundamental analyst to know just how many people are shorting a stock they do own. There are three things to pay attention to when it comes to short interest:

- ✔ **Short interest:** A stock's short interest is a measurement of how many shares of a company's stock have been sold short.

    Just looking at short interest doesn't tell you a whole lot. A company with more *shares outstanding*, or shares in investors' hands, would naturally have more short interest than a company with fewer shares outstanding. You'll want to compare short interest with another measure to get proper perspective, as I describe below.

- ✔ **Average daily share volume:** Remember volume, mentioned above? This data will be helpful again in interpreting how significant short interest is by putting short interest into perspective.

- ✔ **Days to cover:** *Days to cover* tells you how large a company's short interest really is. Days to cover is calculated by dividing a stock's short interest by its average daily volume. This statistic indicates how many days of typical trading it would take for the number of shares being shorted to trade hands.

The higher a stock's days to cover is, the more heavily shorted it is. Fortunately, all three types of shorting data described above are available at Nasdaq.com. Just enter a stock's symbol into the site and a window will pop open. Click on the Short Interest option listed below where it says "Fundamentals."

Determining what short interest means to a fundamental analyst is bit tricky. Some fundamental analysts actually like to see a stock that's heavily shorted. If you're completely confident in your fundamental analysis and know what a company is worth, and believe the stock is *undervalued*, heavy short interest can actually be a good thing. When stocks are heavily shorted, if the company delivers solid earnings, investors who shorted the stock may scurry to buy back the stock.

A rush by nervous short sellers to buy back a stock they wrongly bet against is called a short squeeze. Short squeezes can cause powerful stock rallies.

But fundamental analysts tend to view a heavily shorted stock as a warning sign. After all, an investor who shorts a stock is exposed to a theoretically infinite loss, since there's no real limit to how high a stock can rise. If investors are that confident a stock is going to fall, you want to make absolutely sure you've done a complete job with your fundamental analysis.

Keeping a Close Eye on Options

To be sure, fundamental analysis is all about knowing how to study a company from top to bottom and understand what it's really worth. A classic fundamental analyst only pays attention to a market price for a stock when deciding whether it's undervalued and should be bought, or *overvalued* and should be sold.

And for the most part, looking at the stock's current price is enough to tell you what the market measures a stock's value to be. A stock price is the result of a vigorous back-and-forth between buyers and sellers. Through an auction, conducted largely over vast and rapid electronic trading networks, a stock's price rises and falls until buyers are satisfied with the price they're paying, and sellers are OK with the price they're getting.

But there's an entirely separate layer of trading that takes place beyond the buying and selling of the stock itself in the *options market*. Options are financial contracts that give investors the right, but not the obligation, to buy or sell stocks at a prearranged price at a set time in the future.

 Watching the prices of stock options can give you a better idea of not only what investors are willing to pay for stocks now, but their belief of where a stock might be in the future. You might want to factor in the prices of options in your fundamental analysis.

Understanding the types of options

Options come in two most basic forms, *put options* and *call options*. Put options give investors the right, but not the obligation, to sell a stock at a predetermined price at a set time in the future. Call options, on the other hand, give investors the right, but not the obligation, to buy a stock at a predetermined price at a set time in the future.

Investors may buy and sell both put and call options, driving their prices up and down, just as they would trade stocks. Table 19-2 shows you the four most basic options strategies, which you'll want to understand in order to know how to interpret prices on options.

Table 19-2	The Four Basic Options Strategies	
	Calls	*Puts*
Buy	A bet the stock price will rise.	A bet the stock price will fall
Sell	A bet the stock price will fall.	A bet the stock will rise

Paying attention to put and call price levels

If you want to get an idea of what investors are expecting from a stock, you'll want to take a look at its *option chain.* An option chain tells you how much investors are paying for both put and call options that *expire,* or come due, at different times in the future.

Option chains are usually sorted by *strike price,* or the price at which the option kicks in. For instance, imagine you bought a call option for stock ABC at a strike price of $25 that expires in December. That means you have the right, but not the obligation, to buy the stock at $25 a share in December.

Fast-forward to November. Imagine the stock is now trading at $100 a share. Suddenly, having the right to buy a $100-a-share stock for just $25 a share is valuable, or *in the money.* However, if instead of trading for $100 a share, what if the stock is trading for $2.50? Not many people would want the right to buy a $2.50 stock for $25. At that point, your option is considered to be *out of the money.*

If you start noticing the price of call options with strike prices above the current market price going up, that's an indication investors are expecting good things from the stock in the future.

Some technical analysts also pay attention to the volume, or level of trading activity, in options, too. In fact, the amount of trading in put and call options is the basis of another thing technical analysts watch, the *put-to-call ratio,* discussed below.

Watching the put-to-call ratio

Now that you understand what puts and calls are, you might wonder how you might put the information to use. Again, as a fundamental analyst, you're much more concerned about a company's revenue and earnings rather than short-term trading noise. But, monitoring the level of puts and calls can tell you how many other investors either agree, or disagree, with your assessment of a company's value.

The put-to-call ratio gives investors a quick look at how bullish or bearish investors are on a stock's prospects. The ratio is simply the number of puts (which are bearish) divided by the number of calls (which are bullish).

The higher a stock's put-to-call ratio, the more pessimistic investors are about a stock's future.

You could calculate a stock's put-to-call ratio yourself, but it's easier to use online resources that do it for you. You can get the put-to-call ratio from Schaeffer's Investment Research at `www.schaeffersresearch.com`. Enter the stock's symbol in the upper right-hand corner and click the 'get quote' button. Scroll down and click on the Put/Call Open Interest Ratio option, and you'll see the put-call ratio plotted for you.

Using the market's fear gauge: The Vix

One of the great strengths of fundamental analysis is that it gives you a framework to assess how much a business is worth. That way you can make an intelligent decision on whether the stock's price is higher or lower than the business' value. Fundamental analysts, in fact, often get their best deals when other investors are afraid to buy stocks and push stock prices down. Warren Buffett, in his 1986 letter to shareholders, put it this way: "We simply attempt to be fearful when others are greedy and to be greedy only when others are fearful."

One of the biggest reasons why fundamental analysts might choose to pay attention to technical analysis and options is that they may help you see when other investors are feeling greedy and when they're feeling nervous. And when they're nervous, you can be greedy.

There are many ways to get an idea of when other investors are fearful, which is valuable information for fundamental analysts. One popular indictor of investors' fear is based on options trading. This indictor, called the *Chicago Board of Options Exchange Volatility Index* or *Vix*, is often looked at as a pretty valuable measure of investors' fear. When the Vix is rising, that means investors are getting increasingly nervous. And when the Vix is falling, that means investors are getting complacent.

You can obtain current values of the Vix from the CBOE at `http://www.cboe.com/data/mktstat.aspx`. Historical values of the Vix are available at `http://www.cboe.com/micro/vix/historical.aspx`. Most financial Web sites will also let you plot the Vix, if you enter the symbol. For instance, if you enter $vix.x in MSN Money, you can view its value over time.

Applying Technical Analysis Techniques to Fundamental Analysis

As you've probably picked up from earlier in the chapter, fundamental analysts and technical analysts take very different approaches when checking out stocks. If you put technical analysts and fundamental analysts in a room, while a fight not break out, there certainly would be some dirty looks being exchanged.

Perhaps you're reading this book because you disagree with technical analysis for the reasons highlighted above. Maybe you've tried technical analysis before and gotten burned. Still, even if you're primarily interested in a company's fundamentals, don't assume this chapter doesn't apply to you. While technical analysis is often a dirty word among fundamental analysts, there are some techniques used by technical analysts that can easily be carried over to fundamental analysis.

In the sections above, you find out how to add technical analysis to your investment style. You may have skipped that section, figuring you want nothing to do with technical analysis.

But in this section, I attempt to show you ways to some tricks and techniques used by technical analysts directly to fundamental analysis. This isn't as strange as it might seem. After all, realize one of the most valuable things technical analysts do is turn mountains of complex numerical data into charts and graphs. Numbers that are indecipherable in huge spreadsheets can suddenly become enlightening when turned into a chart. Suddenly, charts can help investors quickly spot trends in data they might have otherwise of missed.

Even if you're a die-hard fundamental analyst, there is something to be said about placing investment data on charts that can be closely studied. In fact, the technical analysts are onto something when it comes to a few of their techniques, which can be applied to fundamental analysis.

One of the great drawbacks of fundamental analysis is timing. A cheap stock, based on fundamental analysis, can get even cheaper if it has technical trends working against it. By applying some of the tricks of the technical analysis trade to fundamental analysis, you might spot trends you might have overlooked if you were just focusing on the income statement and balance sheet.

Giving fundamental data the technical analysis treatment

Some technical analysts love charts so much, they might even plot out some data that are traditionally considered to be for fundamental analysts. Even if you're not onboard with technical analysis, there's no question that sometimes, seeing fundamental data presented graphically may help you spot trends.

Plotting fundamental information, rather than just looking at table stuffed with data, may give you a unique perspective and help you to spot trends you didn't notice before.

Price-to-earnings ratios, or _P-E_s, and dividend yields are two of the fundamental pieces of data that technical analysts most often will place on a chart. Looking at how P-E ratios are rising, or falling, over time can help you determine whether or not investors are getting overly giddy or cautious about a stock. You can read about the P-E ratio in more detail in Chapter 8 and the dividend yield in Chapter 10.

Slapping fundamental information on a chart may bring to light trends your eyes glanced over. And there are online tools that make this pretty easy to do. Nasdaq.com, for instance, provides a free charting service that allows you to plot both P-E ratios and dividend yields. You can do this by following these steps.

1. **Log onto Nasdaq's site at www.nasdaq.com.**

2. **Enter the symbol of the stock you're interested in.**

   After you enter the stock symbol into the blank, click on the Company Charts button.

3. **Select the fundamental data you would like to see plotted.**

   Hover your mouse pointer over the Technical Indicators button, then choose Lower Indicators, and then P/E ratio. If you want to plot dividend yield instead, choose dividend yield.

4. **View the data.**

   The data are then plotted for you in a rectangle below the stock's price chart.

Following the momentum of fundamentals

Technical analysts are often interested in following the *momentum* of stock prices, meaning the prevalent trend either upward or downward. Just as college basketball teams often get momentum during big games and start going on a hot streak, technical analysts believe stocks can turn hot and have the gust of investor enthusiasm at their backs. *Momentum investors* hope to pile into a stock while it's still soaring, grab a quick gain and get out.

Classic momentum investing is contrary in most ways to fundamental analysis. But fundamental analysts might consider borrowing a bit from this concept, as strange as it sounds, when examining fundamental data.

By watching for momentum in a company's fundamentals, you might get a tip-off that something meaningful is taking place at a company.

One way to apply the concept of momentum to fundamental analysis is by studying *earnings acceleration*. Here, you're not just looking for companies that are increasing their profitability every quarter or year. You're being even pickier. You want to find companies that are increasing the rate at which earnings are growing.

Fundamental analysts generally use quarterly earnings as their gauge for a company with momentum. Momentum, by its nature, is short-term focused so it makes sense to use short-term data.

To perform an earnings-acceleration analysis, you just need to have a company's earnings growth rate for the last few periods. While it's usually done using quarterly results, the analysis can be done using quarters or years. Below is an example of how you might do this analysis using Oracle's net income for four past years, shown in Table 19-3.

Table 19-3	Oracle's Annual Net Income
Fiscal year	*Net income ($ millions)*
2008	$5,521
2007	$4,274
2006	$3,381
2005	$2,885

Source: Standard & Poor's Capital IQ

Your first step is calculating the growth rate between each period. A growth rate is the difference between the most recently reported quarter and the same period in the previous year's quarter. You can review how to calculate growth rates in Chapter 4. Once you measure each year's growth, you get a chart that looks like what you see in Table 19-4.

Table 19-4	Oracle's Annual Net Income Growth
Fiscal year	_Annual Growth_
2008	29.2%
2007	26.4%
2006	17.3%

As you can see from Table 19-4, what's interesting is that Oracle's annual growth rate is accelerating. In other words, the growth of the most recent period is greater than the one before it. This is the kind of trend that a fundamental analyst, looking for momentum, would be on the search for.

Fundamental analysts often look for quarterly earnings momentum, for instance, when trying to figure out how successful a _new product_ is. New products can be critical to a company's sustained earnings growth. And if something a company introduces is catching on with customers, an earnings-acceleration analysis might show something exciting is going on at the company.

Part V
The Part of Tens

The 5th Wave   By Rich Tennant

"I like the numbers on this company. They show a very impressive acquittal to conviction ratio."

In this part . . .

No *For Dummies* book would be complete without a Part of Tens. In this part, I've saved a few of my favorite real-life examples of how fundamental analysis might have alerted you to potential concerns as an investor (Chapter 20). You can also read a list of the ten things you should always do when analyzing the fundamentals of a potential investment (Chapter 21). And as important as fundamental analysis is, there are weaknesses that you should be aware of, and I point those out in this part, too (Chapter 22).

Chapter 20

Ten Examples of Fundamental Analysis Unearthing Financial Secrets

. . . .

In This Chapter

▶ Seeing how fundamental analysis can help pinpoint troubles at a company

▶ Applying the techniques common in fundamental analysis to actual examples

▶ Discovering some of the research required to carefully examine a company's financials

▶ Using the Altman's Z-score measure to spot a company that might not make it

. . . .

*L*et's face it. Curling up with a warm cup of coffee and a stack of financial statements just isn't quite as appealing as cracking open a great book. Sure, you might find some salacious details in some company reports – some are even famous, including one financial statement discussed in this chapter. Overall, though, a company's annual report filed with regulators, called the *10-K,* probably isn't going to be something you pass around in your next book club meeting.

But, with that said, reading financial statements is still worthwhile. I've found that investors appreciate the importance of reading financial reports when they see real-life examples of how they could have pinpointed major issues at companies well before they were known to the public.

This chapter highlights several actual examples of how investors could have been tipped off to important developments at a company by reading the financial statements. A couple of the examples in the chapter are fraud. And certainly, knowing when a company is cooking its books is important, since that means you cannot rely on the financials.

But a vast majority of the time, fundamental analysts aren't looking for executives that are lying. Rather, fundamentals analyst are looking for numbers that are lying. Sometimes, the numbers might be completely accurate but don't paint a true picture of the condition a company is in. This chapter shows you how to closely analyze a company's fundamentals by using easy-to-follow examples.

Spotting One-Time Charges That Aren't

Spotting outright corporate fraud using just the publicly available financial statements can be very difficult. If a company lies to you and fabricates portions of the financial statements, you are at a huge disadvantage as a fundamental analyst. Fortunately, corporate fraud, while more common than I'd like to see, still remains rare overall.

What's much more common, though, are companies that pad results using perfectly legal tricks you need to watch out for.

My top suggestion on detecting when a company is using little tricks to boost earnings is by comparing a company's *net income* with its *free cash flow*. I step you through this very important analysis, in detail, in Chapter 11. If you didn't read that section during the first swing through this book, you might want to flip back and check it out now.

Another thing to be aware of as a fundamental analyst is when companies routinely take so-called *one-time* or *restructuring charges*. By classifying a charge as one-time or *nonrecurring*, some analysts might overlook the costs, assuming they are unusual and not indicative of the company's core business. But when you see a company constantly taking one-time charges, be careful.

One of the companies that seemed to make one-time charges a regular phenomenon was technology firm, i2 Technologies. As of late 2001, the company made reporting one-time charges a quarterly event. And these charges were significant. In fact, at some points the company's nonrecurring charges were larger than its revenue.

Detecting companies reporting incessant one-time charges can tip you off to an overly aggressive management team.

And certainly at i2, the chronic one-time charges were a red flag worth paying attention to as they were symptomatic of deeper problems. In June 2004, the company agreed to pay $10 million to wronged investors for a pattern of misstating its results for a five-year period ended in 2002, according to the

Securities and Exchange Commission. The company's improper accounting techniques gave investors the impression the company's revenue and profits were rising, when in fact, its results were "increasingly negative," the SEC says.

You can spot a company reporting excessive one-time charges yourself in the earnings press release or the income statement, as described in Chapter 5. But MSN Money, a Web site that consolidates financial information, makes it even easier to find one-time charges. Enter a stock symbol at money.msn.com, click the Get Quote button and choose the Financial Results option, and then Statements. You'll see a row called "Total Extraordinary Items." If that item is consistently high relative to revenue, be wary.

Spotting Financial Distress a Mile Away

There are many ways to protect yourself from buying a car that's a lemon. You can look up the company's history and even get a warranty. When it comes to avoiding a dud in investing, though, fundamental analysis is one of your best weapons.

The best way to know whether a company is unlikely to survive is by carefully studying the financial statements, covered in Chapters 5, 6 and 7 and the financial ratios, discussed in Chapter 8.

There's a shortcut, though, to finding whether a company is unlikely to make it. It's called the *Altman's Z-score*. The Z-score is a long formula that crunches down many of the things you look for and puts it into a single number.

$$\text{Z-Score} = (0.717 * A) + (0.847 * B) + (3.107 * C) + (0.42 * D) + (0.998 * E)$$

Where:

A: (Current assets – current liabilities) / total assets

B: Retained earnings / total assets

C: Earnings before interest and taxes / total assets

D: Shareholders' equity / total liabilities

E: Revenue / total assets

Calculating the Z-score is just a matter of mostly pulling the data off the financial statements and plugging them into the formula. You can find out how to obtain all the data listed above from a company's financial statements in Chapters 5 through 7. But to make it easy, I've listed their locations in Table 20-1.

Table 20-1	Where To Find The Numbers You Need For Z-Score
You will find . . .	*. . . on the . . .*
Current assets	Balance sheet
Current liabilities	Balance sheet
Total assets	Balance sheet
Retained earnings	Balance sheet. This is the amount of a company's earnings that it keeps, rather than distributing them to shareholders as *dividends*.
Earnings before interest and taxes (or EBIT)	Income statement. You'll need to calculate EBIT. Chapter 8 tells you how.
Shareholders' equity	Balance sheet
Revenue	Income statement

Once you calculate the Z-score, you might wonder what it means. One of the beauties of the Z-score is that you just see where it fits on a chart, as shown in Table 20-2, and get a quick interpretation.

Table 20-2	Reading the Z-Score
If a company's Z-Score is . . .	*. . . Then it's considered . . .*
Less than 1.2	Highly likely to fail
Between 1.2 and 2.9	In so-so condition
Higher than 2.9	Unlikely to fail

Consider the example of Nortel Networks. The telecommunications company stunned many long-term investors who figured the company was too big to fail, when it became the second largest public company bankruptcy in January 2009, says BankruptcyData.com.

But fundamental analysts monitoring the Z-score saw this colossal wipeout coming. Nortel's Z-score dipped below 1.2 in the second quarter of 2001, coming in at a -1.74, says Capital IQ. The Z-score never pulled above 1.2 again. Talk about a huge warning.

The Z-score is really a quick-and-dirty way to assess a company's health. Don't rely on it solely when making a financial decision, instead, be sure to fully analyze the company's health.

Sidestepping the Financial Crisis

Every once in a while, perhaps once every generation, there comes a shock to the financial and economic system so severe, you really don't want to get caught in the middle of it. The banking crisis that began in 2007 with the sub-prime mortgage crisis was one of those brutal economic events you didn't want to have anything to do with.

The crisis stunned many investors because much of the damage hit shares of banks, which for many years, had been considered safe and steady investments. While the severity of the crisis caught many investors off guard, there were some clues available to fundamental analysts that at least showed there were problems brewing.

 A good place to have noticed the financial crisis gaining steam was reading the risks section of the 10-Ks filed by top financial institutions. Chapter 12, for instance, shows how AIG was taking blatant risks that caused the firm to implode.

But there were other tip-offs for fundamental investors. Consider the fate of Cleveland's National City Corp. The regional bank, founded in 1845, grew into one of the nation's largest originators of mortgages. National City's dividends and earnings were all steady. So was the stock for many years, as it marched to nearly $37 a share at the end of 2006.

Turns out the steady results were a mirage. National City was eventually bought by rival bank PNC in a distress situation in 2008, for just $1.92 a share. Investors were shocked at how a seemingly strong bank could weaken so quickly.

But they shouldn't have been so surprised. Basic industry analysis provided a clue, had investors picked up the regulatory filings released by National City's nearby Akron, Ohio-based rival FirstMerit. As far back as 2003, FirstMerit, which serves many of the same communities as National City, constantly alerted investors it was aware of some shaky mortgages on its books and was taking action to get rid of them.

Back in 2003, FirstMerit told investors it was selling off some of its most risky loans. And again, in the 2006 letter to shareholders, the CEO of FirstMerit said the company was actively identifying potentially problematic loans and dealing with them immediately. All these warnings came well before the mortgage crisis hit in force in 2007.

But even as FirstMerit was paring troubled assets, National City's 2006 annual report to shareholders was glowing. "Our competitors face the same issues as we do, but we believe we're better-positioned than most in this tougher environment," then-CEO David Daberko wrote in a letter to shareholders in the 2006 annual report.

Savvy fundamental analysts might have wondered why FirstMerit was making such a dramatic effort to reduce its risk, while nearby rival National City hardly made a mention of troubles until it was too late.

Seeing Companies with Potential Environmental Issues

Rising concerns about the environment are increasing awareness by consumers, regulators and investors about how companies are treating the planet. Without getting into the ethical issues connected with how companies use natural resources, investors need to be aware of the potential for financial risk connected with pollution or other environmental factors. Companies might face large fines or consumer backlashes if caught violating environmental rules and regulations.

Don't expect a company to give you a nice neat list of all the potential sites they may have polluted that could come back to haunt it. However, again, the 10-K can give fundamental analysts a head's-up of potential environmental concerns.

My favorite example of this is Pacific Gas & Electric's 1994 10-K. Buried deep in this filing are the allegations from a lawsuit claiming the company's power station in San Bernardino County, California, was causing serious contamination. The suit alleged the plant was exposing residents to chromium. The company also disclosed a number of environmental measures that would cost it up to $55 million over five years. Does this sound familiar? Well, these allegations were the basis of the movie *Erin Brockovich*. Of all the 10-Ks in the world, this might be one of the most famous ones.

Staying Away from Investment Fads, Like the Dot-Bombs

Up until the financial crisis, the biggest implosion of the financial markets had to be the Internet bubble. Investors ignoring the fundamentals of companies rushed to buy stock of companies that didn't make any money and sometimes didn't even have revenue.

Even to this day, the absurdity of the dot-com bubble remains one of the best reasons why anyone who buys individual stocks should take the time to understand the fundamentals. Investors who blindly jumped into technology and Internet stocks blindly got a beating of a lifetime.

More than 117 dot-com companies collapsed between September 1999 and October 2000, according to Boston Consulting Group. Of those, 12 of the failures resulted in bankruptcies, 63 shut down their Web sites completely, and the rest struggled in various forms. But in each case, investors lost nearly all, if not all, their money.

Online pet supply store Pets.com, in hindsight, provides some of the best lessons on how fundamental analysis can help you avoid getting sucked into investment fads. The company's story sounded great. The site allowed consumers to buy things they needed for their pets over the Internet. Great, right?

But fundamental analysis revealed the true story. Turns out the company's survival was nearly impossible. Pets.com lost 19 cents on every $1 in revenue it posted in the third quarter of 2000, reported USA TODAY. And that didn't even include *overhead costs*. In other words, the more product the company sold, the more money it lost. You can't do that very long before going out of business. And it didn't. Pets.com liquidated itself roughly one year after going public.

It turns out that Pets.com wasn't alone. Nearly 60 of the 729 Internet companies in late 2000 were selling products for less than what they paid for them, USA TODAY found. If you want a telltale sign of a mania, this is it.

Pinpointing Companies Fooling Investors

When trying to detect accounting fraud, there's only so much a fundamental analyst can do. After all, you have to believe the numbers to some degree, since you don't have the authority to go inside a company to verify its books and records yourself.

But there are some aspects of accounting that are so commonly abused, they are worth constantly being on a lookout for. So-called *channel stuffing* would be at the top of my list of early fraud warnings.

A company can boost its revenue and profit by enticing customers to buy products now, even thought they don't want them yet, in order to boost results in the short term. Often, a company might cut customers slack in how quickly they must actually pay for the merchandise. That way, the company may book the revenue, even though no cash is collected. Clearly, this practice causes a problem for the company in the future, since consumers don't order because they have more than enough product.

Sunbeam is a classic example of alleged channel stuffing. The SEC accused the company's management of providing customers with lucrative deals in 1997 to coax them to buy product ahead of time. And the channel stuffing technique wasn't enough to keep the fraud going, so the company resorted to even more aggressive means to prop up results, the SEC says.

Again, techniques in this book could have at least shown you something was amiss. Fundamental analysis of the company's *accounts receivable turnover in days*, discussed in Chapter 8, would have provided clues. This financial ratio tells you how many days it takes for a company to collect amounts owed to it by customers. In 1996, Sunbeam collected its accounts receivable in 79 days. But that period shot up to 92 days in 1997, which was a gigantic red flag.

Always be suspicious when you see accounts receivable turnover in days jump up like that.

Seeing through Distortions Caused by Stock Buybacks

Stock buybacks occur when a company uses its cash to buy back shares of its own stock. There are many reasons why companies might do this, as explained in Chapter 18.

But these buybacks can create enormous distortions to financials. While there's nothing nefarious about stock buybacks, investors might come to false conclusions unless they use fundamental analysis. Since buybacks reduce a company's number of shares outstanding, they can inflate a company's earnings per share. Remember earnings per share is calculated by dividing net income by the number of shares outstanding. So if the number of shares falls, the denominator falls, and the earnings per share rises.

The distortions caused by stock buybacks to a company's earnings per share aren't fraudulent. They're merely the result of mathematics. Still, the effect can dramatically alter how investors perceive a company's results.

Take, for instance, Automatic Data Processing. The company has been financially strong for a long time, and is one of the few nonfinancial firms to earn the coveted AAA-credit rating from Standard & Poor's. The company had been long known for its unstoppable consistency. Back in January 2003, the company touted it had extended its "streak" of posting higher earnings per share for 166 straight quarters. ADP's streak gave it the reputation of being a solid and dependable generator of consistent growth.

But fundamental analysts who took a closer look saw that while the company was telling the truth, there was more to the story. Certainly, the company's earnings per share indeed rose 2% to 43 cents a share during the December 2002 quarter. However, that increase in earnings per share was largely due to the fact the company reduced its number of shares outstanding by spending $80 million buying back 2 million shares of its stock during the quarter. Stripping out the effect of buybacks, by looking at net income, tells the real story. ADP's net income fell 1.1% in the quarter to $262 million. No, it wasn't a big drop, but the number puts ADP's streak into more context.

Knowing a Trend Will Come to an End

It never fails. Every couple of years, there's a company that captures the imagination of investors. Crocs, the maker of plastic shoes that had been used mainly by gardeners and boaters, became that new darling. After debuting its shares as an initial public offering in February 2006, the company could do no wrong.

Crocs' revenue soared at a neck-turning pace, rocketing from just $1.2 million in 2003 to $847.4 million in 2007. And investors didn't miss a step, driving shares from their first day's closing price of $14.28 in Feb. 2006 to $74.75 on Oct. 31, 2007. Investors figured the company could expand into all sorts of new footwear and keep up the growth.

Fundamental analysts, though, knew better. For one thing, Crocs' compound average annual growth rate of 415.5% between 2003 and 2007 wasn't sustainable, just by using logic. If Crocs were to grow keep growing that fast, it would have exceeded the revenue of Nike in two years. You can find out how to calculate compound average annual growth rates in Chapter 17.

But fundamental analysis also gave investors clues the momentum at Crocs was petering out. As early as the first quarter of 2007, the company's revenue and earnings growth both fell, breaking a streak of quarterly increases in growth. Even if investors missed this first sign of trouble, there were more, including when the company posted a net loss of $4.5 million in the first quarter of 2008. Even at that time, fundamental investors could get out, as Crocs' stock was still trading for $17.47 a share in March 2008.

But ignoring the fundamentals proved to be very hazardous. While Crocs posted a small profit in the second quarter of 2008, it swung to large losses in the third and fourth quarters. At the end of 2008, Crocs shares fell to $1.24. And then, in 2009, the company's auditor publicly questioned whether Crocs could survive as the company's revenue fell to $126.1 million in the fourth quarter of 2008, down from $224.8 million in the fourth quarter of 2007.

Separating the Strong from the Weak Players

Savvy fundamental analysts know economic downturns can be as much as an opportunity as it is a threat.

If a company can survive, while its key rivals do not, it will likely be better off once the economy heals. A great example of this occurred in the consumer electronics business in 2008. Clearly, the slowdown in the economy caused consumers to cut back their spending on big-screen TVs and MP3 players. And that caused a big problem for archrivals Circuit City Stores and Best Buy.

But fundamental analysis removed any doubt which company would survive. A free cash flow analysis, as described in Chapter 11, told the story. During the fiscal year ended Feb. 2007, Circuit City's free cash flow was just $34 million, and it actually burned $355 million in cash in the fiscal year ended Feb. 2008. Considering the company only had $296.1 million in cash in February 2008, fundamental analysis told you Circuit City had a big problem. Circuit City filed for bankruptcy protection on Nov. 10, 2008, making it the 13th largest public company bankruptcy in 2008, says BankruptcyData.com.

Contrast Circuit City's standing with the situation at Best Buy. Best Buy had a sizeable chunk of cash, $1.4 billion, in the bank at the end of its fiscal year in March 2008. And while Best Buy felt the negative impact of the economy, as did Circuit City, it still generated $1.2 billion in free cash flow in its fiscal year ended March 2008. Clearly, Best Buy was in a position to survive.

Correctly choosing which company can withstand a tough economic period can be lucrative once the weaker rivals drop off. With Circuit City out of the way, Best Buy reported better-than-expected 9.7% revenue growth in the quarter ended Feb. 28, 2009.

Watching for Market Saturation

When companies start out, investors can't help but expect limitless growth. Many of the most successful stocks in history include brand-new concepts for stores, such as Home Depot and Starbucks, which seemed to have no end in sight as to where they could open stores.

Guess what? There were limits. Especially in retail, investors at first get overly optimistic about how many cities and communities can support a new concept. Investors rush into the stock, assuming its blistering pace of opening new stores will never end. But inevitably, as fundamental analysts know, it's possible to build one too many locations. After time, *market saturation* sets in.

Starbucks remains a classic example of a chain which has tremendous growth prospects, but there were still limits. Since being founded in 1971 with its first store, Starbucks seemed able to open as many stores as it wanted, and then open even more. The company added hundreds of stores a year starting in 1994 and by 2007 there were nearly 16,000 Starbucks locations worldwide.

But in July 2008, the first signs of market saturation become apparent when the company said it would close about 600 company-owned stores in the U.S. Investors, used to Starbucks turning coffee into liquid gold by constantly opening new stores, didn't like what they heard. Shares of Starbucks fell nearly 40% from the July announcement through the end of 2008, trailing the rest of the stock market by about 10 percentage points amid a tough time for the economy.

Fundamental analysts, though, saw this market saturation coming. And it didn't take any fancy financial formulas to spot these warnings. In the quarter ended March 2008, Starbucks reported its largest decline in net income growth, 28%, since 1998.

And even more alarming, the company's return on assets fell to an uncharacteristically low 7% for Starbucks. That was half the return the company earned on its assets in the quarter ended Dec. 2007. It was clear the company wasn't getting the kinds of returns it traditionally did from its stores and assets.

Chapter 21

Ten Things to Look at When Analyzing a Company

· ·

In This Chapter

▶ Running through ten of the most basic things fundamental analysts should check for

▶ Reinforcing some of the fundamental analysis techniques that matter most

▶ Showing how several of the types of fundamental analysis may complement each other

▶ Considering some signs that a company is beginning to lose its competitive edge

· ·

*W*hen you see that pile of dirty dishes in the sink, you probably feel a tinge of guilt telling you that you really should wash them. But you just might not be in the mood.

And that same sense of reluctant obligation might also apply to your portfolio. You might own some individual stocks and realize you really should be analyzing their fundamentals, but other things just seem more interesting. So the annual reports and proxy statements just pile up.

Certainly, performing a complete financial analysis of a company takes time as you run through all the financial statements, calculate dozens of financial ratios and study the industry, just to name a few things. Fundamental analysis can take a bit of effort, seeing that Wall Street analysts and credit rating experts get paid to do this kind of thing all day long.

Just because you might not have time to do a complete financial analysis doesn't mean you should let your financial dishes sit in the sink. This chapter will tell you what ten types of fundamental analysis you should always make time for. You'll find out which types of fundamental analysis you should prioritize for when looking to dig into a company's financials but have limited time. If you conduct these ten aspects of fundamental analysis, you will be well ahead of many investors who just blindly buy stocks on a whim.

Measuring How Much of a Company's Earnings Are "Real"

If you're not a full-time fundamental analyst, and you own more than a handful of stocks, it would be a full-time job to constantly monitor in real-time every bit of financial data you'll want to be aware of.

So here it is. My suggestion on the one form of fundamental analysis you should never skip is the measurement of a company's *quality of earnings*. As soon as you can get your hands on a company's *income statement* and *statement of cash flows*, you want to make sure a company's *cash from operations* is greater than or equal to its *net income*. When a company is generating cash flow, you have some proof the earnings are real, not just smoke and mirrors allowed by accounting. You can review how to conduct this analysis in Chapter 11.

Comparing a company's cash from operations to its net income only takes a few moments. The payback for this small investment of time is huge. If you avoid investing in companies with weak cash flow relative to their net income, you may sidestep many bum investments or even outright frauds.

Considering How Much Cash the Company Has

It would be pretty rude to ask strangers you meet at a cocktail party how much money they have in their savings accounts. But you don't have to worry about such etiquette when it comes to companies. Before you invest a dime in a company, you want to make sure you not only know how much companies have, but also what they owe. You should know:

- ✔ How much cash a company has on the balance sheet.
- ✔ How much the company owes to lenders in the short term and long term.
- ✔ How much cash a company generates.

Paying close attention to these four variables will help you avoid plunking your money down in a company that may not survive.

Looking for a quick way to see if a company's survival is in question? Don't forget to calculate the company's Altman's Z-score, described in Chapter 20.

Making Sure You Don't Overpay

Investors are constantly surprised when they spend hours and hours analyzing a company's fundamentals, only to buy a stock and still lose money.

There are countless forces at work to determine a stock's price. Remember, stock prices are set by the constant tug of war between buyers and sellers trading shares back and forth until settling on a price everyone can agree upon. And that's why it's critical for you to not only evaluate how solid a company is, but also how profitable it is and whether it has staying power. It's imperative not to pay too much.

Studies have shown that *growth stocks*, or shares of companies with the highest valuations measured by price-to-book ratios, are often the biggest disappointments for investors. This means that the more you pay for a stock, the lower your future return is likely to be.

Evaluating the Management Team and Board Members

As an investor in a company's *common stock*, or the shares issued to the public representing standard ownership in the company, you're at the mercy of the management team to make the correct decisions with your money. And you're counting on the board of directors to keep a watchful eye on the management team. If you can't trust the management team and board of directors, you shouldn't trust them with your investment.

If you don't look at anything else in the proxy statement, always be sure to look for related party transactions between executives or board members and the company. These are side business dealings with the potential to corrupt the ability of executives or board members to represent the interests of investors like you. And even if a CEO is doing an excellent job, be watchful of excessive pay packages. CEOs that aren't ashamed to lavish themselves with excessive pay probably aren't afraid to take other liberties with your money. Review Chapter 9 for tips on how to dig into the proxy statement.

Examining the Company's Track Record of Paying Dividends

Day traders used to scoff at investors who paid attention to *dividends*. During stock market booms, these small cash payments some companies pay to their shareholders seem almost insignificant.

But fundamental analysts know better. For one thing, dividend payments account for a big portion, roughly 4 percent, of the returns generated by stocks over time. Miss out on those payments, and you're leaving quite a bit of cash on the table. Also, steady dividends can make sure you're earning something on your money even if a stock is flat. Dividend payments can also be helpful in helping you decide how much a stock is worth, as described in Chapter 10.

Lastly, while companies can fudge or pad their earnings, dividends can't be faked. Dividends are usually actual cash payments you can deposit in a bank account or spend. Companies paying dividends are at least showing you a tangible sign of their profitability.

Comparing the Company's Promises with What It Delivers

It's easy to simply take a company management's word as gospel. Financial television is especially infamous for practically turning corporate CEOs into royalty and taking everything they say at face value.

That's not to say you, as a fundamental analyst, need to treat CEOs as crooks or liars. But it is up to you to verify claims made by a CEO. If a company's CEO says a new product is selling like crazy, take the time to look at its *revenue growth* and also the *accounts receivable turnover* in days to ensure customers are buying and actually paying for the goods. If a company claims to have posted record profits, it's up to you to not only verify the claim, but also make sure it wasn't the result of accounting puffery.

Always compare the promises made by a CEO in one year's *annual report to shareholders* with the reality delivered in the following year's financial statements. Professional fundamental analysts often read a company's latest 10-K with the previous one, side-by-side.

Keeping a Close Eye on Industry Changes

Fundamental analysis is powerful, but there is a great deal of emphasis placed on financial statements. And the big weakness of financial statements is that they're historical documents telling you how a company did, as opposed to how it will do.

Trend analysis, described in Chapter 17, is one way fundamental analysts look beyond historical numbers to assess the future. But you need to be especially mindful of game-changing technologies or new ways of doing things in business that can render a company's way of making money, or *business model*, obsolete.

The constant danger that a new technology may wipe out a company is one reason why some fundamental analysts stick with easy-to-understand and basic businesses, where consumers keep coming back. Consumer products companies, for instance, don't have to worry that people will stop buying deodorant (at least your nose hopes so).

Understanding Saturation: Knowing When a Company Gets Too Big

Eventually, for most companies, the early days of easy growth evaporate as the product and business matures. A product, which might have been so new that everyone had to buy one, eventually becomes so prevalent that growth slows. And when a company expands so much, it becomes more difficult to grow further. These growing pains and maturity present great challenges to both management teams and fundamental analysts. Companies often struggle with the transition from a fast-growth company to a slower growth one, and sometimes need to change their entire strategies. Fundamental analysts, too, much change the way they evaluate a company and measure its valuation.

Keep a close eye on a company's *operating profit margin*, or how much of revenue the company keeps in profit after paying direct and indirect costs. When you see the operating profit margin deteriorate, that can be a heads-up that the business' glory days are fading. That doesn't mean you shouldn't invest in a mature business. In fact, the contrary is often true. But you need to be aware that the business' fundamentals have changed. Review Chapter 5 for methods on how to monitor profit margins.

Avoiding Blinders: Watching the Competition

It's often tempting to buy stock in a company you think is the best in a business, and assume that your work is done. But companies are constantly changing and evolving. Sometimes a company's rival might rise up from near death with a killer product and pose a huge threat. Meanwhile, the valuations of so-called leading stocks are often driven up so high that its future returns are often disappointing.

When looking to invest in a company, take the time to read statements and documents released by a rival company you might consider to be weaker. Paying attention to statements made by the CEO of a rival company in a letter to shareholders, for instance, might tip you off to industry trends the CEO of the leading company may not have noticed yet.

Watching Out When a Company Gets Overly Confident

Some athletes get themselves into trouble when they decide to showboat. The temptation to do that one extra and unnecessary back flip or victory dance sometimes lets a quiet competitor sneak up and steal the win.

Companies, too, can sometimes get full of themselves. Figuring that their fat days will never end, some companies build opulent headquarters, send employees on overly lavish business trips or even spend cash on vanity promotions.

Perhaps one of the ultimate forms of business vanity is when a company pays millions of dollars for the right to slap its name on a professional sports team's stadium. During the 1990s, it became fashionable for companies to pony up millions of dollars to sponsor venues hosting a professional team in sports including football, baseball and basketball. Several academic studies, though, have shown there to be very little to no benefit to companies, on average, for making these large investments. One of these studies lists a number of the classic examples of companies that ran into extreme financial difficulty after paying to put their names on sport facilities, including Adelphia, Enron and PSINet, which all filed for bankruptcy protection. You can read the full study here: http://jse.sagepub.com/cgi/content/abstract/8/6/581.

Chapter 22

Ten Things Fundamental Analysis Can't Do

I'd love to tell you fundamental analysis will make you instantly rich beyond your wildest dreams. Heck, I'd love to tell you that fundamental analysis will make you look 15 years younger, too.

And certainly, fundamental analysis is a very valuable tool. It can be used by all sorts of investors, or even by employees, members of the public, or just about anyone interested in knowing how to gauge the health of companies.

But, fundamental analysis also has its limitations. And rather than trying to ignore the shortcomings of fundamental analysis, it's important to recognize upfront what they are and adjust your strategy accordingly. If you don't approach fundamental analysis with reasonable expectations and knowing what the risks are, you may certainly be disappointed with the results.

In this chapter I outline some of the primary drawbacks to fundamental analysis. I hope you don't let these shortcomings turn you off completely from fundamental analysis. After all, understanding how companies work, how stocks are valued and how to measure how profitable a business is are skills that can only benefit you. But again, you need to know what fundamental analysis can do, and what it cannot, before making ill-informed decisions.

Ensure You Buy Stocks at the Right Time

The biggest knock against fundamental analysis is that it doesn't necessarily help you time your investment decisions just right. You might do a beautiful job analyzing a company's financials, identify an undervalued stock, buy it and wait to make money. And then, 10 years later, you're still waiting and waiting.

Just because a stock is fundamentally cheap doesn't mean it must soar in value anytime soon; in fact, it can become even cheaper. Sometimes a stock is cheap for a reason that will reveal itself in its financial statements in the future.

Guarantee You'll Make Money

I wish I could tell you that if you use fundamental analysis, you'll make money on every stock you buy. But the fact is, during a bear market, even the most skilled fundamental analyst will likely suffer losses, at least on paper. During times of extreme stock market stress, some investors might wonder why they even bothered with fundamental analysis.

One investor, who submitted a question for my daily Ask Matt investment column at USATODAY.com, stated this frustration very well. "I've learned how to read the fundamentals, including earnings per share, price-to-earnings, return on equity and the stock price chart. But I'm still losing money. How are you supposed to research stocks anyway?"

Hopefully this book shows you that fundamental analysis requires taking a close look at many aspects of a company. And even after this, fundamental analysts can make mistakes.

Being wrong from time to time is just one of the aspects of fundamental analysis you need to be aware of and live with. Don't beat yourself up too badly when you make a mistake. Consider some of the admissions made by Warren Buffett in his 2008 letter to Berkshire Hathaway investors. Buffett bought a large position in oil company ConocoPhillips during the year, when oil and gas prices were near peak levels. Buffett was thinking energy prices would go higher. But in the letter, he wrote "I have been dead wrong." He added: "Even if (energy) prices should rise, moreover, the terrible timing of my purchase has cost Berkshire several billion dollars."

Save You Time When Picking Stocks

Some investors like to refer to fundamental analysis as an art. There's at least one key difference, though, between art and fundamental analysis. After an artist is done chiseling a statue or creating a painting, he or she is done. The work stands as a completed masterpiece of enduring value.

Fundamental analysis, though, doesn't age well. Even after you spend hours completely studying all public information about a company, its stock and industry, you're not done. New information continuously flies at you and may have an influence on your analysis. If fundamental analysis is art, it's definitely a work in progress.

Performing fundamental analysis takes time, patience and determination. You'll need to take the time to gather, analyze and process new financial information as it comes in. Fundamental analysis can be somewhat time-consuming, as you'll need to make sure you are studying every aspect of a company that you possibly can.

Reduce Your Investing Costs

There's no question the cost of buying and selling individual stocks has fallen dramatically. If you open an account with an online discount brokerage firm, you might expect to pay $10 a trade or less as a *trading commission*. And certainly, at $10 a trade, the trading commissions you pay won't make a big dent in your portfolio's return.

But many investors make the mistake of assuming the trading commissions are the only tolls you pay when you buy and sell individual stocks. Other costs include:

- ✔ **Your time:** Imagine if you decided to invest $100,000 in 10 different stocks using fundamental analysis. And presume that you need to spend at least an hour a week researching each stock. If you're very good, you might happen to pick ten great stocks that wind up beating the market by two percentage points a year. Sounds great. But that additional return works out to $2,000 a year, which means you've only made about $4 an hour for all the work you put in, according to an analysis by Mark Hebner of Index Funds Advisors.

- ✔ **Research:** It's true you can obtain a vast majority of the data you need for fundamental analysis for free. The Securities and Exchange Commission, for instance, provides free access to companies' regulatory filings. And there's no shortage of helpful, free sites that provide fundamental data on companies.

But if you really get into fundamental analysis, you might be tempted to subscribe to fundamental data and research services that will cost you money.

✔ **Being wrong:** By taking on fundamental analysis, you're saying you think you can outsmart the market. By using your ability to read financial statements and make intelligent forecasts, you may load up on shares of individual companies. And if you choose correctly, then you may benefit. However, being wrong can be costly. Remember that large U.S. stocks, on average, gained 9.2% a year between January 1928 and December 31, 2008, says IFA.com. If you pick the wrong stocks or buy or sell at the wrong time, you might sabotage the nearly 10% return you could have had for just buying a diversified basket of stocks and holding on.

✔ **Tax hits:** Buying and selling individual stocks may generate tax events, which could eat into your return. You can read more about the role taxes play below.

While fundamental analysis has its costs, picking your own stocks could actually save you money versus investing in *actively managed mutual funds*. Actively managed mutual funds employ professional money managers who select stocks and decide when to get in and out. Some of these mutual funds charge large fees. These fees, disclosed as part of a mutual fund's *expense ratio*, can cost you 1% of your investment a year or even more. If you're convinced you don't want to put your money in a low-cost index fund, and instead are invested in a fund that charges a large expense ratio, it's possible you might save money by picking stocks yourself.

Getting started with investing

In this book, I assume you're already familiar with setting up a *brokerage account* or may already have a relationship with a brokerage. But if you don't already have a brokerage account, don't underestimate the importance of this decision. In fact, choosing the right type of account to use for investing can be as important or even more important than choosing stocks using fundamental analysis.

The first thing you need to decide is whether you plan to do your investing from a *taxable account* or a *retirement* account. When you buy and sell stocks in a taxable account, you will need to pay attention to rules on capital gains and losses. For instance, if you sell a stock for a profit inside a taxable account, you may need to pay tax on that gain. However, if you trade from inside a retirement account, such as an individual retirement account or IRA, you may defer your gains when you sell winning stocks.

You'll also want to make sure you take the time to fully investigate what kind of brokerage firm is right for you. Some brokerage firms charge rock-bottom commissions, but you're completely on your own when it comes to handling your accounts. Other firms charge more for commissions, but provide you access to branch offices and financial advisers, if that's something you're interested in.

You can read more about how to choose the type of account and brokerage firm that's right for you in my other book, *Investing Online For Dummies*.

Protect You from Every Fraud

There's no question fundamental analysis is one of your biggest shields from getting sucked into the next Enron or Sunbeam accounting scandal. As you discovered throughout this book, there are tricks and techniques to fundamental analysis that help you spot suspicious activity going on at a company. And while you may not be able to pinpoint the specifics of a fraud using a company's financial statement, you'll probably see enough red flags to make you suspicious of the company and the way it operates.

With that said, fundamental analysts must accept, to a certain degree, the fact they must take financial statements somewhat at their face value. If a company completely fabricates the numbers on the financial statements while the board of directors and auditing firm aren't paying attention, there's only so much a fundamental analyst can do.

Easily Diversify Your Risk over Many Investments

Given the costs of fundamental analysis, discussed above, generally you will need to focus your efforts on a few stocks. It's true that even fundamental analysts have tools that allow them to scan many companies. For instance, you can sift through thousands of companies' fundamentals using *computerized stock-screening tools*, as described in Chapter 17.

But generally speaking, if you're going to go to the trouble and expense of digging into the bowels of individual companies, you will likely only be able to keep up with so many stocks. In fact, if you own too many stocks, you might miss some important fundamental details and derail your success.

Being concentrated in a few stocks, though, presents risks, too. A big and unexpected decline in revenue or earnings at one of the companies you're invested in could depth-charge your returns. Worse yet, a massive decline by one of your holdings might make a dent in your portfolio that will be difficult to overcome.

Predict the Future

Fundamentals can be poor indicators of the future. Financial statements are backward-looking, meaning they tell you how a company did in the past, not necessarily how it will do in the future.

The easiest way to understand the lagging nature of fundamentals is by studying the collective earnings of the companies in the Standard & Poor's 500. Fundamental analysis rarely signals a recovery in stock values or the economy. In fact, fundamentals continue to deteriorate for an average of five months even after the stock market bottoms, according to S&P data.

Rewind back to October 11, 1990. Stocks had been falling for more than a month in what had been a nearly 20% pullback. October 11, 1990, though, was the market's bottom and the beginning of a powerful rally. But you wouldn't have known it by looking at the fundamentals. Companies' reported earnings would remain weak for another 15 months after October 1990. Investors who waited for the fundamentals to improve before getting back into the stock market would have missed a powerful bull market.

Fundamentals, though, can sometimes be decent predictors. During the bear market that ended in October 2002, companies' earnings actually started to heal nine months ahead of the stock market's bottom, S&P says. This was a pretty unusual occurrence, though. Companies' fundamentals have been poor predictors of market and economic recoveries in eight of the past 10 downturns, S&P says.

Make You the Next Warren Buffett

Giving the success Warren Buffett has enjoyed at the helm of Berkshire Hathaway, it's natural to want to take a page from his playbook. And clearly, Buffett is a master at using fundamental analysis to identify businesses that generate strong returns over the long term. There are many things to be learned from Buffett's long-term and patient approach.

But don't assume that just by reading about fundamental analysis, you can expect to have the same kind of success. Remember, Buffett has an army of analysts to assist him in studying companies. Also, know Buffett's cache allows him to get deals on stocks you, as an individual investor, would never get. For instance, in 2008, General Electric gave Buffett the opportunity to invest $3 billion in the company and get preferred shares generating 10% annual returns. If only you and I could be so lucky.

Protect You from Your Own Biases

The discipline of fundamental analysis can keep you relatively level-headed when it comes to your investing. Instead of blindly following stock tips from a neighbor or from a guru on TV, fundamental analysts take the time to do their own due diligence. By scanning through a company's financials, you can get a pretty decent idea of a company's intrinsic value and how healthy the company is.

And because fundamental analysis is rooted in business and mathematics, it portrays a sense of precision. After all, some of the formulas in this book might look like something Einstein scrawled on a blackboard. How could those lead you astray?

There's still a healthy dose of judgment and estimation that goes into fundamental analysis.

In *trend analysis*, for instance, it's up to you to determine whether or not an interruption in a company's long-term earnings track record is a major shift or just a short-term blip. And when it comes to *valuation*, including using the *discounted cash flow analysis*, the answer you get largely depends on assumptions that you make.

Some may say the fact that fundamental analysis allows for human judgment makes it more flexible than some sort of computer program that spits out a generic opinion on a stock. That's true. But it's also important to keep in mind that your own biases can work their way into your fundamental analysis.

Overcome the Danger of Thinking You're Always Right

One of the things that has always surprised me about investors is how most assume they're skilled at choosing stocks, even when they don't have any factual basis to believe that. Many investors buy and sell individual stocks, and conveniently remember their winners while somehow forgetting about all the bum investments they've made.

Fundamental analysis can give some investors, sadly, even more ammunition to pad their imaginary stock-picking track records. You might, for instance, accurately forecast a company's future earnings, which is pretty difficult to do. You might, in hindsight, applaud your excellent trend analysis, and somehow forget that you actually lost money on the investment because you overpaid for the stock.

And that's why if you're going to attempt to pick individual stocks using fundamental analysis, you owe it to yourself to also learn how to track your performance. Every year, you should know how to calculate what your portfolio's return was and how much risk you took on in order to achieve that risk.

Being able to measure your portfolio's return and risk and compare it against the stock market is critical. If you're spending lots of time and money searching for stocks, and lagging the stock market, you might want to try a different strategy.

How to measure your portfolio's return

Measuring your portfolio's return is pretty straightforward. Assuming you didn't add any fresh cash to the account during the year, simply subtract your portfolio's value at the end of the year from its value at the start of the year. Divide that difference by your portfolio's value at the beginning of the year and multiply by 100, and voila, that's your percentage gain for the year. Table 22-1 provides a simple example of returns.

Table 22-1	Here's a Sample Portfolio
Quarter ended	*Portfolio value*
December 2008	$10,000
March 2009	$10,050
June 2009	$10,500
September 2009	$10,501
December 2009	$11,000

Using Table 22-1, you would measure your portfolio's return this way:

($11,000 – $10,000) / $10,000 = 0.10. Multiply by 100 to convert the answer into a percentage, or 10%. That is your annual return.

Be sure to compare the return of your portfolio to that of the Standard & Poor's 500 or another *stock market index* to find out if you're beating, or getting beaten by, the market.

How to measure your portfolio's risk

Putting a number on your portfolio's risk is a little trickier than measuring your return. You'll need to figure out how volatile your returns are using a statistical measure called standard deviation.

To calculate your portfolio's standard deviation, you will first need to tabulate the percentage changes for each period. You can do this analysis based on any period of time, but since Table 22-1 is quarterly, you can practice with that. You just use the formula above and calculate the returns for each quarter. When you're done, you'll see a table that looks like what you see in Table 22-2.

Table 22-2	Sample Portfolio of Returns
Quarter ended	*Return*
March 2009	0.5%
June 2009	4.5%
September 2009	0.01%
December 2009	4.8%

Lastly, you'll need to calculate the standard deviation. If you want to understand the gory details of standard deviation and how to calculate it by hand, check out *Statistics For Dummies* (Wiley).

Otherwise, you'll want to enter the row and columns into Microsoft Excel just as you see it in Table 22-2. You can then use the "=stdev" function. For more help on ways to use your computer to calculate standard deviation, especially when returns are negative, that's also covered in *Investing Online For Dummies* (Wiley).

If you have an HP 12C financial calculator, you can enter each return followed by the Sigma + key. When you're done entering all the returns, press the g key and the s key to see your portfolio's quarterly standard deviation. The answer you get is 2.55 percentage points.

You're almost done. You must now convert the quarterly standard deviation into an annualized number. You do that by multiplying the period's standard deviation by the square root of the number of periods in a year. Yikes, I know. But in this case, since you are measuring quarterly standard deviation, there are four quarters in a year. That means you take the square root of 4, which is 2. So to convert your quarterly standard deviation to an annualized figure, just multiply the 2.55 standard deviation by 2.

Sizing up your portfolio's risk and return

Just knowing your portfolio's return and risk doesn't tell you much. It's important to compare those data with a benchmark, or a set of investments that you want to size yourself up against. The IFA Risk and Return Calculator (www.ifa.com/portfolios/PortReturnCalc/index.aspx) lets you see the returns and standard deviations of several measures of stocks to see how you're doing.

Be careful of drawing too much from just one year. Don't assume that if you had one good year your luck will continue.

If all these measurements just give you a headache, but you still want to see how you're doing with fundamental analysis, there are Web sites that do much of the crunching for you. A few performance tracking sites include RiskGrades (`www.riskgrades.com`), Icarra (`www.icarra.com`), and Stockalicious (`www.stockalicious.com`).

Index

• *C* •

• *Q* •

• *R* •

• *U* •

• *V* •

• *W* •

Business/Accounting & Bookkeeping

Bookkeeping For Dummies
978-0-7645-9848-7

eBay Business
All-in-One For Dummies,
2nd Edition
978-0-470-38536-4

Job Interviews
For Dummies,
3rd Edition
978-0-470-17748-8

Resumes For Dummies,
5th Edition
978-0-470-08037-5

Stock Investing
For Dummies,
3rd Edition
978-0-470-40114-9

Successful Time
Management
For Dummies
978-0-470-29034-7

Computer Hardware

BlackBerry For Dummies,
3rd Edition
978-0-470-45762-7

Computers For Seniors
For Dummies
978-0-470-24055-7

iPhone For Dummies,
2nd Edition
978-0-470-42342-4

Laptops For Dummies,
3rd Edition
978-0-470-27759-1

Macs For Dummies,
10th Edition
978-0-470-27817-8

Cooking & Entertaining

Cooking Basics
For Dummies,
3rd Edition
978-0-7645-7206-7

Wine For Dummies,
4th Edition
978-0-470-04579-4

Diet & Nutrition

Dieting For Dummies,
2nd Edition
978-0-7645-4149-0

Nutrition For Dummies,
4th Edition
978-0-471-79868-2

Weight Training
For Dummies,
3rd Edition
978-0-471-76845-6

Digital Photography

Digital Photography
For Dummies,
6th Edition
978-0-470-25074-7

Photoshop Elements 7
For Dummies
978-0-470-39700-8

Gardening

Gardening Basics
For Dummies
978-0-470-03749-2

Organic Gardening
For Dummies,
2nd Edition
978-0-470-43067-5

Green/Sustainable

Green Building
& Remodeling
For Dummies
978-0-470-17559-0

Green Cleaning
For Dummies
978-0-470-39106-8

Green IT For Dummies
978-0-470-38688-0

Health

Diabetes For Dummies,
3rd Edition
978-0-470-27086-8

Food Allergies
For Dummies
978-0-470-09584-3

Living Gluten-Free
For Dummies
978-0-471-77383-2

Hobbies/General

Chess For Dummies,
2nd Edition
978-0-7645-8404-6

Drawing For Dummies
978-0-7645-5476-6

Knitting For Dummies,
2nd Edition
978-0-470-28747-7

Organizing For Dummies
978-0-7645-5300-4

SuDoku For Dummies
978-0-470-01892-7

Home Improvement

Energy Efficient Homes
For Dummies
978-0-470-37602-7

Home Theater
For Dummies,
3rd Edition
978-0-470-41189-6

Living the Country Lifestyle
All-in-One For Dummies
978-0-470-43061-3

Solar Power Your Home
For Dummies
978-0-470-17569-9

Internet
Blogging For Dummies,
2nd Edition
978-0-470-23017-6

eBay For Dummies,
6th Edition
978-0-470-49741-8

Facebook For Dummies
978-0-470-26273-3

Google Blogger
For Dummies
978-0-470-40742-4

Web Marketing
For Dummies,
2nd Edition
978-0-470-37181-7

WordPress For Dummies,
2nd Edition
978-0-470-40296-2

Language & Foreign Language
French For Dummies
978-0-7645-5193-2

Italian Phrases
For Dummies
978-0-7645-7203-6

Spanish For Dummies
978-0-7645-5194-9

Spanish For Dummies,
Audio Set
978-0-470-09585-0

Macintosh
Mac OS X Snow Leopard
For Dummies
978-0-470-43543-4

Math & Science
Algebra I For Dummies
978-0-7645-5325-7

Biology For Dummies
978-0-7645-5326-4

Calculus For Dummies
978-0-7645-2498-1

Chemistry For Dummies
978-0-7645-5430-8

Microsoft Office
Excel 2007 For Dummies
978-0-470-03737-9

Office 2007 All-in-One
Desk Reference
For Dummies
978-0-471-78279-7

Music
Guitar For Dummies,
2nd Edition
978-0-7645-9904-0

iPod & iTunes
For Dummies,
6th Edition
978-0-470-39062-7

Piano Exercises
For Dummies
978-0-470-38765-8

Parenting & Education
Parenting For Dummies,
2nd Edition
978-0-7645-5418-6

Type 1 Diabetes
For Dummies
978-0-470-17811-9

Pets
Cats For Dummies,
2nd Edition
978-0-7645-5275-5

Dog Training For Dummies,
2nd Edition
978-0-7645-8418-3

Puppies For Dummies,
2nd Edition
978-0-470-03717-1

Religion & Inspiration
The Bible For Dummies
978-0-7645-5296-0

Catholicism For Dummies
978-0-7645-5391-2

Women in the Bible
For Dummies
978-0-7645-8475-6

Self-Help & Relationship
Anger Management
For Dummies
978-0-470-03715-7

Overcoming Anxiety
For Dummies
978-0-7645-5447-6

Sports
Baseball For Dummies,
3rd Edition
978-0-7645-7537-2

Basketball For Dummies,
2nd Edition
978-0-7645-5248-9

Golf For Dummies,
3rd Edition
978-0-471-76871-5

Web Development
Web Design All-in-One
For Dummies
978-0-470-41796-6

Windows Vista
Windows Vista
For Dummies
978-0-471-75421-3

How-to?
How Easy.

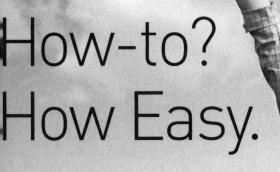

From hooking up a modem to cooking up a casserole, knitting a scarf to navigating an iPod, you can trust Dummies.com to show you how to get things done the easy way.

Visit us at Dummies.com

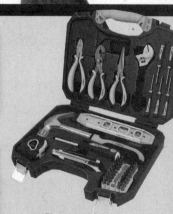